EMINENT
GEORGIANS

EMINENT GEORGIANS

The Lives of
King George V,
Elizabeth Bowen,
St. John Philby,
& Nancy Astor

JOHN HALPERIN

St. Martin's Griffin
New York

EMINENT GEORGIANS
Copyright © John Halperin, 1995, 1998.
All rights reserved. Printed in the United States of America. No part
of this book may be used or reproduced in any manner whatsoever
without written permission except in the case of brief quotations
embodied in critical articles or reviews. For information, address
St. Martin's Press, 175 Fifth Avenue, New York, N.Y. 10010.

ISBN 0-312-17685-6 paperback

Library of Congress Cataloging-in-Publication Data

Halperin, John, 1941–
    Eminent Georgians : the lives of King George V, Elizabeth
Bowen, St. John Philby, and Nancy Astor / John Halperin.
        p. cm.
    ISBN 0-312-12661-1 (alk paper) (cloth) ISBN 0-312-17685-6
(pbk)
    1. Great Britain–History–George V, 1910-1936–Biography.
2. George V, King of Great Britain, 1865-1936. 3. Great Britain-
-Kings and rulers–Biography. 4. Bowen, Elizabeth, 1899-1973-
-Biography. 5. Women novelists, Irish–20th century–Biography.
6. Philby, H. St. J. B. (Harry St. John Bridger), 1885-1960.
7. Explorers–Arabian Peninsula–Biography. 8. Orientalists–Great
Britain–Biography. 9. Astor, Nancy Witcher Langhorne Astor,
Viscountess, 1879-1964. 10. Women politicians–Great Britain-
-Biography. I. Title.
DA568.A1H35 1995
941.083'093--dc20
[B]   95-2269
                                                                CIP

Book Design by Lynn Newmark

First published in hardcover in the United States of America in 1995
First St. Martin's Griffin edition: January 1998
10 9 8 7 6 5 4 3 2 1

PERMISSIONS

The quotation from Louis MacNeice's "Autumn Journal" in the Introduction is by permission of Faber and Faber Ltd, publishers of *The Collected Poems of Louis MacNeice*, ed. E. R. Bobbs.

Quotations in Chapter 1 from King George V's unpublished diary in the Royal Archives are by the gracious permission of Her Majesty Queen Elizabeth II.

Excerpts in Chapter 1 from *King George V* by Kenneth Rose, copyright © 1983 by Kenneth Rose, are reprinted by permission of Alfred A. Knopf, Inc.

Quotations in Chapter 1 from Harold Nicolson, *King George V: His Life and Reign*, are by permission of Nigel Nicolson.

Sir John Betjeman's "Death of King George V" is reproduced in Chapter 1 by permission of John Murray (Publishers) Ltd.

Quotations in Chapter 2 from the unpublished letters of Elizabeth Bowen are by permission of the Curtis Brown Group. Additionally, letters from Elizabeth Bowen to Virginia Woolf are quoted in Chapter 2 by permission of the Librarian of the University of Sussex at Brighton, where the Monks House Papers are collected. Letters from Elizabeth Bowen to William Plomer are quoted in Chapter 2 by permission of the University Librarian at the University of Durham, Palace Green.

Excerpts in Chapter 2 from the following works by Elizabeth Bowen are by permission of the Estate of Elizabeth Bowen and Jonathan Cape, Ltd.: *The Collected*

For Prentice, Rita, Eric, Michael, and Amanda Elaine

CONTENTS

ACKNOWLEDGMENTS

For aid, advice, information, and encouragement, I am grateful to Janet E. Dunleavy, Ruth Fainlight, Victoria Glendinning, Elizabeth Jenkins, Molly Keane (M. J. Farrell), Phillip Knightley, Michael Kreyling, the late Rosamond Lehmann, Robert B. Martin, the late May Sarton, Gillian Tindall, and Joseph Wiesenfarth. Joanne Harris of the National Portrait Gallery and Alan Williams of the Imperial War Museum gave me crucial help with photographs, Elizabeth Stevens of the Curtis Brown Group with permissions. Omissions, errors or failures of mine should not be blamed on them.

A small section of Chapter 2 appeared in different form as "Elizabeth Bowen and Henry James," in the *Henry James Review*, Vol. 7, No. 1 (Autumn 1985), and is reprinted here by permission of The Johns Hopkins University Press. I am also indebted to the Department of English at the University of Wisconsin, Madison, for permission to quote from correspondence between the Department and Elizabeth Bowen in the 1960s; and to the Betjeman Estate for permission to reprint "On the Death of King George V" at the end of Chapter 1.

I would also like to thank Carolyn Levinson for preparing the manuscript of this book for publication and Daniel Hipp for preparing the index.

J. H.
La Jolla, California, February 1995

LIST OF ILLUSTRATIONS

I am getting to know quite a lot of the Young Georgians, &
have a paternal feeling . . . towards them.
—Thomas Hardy to Florence Henniker (2 July 1921)

In the Twenties, I learned to value courage and sportsmanship
above a nice culture.
—Warwick Deeping

INTRODUCTION

THE ATTITUDE OF the post-Victorian generation to its own past may be glimpsed in a letter Thomas Hardy wrote to Lytton Strachey in April 1921. Having just read Strachey's latest biographical volume, *Queen Victoria* (1921), Hardy declared that he had been "deeply interested" in it "notwithstanding that your subject was a most uninteresting woman." He added: "I often wished you could have had a more adequate & complicated woman to handle, such as Mary Stuart or Elizabeth. However, Victoria was a good queen, well suited to her time & Circumstances, in which perhaps a smarter woman would have been disastrous." Strachey would publish his *Elizabeth and Essex* in 1928.

Queen Victoria died, along with the old century, in January 1901. Samuel Butler's *The Way of All Flesh* (1903), though written earlier, memorably attacked Victorian coldness and hypocrisy and became a kind of underground cult hit upon publication. Teenagers read it surreptitiously late at night and delighted in its attack on their parents' generation. Somerset Maugham, D. H. Lawrence, and James Joyce, among others, pilloried nineteenth-century morality, mendacity, and pretense in their fiction. Bloomsbury's appetite for the assault upon its parents and grandparents was insatiable; Strachey's *Eminent Victorians* (1918) bore witness to the hatred many postwar Britons harbored for, as they saw it, the muddled, bungling, proud, bourgeois, unfeeling, repressed ancestors who dealt them into the Great War and all of its horrors.

No one's reputation suffered more unfairly as a result of anti-Victorianism in the twentieth century than King George V's. Though beloved by his contemporaries, until quite recently he has been remembered primarily as Victoria's grandson, which he could not help being, and as a continuation of Victorianism after the brief (1901–1910) reign of his father, Edward VII. But this isn't fair. George V, it is true, was brought up as a Victorian gentleman, but the duties he inherited unexpectedly (he had an older brother) turned out to be those of a world altogether different from that in which he grew up. Within months of his accession he had to face a riveting constitutional crisis that placed the old way of doing business in Whitehall squarely in confrontation with an entirely new and more radical view of government. Faced with the struggle between socialists and reactionaries for control of Westminster, the new king astonished the country by cooperating in the abolition of the power of the House of Lords, and England has never been the same since. Everyone knows that the Lords cannot veto a money bill or any other bill passed by the Commons in three successive sessions; it is by no means a commonplace of historical memory, however, that the Lords lost the veto in 1911, when George V backed this revolutionary change as a way out of a paralyzing political stalemate. The decision he made on the Parliament Bill was one that his grandmother, and probably his father too, would have died or abdicated rather than make. Much of the rest of his reign, though by no means all of it, was flavored by this early and instinctive liberalism. He could be reactionary too, as we shall see. In being both the old-fashioned country squire that he was, the man who shot an obscene number of birds every weekend, and the forward-looking progressive interested in technology and the improvement of his subjects' lives, as he also was, he combined in himself much that was "Georgian."

The term is used here in reference to George V—that is, to specify the period from, roughly, 1910, when he came to the throne, to 1940, four years after his death. Nancy Astor, Elizabeth Bowen, and St. John Philby all lived well beyond the reign of George V, but in many ways they are creatures of the 1920s and 1930s and did their best work, led the most interesting parts of their lives, during the interregnum between the two world wars. The term "Georgian" in its twentieth-century incarnation has often been employed to refer to a school of poets—as in, to take just one example, the phrase "Georgian Revolt," sometimes used to describe postwar English poetry. Adoption of the word "Georgian" became general after the appearance, in 1912, of a volume called *Georgian Poetry*, and the controversies surrounding its publication. This was an anthology of new poems by, among others, Rupert Brooke, John Drinkwater, and Edward Marsh. Five volumes of *Georgian Poetry* appeared between 1912 and 1922, and the list of poets whose work was published in them expanded to include W. H. Davies, Walter de la Mare, D. H. Lawrence, John Masefield, Robert Graves, and others. These men were born in the last third of the nineteenth century; by the time George V came to the throne they had, if they lived, reached the age of influence. The subjects of the present study, though not poets, were "Georgian" in the same sense: they reached maturity, productivity, influence, during this era.

At the heart of this discussion of the term "Georgian" is the question of modernity. Differences between the literature of the 1880s and 1890s and that of the 1920s and 1930s often have been seen as the differences between the Victorian and the modern ages. But what is especially interesting about the Georgians, beginning with George V himself, is the simultaneous allegiance so many of them had to tradition and to change, to the status quo and to the future. As we shall see, George V embodies in himself many of these apparent contradictions—but in their own ways so do Nancy Astor, Elizabeth Bowen, and St. John Philby. Perhaps the term "Georgian" has something to do with both looking forward and looking back—with an ambivalence about the present born of uncertainty as to whether it is going by too quickly or too slowly. David Lodge has characterized 1930s writing as "anti-modernist, realistic, readerly and metonymic"; it was a time, he says, when bourgeois writers often felt obliged to identify with the proletariat, and experimentalism was not as fashionable as it had been in the 1920s. A mixed decade, indeed. Writers of the 1930s were often interested in politics and frequently in Russia; it was in the 1930s that Philby's son, Kim, was recruited to spy for the Soviets. Perhaps no time so quickly and thoroughly repealed and stigmatized the values of the past. And yet today, looking back, this period also seems astonishingly reactionary, yearning for the good old days, while all innovations and changes—that is, everything contemporary—were condemned. The 1930s, after all, was the decade of the dictators, of the politics not of the left but of the right.

In the context of these apparent contradictions, the lives of the four subjects of this book are exemplary and revealing. Their spiritual and historical ambivalence defines the age they lived in; and the age they lived in, it may be, was defined in some small way by the lives they led.

Perhaps no one has captured so well as Alan Pryce-Jones (born 1908), in *The Bonus of Laughter* (1987), what it meant to be a twentieth-century Georgian:

> by the time I was sixteen I worried my father by choosing the five tree-calf bound volumes of Eddie Marsh's Georgian Poetry for a school prize, because he feared they might affect for the worse my little talent. I deduced that at first he suspected Marsh of compiling an eighteenth-century anthology, and my father well knew that the eighteenth century was no good. Later, when he discovered the George in question to be George the Fifth, he became even warier. Why, when Keats and Shelley were available, waste time on writers who could be lumped together with the cacophonous Debussy and the incompetent

post-Impressionists, as 'modern'? My father was a Meissonier man: he liked pictures of quaffing cardinals only a little less; he had not opened Keats or Shelley in the twentieth century, and he thought them both foolish fellows at best. But at least they were not modern.

There is always some automatic resistance to the contemporary, no matter how tame. Here the issue is poetry rather than politics, with *Georgian Poetry* cast as the satanic verses.

For those determined to divide everything into old and new as well as good and bad, the Great War was the inevitable dividing line. Pryce-Jones recalls:

> We could faintly remember from experience the world of Before-the-War, and we perceived that that world had gone for ever. Our elders, having known it for longer, grew up in it and accepted it as perfectly natural and right, were usually more optimistic than we. They believed in the League of Nations, in the liberal values, in the perfectibility of man; they could not bear to be cut off from the nineteenth century by vulgar barriers such as Fascism, Nazism, Leninism, which is why they often denied the existence of such barriers and claimed one or other of them, according to their own inclinations, as useful props the fault of whose architects was merely to be a little vexatious at times.

Pryce-Jones concludes this section of his memoir with an account of the spiritual schizophrenia of his generation in Britain:

> We who came of age in the late Twenties, finding the post-War world in fragments, clung to whatever offered a sense of order. It might be the world of G. E. Moore, as filtered through Bloomsbury; it might be the Catholic Church; it might be some disciplinary enterprise like money-making or sport. Or it might be the inversion of order, exemplified by Dada and Surrealism. . . . It was already a tragedy that the manipulators of our society were imprisoned by the past, like bees in amber. Our leaders, Baldwin and Chamberlain, had been born before the Franco-Prussian War; they had always been on the winning side; they knew almost nothing at first hand of other countries than their own. Like their immediate subalterns they operated within the framework of an indomitable empire: how could they make any accurate assessment of a foreign enemy? . . . We found ourselves bottled up by our elders, and bored to extremity by their tales of Passchendaele and Mametz Wood. And so part of our silliness was in sheer reaction against the repetition of abstracts like victory, patriotism, never-say-die endeavour.

Georgian ambivalence indeed! And incidentally, or perhaps rather coincidentally, the fatal blundering of the political leaders of the 1930s in Britain runs like a ribbon through the brief lives constituting the present volume.

By the end of the 1930s—that is, by the end of what has been called the *entre deux guerres* period—Bloomsbury had lost much of its influence and its fashion among intellectuals. War and communism were in the air. One of Lady Astor's neighbors went off to fight in Spain on the republican side. "Hitler yells on the wireless," Louis MacNeice wrote in his journal in 1938:

The night is damp and still
And I hear dull blows in the wood outside my window;
They are cutting down the trees on Primrose Hill . . .

They were indeed. The top of Primrose Hill, MacNeice added,

Once was used for a gun emplacement
And very likely will
Be used that way again.

In her novel *Over the Frontier* (1938), Stevie Smith referred to a sort of "nervous irritability that has in it the pulse of our time." There was plenty to be nervous about in 1938; it didn't end with Hitler yelling on the wireless. Virginia Woolf used the image of the leaning tower to characterize the 1930s, the critic Patricia Craig points out, as a time of "disorder, malaise and a sense of the impending abolition of class."

The simultaneity of traditionalism and experimentation, of the Victorian and the modern, the nineteenth century and the twentieth, and the hostility of each perspective to the other is perhaps the most noticeable intellectual hallmark of the interregnum, the period between the world wars. For some, everything that led to the Great War was anathema, that war having changed everything; on the other hand, nostalgia for the old prewar days grew in some quarters where the new seemed emptier, more hollow, than the old. This doubleness, this schizophrenia, is typical of the era.

And it may be seen as well in the lives of the four protagonists of the present study. Lady Astor was a reactionary American who broke the gender barrier of the British parliament, becoming the first woman to sit there. St. John Philby was another conservative who evolved into a rebellious British civil servant, later producing a son who betrayed the Establishment his father, sometimes mutinously, served. King George V, raised as a Tory squire and trained as a sailor, turned out to be in tune with many of the radical ideas and politics of his day—more so, at least, than Nancy Astor, M.P. Elizabeth Bowen wrote novels in the 1920s and 1930s satirizing contemporary values, but those very values turned out to be, in her later years and books, what she missed most. Her last novels are less satirical than nostalgic.

Does an age shape the people who live in it, or do the people who live in it shape an age? Does the impulse of influence travel in one direction, or both directions, or neither? Can this be measured? What is the connection, exactly, between the play and the actors? Can you have one without the other?

The stories of our four eminent Georgians may help to answer these questions—or they may not. But in a sense these are exemplary lives, reflecting some aspect of the world inhabited by each and by all.

1

THE FIRST WINDSOR: GEORGE V

I

"ARE YOU AWARE," Queen Victoria wrote to her eldest daughter in 1862, "that Alexandra has the smallest head ever seen? I dread that—with Bertie's small empty brain—very much for future children." Thus were the parents of George V characterized by his grandmother.

Could this Victorian grandson, a child of the mid-nineteenth century, possibly be equipped to deal with such "modern" convulsions as the Great War, Irish Home Rule and Indian independence, the question of the future of the House of Lords and of constitutional monarchy itself, the demands of suffragettes, the end of Empire, the rise of the Labour party, the General Strike, the Depression, establishment of an all-party National Government, and indeed the very survival of the royal house to which he belonged? Could a man born out of the direct line of succession to the throne and trained for nothing but sailing, whose chief daily leisure-time occupation was the murdering of hundreds of birds and who possessed no interest in politics, history or art—among other things—survive, prosper, even distinguish himself as King of England? How would a man whose life touched that of Lord Palmerston at one end and that of Sir Anthony Eden at the other conduct himself in times not only changing but virtually unrecognizable pole to pole? Born two months after Lee surrendered to Grant at Appomattox and living to see the rise of Hitler, would this man grow with the times and understand them? Or would he be mired in the past, a product of the allegedly small brains of his parents?

To H. G. Wells's disparaging reference to "an alien and uninspiring court," George V replied: "I may be uninspiring but I'm damned if I'm an alien." And yet this uninspiring man inspired the British people with possibly the greatest respect, reverence, and affection felt for any British monarch. How did this happen?

"In the end it is character not cleverness that counts," Violet Markham wrote of George V after his death, "goodness and simplicity, not analytical subtlety and the power to spin verbal webs." The key to understanding this king lies in his character—his common sense, his compassion, his kindliness, his patriotism, his tendency to be considerate rather than condescending, to be without prejudice except on behalf of his humblest subjects, for whom he consistently interceded with less sympathetic minsters. How did it happen that this apparently backward child of the Victorian age, unsophisticated and uncultured, grew into the very modern monarch the early twentieth century cried out for? Or is all of this simply untrue? Posterity has endowed his memory with all sorts of negatives. Wasn't he an appalling father and so mindlessly conventional as to be a sort of reactionary stooge? Isn't it true that his only interests were in the Empire and shooting birds and punctuality and clothes? Isn't that so, after all?

II

The second son of Albert Edward, Prince of Wales, afterward King Edward VII, and Princess Alexandra, eldest daughter of Prince Christian of Glücksborg, afterward King Christian IX of Denmark, was born a month prematurely at Marlborough House in London on 3 June 1865; it was perhaps the last time in his life that he was unpunctual. Princess Alexandra was twenty, the Prince was twenty-three. Gladstone was Chancellor of the Exchequer in 1865; in the same year Mrs. Gaskell and the Prime Minister, Lord Palmerston—preferring to the end, as Denis Judd reminds us, the Belgian Treaty to the Bible as deathbed reading—died; and Dr. Livingstone was writing his book on the Zambesi.

The royal parents wished to name the boy George Frederick but were obliged to consult the Queen, who had definite ideas about names. The Prince of Wales told his mother: "we had both for some time settled that, if we had another boy, he should be called *George,* as we like the name and it is an English one." Victoria, perhaps remembering the unfortunate reputations of her disreputable uncles, King George IV and Frederick, Duke of York, replied:

I feel I cannot admire the names you propose to give the baby. I had hoped for some fine old name . . . George only came in with the Hanoverian family. However, if the dear child grows up good and wise, I shall not mind what his name is. Of course you will add Albert at the end . . . as you know we settled long ago that all dearest Papa's male descendants should bear that name, to mark our line, just as I wish all the girls to have Victoria after theirs.

The Prince's first son had been called, dutifully, Albert Victor. But this time Edward replied to his mother: "We are sorry to hear that you don't like the names we propose to give our little boy, but they are names that we like and have decided on for some time." A compromise, however, was worked out, and the boy was christened George Frederick Ernest Albert. To the public he would be known as Prince George Frederick; to the family he was Georgie.

For all children, royal or not, the most important people in the world are their parents. A great deal has been written about the parents of this little prince, but only a few words are possible here.

Princess Alexandra was devoted to her children and her husband. Graceful, charming, and lovely, she retained all of her life a disarming simplicity and warm-heartedness. She was uncomplicated, unpretentious, and unintellectual; and she was generous and tactful. Always stylish, she scorned fashion. "I know better than all the milliners and antiquaries," she once said. "I shall wear exactly what I like and so shall my ladies." She loved domestic life and liked to stay at home. Even her mother-in-law admired the "great simplicity and an absence of all pride" with which she brought up her children. She adored flowers, animals, and the country, and was fond of raising money for the nursing profession. She read the Bible aloud to her children, and from this Prince George acquired the habit, retained until his death, of reading a biblical passage to himself every day. Her children revered Alexandra and gladly forgave her notorious unpunctuality and general disorganization.

They did not always revere their father, the future Edward VII, but they did trust and confide in him, and Prince George in time came to regard his father as a sort of elder brother. This was something the unbending Prince Albert never managed to achieve with his own Albert Edward. As George V's biographer Harold Nicolson observed about the relationship between the Prince of Wales and the future king, "seldom has so frank and staunch a bond been forged between a Sovereign and his heir." The Prince's tastes and pleasures have been well documented: what is perhaps less well known is that nothing he did weakened or even very much changed the affectionate relations between himself and the members of his immediate family, who continued to respect and defend him no matter what happened. This was because he was an attentive and affable father and even, in his fashion, a loyal husband. At home he was invariably genial and indulgent, relaxed and loving; he did not perpetuate the strict discipline with which he had been brought up, but rather saw its pitfalls as a system and attempted to avoid them with his children. Though he sometimes lost his temper, he never lost it with his children. "Throughout a life that was sometimes selfish and always restless," Kenneth Rose has written, Edward "loved to have his family about him, cared for their happiness, protected their interests."

So Prince George Frederick saw in his domestic life a model he wished to emulate later; and though it was not possible, as it turned out, to have with his own heir the kind of close and trusting relationship he had with his father, he did his best to construct such a relationship. As a husband he would be more uxorious than his father was. If his upbringing lacked anything, it lacked any attention to intellectual pursuits. Neither of his parents was ever seen to open a book; as George V, he was justly but unfortunately known as a man utterly ignorant of the arts. "I am not a professor like my grandfather," he would admit later.

And the rest of the family? Prince Albert Victor was eighteen months older than Prince George. There were three sisters: Princess Louise, two years younger than Prince George; Princess Victoria, three years younger; and Princess Maud (later Queen of Norway), four years younger. Another boy, born in 1871, lived only a day.

The two young princes were tutored at home—Sandringham, in Norfolk—which was the practice among royal families in those days. Their grandmother watched their progress closely. "They are such ill-bred, ill-trained children," she declared when Prince George was seven. "I can't fancy them at all." Probably she saw them as their father's children: we know what she thought of his brain. Prince George as a child was lively and sturdy; his elder brother, called Eddy in the family, was slower and less energetic. Young George was subject, said his tutor, the Reverend Mr. Dalton, to a "general spirit of contradiction," "fretfulness of temper," and "self-approbation." At his mother's urging, Prince George stopped finding fault with the more temperamental and vulnerable Eddy, who was of course next in line to the throne after their father; and over time, again at their mother's urging, the younger brother grew more protective of the elder.

Typically the two young princes read geography and English before their breakfast at Sandringham. After breakfast came Bible study or history, and afterward mathematics. There was a break, followed by a language lesson, usually either French or Latin. The boys were allowed out in the afternoon (riding, cricket). After tea and before bedtime came more English—and, often, music, though study of the latter seems to have left no trace on the future George V. One of his most celebrated remarks as King was that *La Bohème* was his favorite opera because it was the shortest. Dalton complained that Prince George "wants application, steady application" and strove to impress upon his young pupils the importance of tidiness, order, and duty in everything they did. This influence did take on Prince George, as we shall see. From time to time there were also lessons in drawing, dancing, fencing, riding, and gymnastics. And at an early age Prince George was taught to shoot, which would become for him a lifelong passion bordering on obsession.

When Prince George was eight his grandmother gave him a watch— "hoping," the Queen wrote, "that it will serve to remind you to be very

1.1 Prince George as a naval cadet in the 1870s; by permission of the National Portrait Gallery.

punctual in everything and very exact in all your duties. . . . I hope you will be a good, obedient, truthful boy, kind to all, humble-minded, dutiful, and always trying to be of use to others!"

The attributes and virtues the Queen mentions are, among other things, the required qualities of a naval officer. As a second son, not in the direct line of succession to the throne, Prince George had to have a career of some sort, and it was decided in 1877 by the family that he should make his way in the Royal Navy as a sailing officer. Dalton, pointing to the listlessness and self-conceit of Prince Eddy, argued that the elder brother should accompany the younger, that they should train together on the elderly and comfortless Royal Navy training ship *Britannia,* that this would inculcate in both princes "habits of promptitude and method, of manliness and self-reliance," areas in which Prince Albert Victor was rated especially deficient by his tutor. The Prince and Princess of Wales approved this plan, much to the consternation of Queen Victoria. Suppose the ship should go down, she argued: numbers two and three in the succession would be lost. If they lived their positions in life would be very different; they should not both enter the Navy: "The very rough sort of life to which boys are exposed on board ship is the very thing not calculated to make a refined and amiable Prince." The boys should go, said their grandmother, to a public school, preferably Wellington College. She persisted: "Will a nautical education not engender and encourage national prejudices and make [the Princes] think that their own Country is superior to any other? . . . a Prince . . . should not be imbued with the prejudices and peculiarities of his own Country, as George III and William IV were." This, for the Queen, was rather progressive thinking. But the monarch was overruled by the boys' parents, and the two royal princes joined the *Britannia* at Dartmouth in the autumn of 1877, where they were to remain for two years.

Prince George was now twelve. He would spend the next fifteen years in the Navy, advancing from cadet to captain, leaving the service only when Prince Albert Victor died and he became, to his astonishment, heir presumptive to the throne after his father, the Prince of Wales. Obviously his fifteen years as a naval officer helped to shape his habits as well as his outlook on things. In later life, however, the King was prone to recall his naval years diffidently. On the *Britannia,* he said, "It never did me any good to be a Prince. Many was the time I wished I hadn't been. It was a pretty tough place."

In September 1879 the two princes embarked together on the warship H.M.S. *Bacchante,* with their tutor and some other midshipmen, for what would be a three-year cruise around the world. As it turned out, this voyage happened to secure for the future King the beginnings of a personal knowledge of the British Empire that would exceed that of many contemporary statesmen and politicians. Between 1879 and 1882 he and his brother visited the Mediterranean, the West Indies, Ireland, Spain, South America, South

Africa, Australia, Japan, China, Singapore, and Egypt. From this time (age fourteen) he began to keep a diary, and he wrote in it every day until just before his death in 1936. He also would bring back from this extended journey a body more liberally tattooed than that of any other British monarch and a full beard.

Prince George was not an eloquent or loquacious diarist, and his account of these years tells us little of substance about the trip (example: in Cape Town "we . . . passed an ostridge farm, and saw a good many ostridges"). At least he was consistent. Later attempts to develop the Prince's French (in Lausanne) and German (in Heidelberg) came to nothing. In 1913 the British consul-general in Berlin told his wife that King George V "cannot speak a solitary word of German, and his French is atrocious." Though his naval training helped give George V a solidity and steadiness of character and a pronounced sense of duty, it did nothing for his intellect; he may well have been the most formally undereducated of the English kings. The fact that he was not expected to succeed to the throne is a poor excuse for his want of education. During his time on the *Bacchante* he appears to have read nothing but Dickens, which is hardly a preparation for life. He left the ship, with his elder brother, in August 1882. Looking back later, he declared that his naval training to that point in his life enabled him to acquire what he called the sailorly virtues of "truthfulness," "obedience," and "zest."

In June 1883 the two princes were separated when the younger was appointed to a ship of the West Indian and North American squadron, H.M.S. *Canada*. Prince Eddy stayed home to be coached for Cambridge. No brother and no tutor: for the first time Prince George was on his own. The *Canada* visited Niagara, Ottawa, Montreal, and Halifax, and returned to England a year later, in July 1884; Prince George, now nineteen, was a sub-lieutenant. He spent some time at the Royal Naval College in Greenwich, where he did particularly well in Practical Navigation and particularly badly in Mechanics. Then he went off to Portsmouth to take a gunnery course on H.M.S. *Excellent*; here he excelled in Gunnery, Torpedoes, and Seamanship, and nearly failed Pilotage.

Meanwhile he kept getting didactic letters from his grandmama, who worried that he might go down the same paths his father trod at age twenty. But the Prince of Wales had been rebelling against a harsh and loveless regime; Prince George felt neither excluded nor unloved. Nonetheless did the Queen fret. She wrote to Prince George:

Avoid the many evil temptations wh. beset *all* young men and especially Princes. Beware of flatterers, too great love of amusement, of *races* & betting & playing high. I hear on all sides what a good steady boy you are & how you can be trusted. Still you must always be on the watch & must not fear ridicule if you do what is right. Alas! Society is very bad in these days; what is wrong is winked at, allowed even, & as for betting or anything of that kind, no end of young and older men have been ruined, parents hearts broken, & great names and Titles dragged in the dirt. It is in *your* power to do immense good by setting an example & keeping your dear Grandpapa's name before you.

And much more of the same. "What bosh," the Prince was heard to exclaim over one of his grandmother's many letters. He could not have failed to note that the model held up for his perusal was the grandfather he never knew rather than the father he cherished. Victoria was only beginning to see that Prince George was not his father. His chief leisure-time activities were polo, riding, billiards, and stamp collecting—after all not very bohemian, even by the standards of the Queen.

After receiving a good report from his superiors on the *Excellent,* the Prince was promoted to lieutenant in the autumn of 1885. His next posting was to the battleship H.M.S. *Thunderer,* in the Mediterranean fleet. He served for the next two and a half years (1886-89) aboard the *Thunderer* and several other battleships in the Mediterranean. It is clear from his diary that he had little comfort and no special privileges aboard these ships—he complains in one entry that a brother officer has appropriated the ship's only comfortable chair—and that he missed his family and his home acutely. "How I wish I was going to [Sandringham], it almost makes me cry when I think of it," he wrote to his mother. In June 1887 he was given leave to attend the Queen's Jubilee, sailing in the same ship, he noted in his diary, with Lady Randolph Churchill and her thirteen-year-old son.

In April 1889 Prince George completed his tour of duty in the Mediterranean and returned home to England. In June he was given the Freedom of the City of London and had to make a speech. "Was awfully nervous," he wrote in his diary. And now, just twenty-four, he was given his first command, a torpedo boat, in which he was habitually seasick. While commanding this ship he rescued another in trouble in heavy seas off the coast of Northern Ireland, a venture that witnesses said took great skill and some nerve. A few months later he accompanied his father on a state visit to Berlin, one of the highlights of which was a call on Bismarck, who had just been sacked by Kaiser William II. "He speaks English perfectly," the Prince wrote of Bismarck. During this visit the Kaiser presented his cousin George with the honorary command of a Prussian regiment. The Princess of Wales, who hated the Germans, commiserated with her second son: "it was your misfortune and not your fault," she wrote, to have become "a real life filthy blue-coated Picklehaube German soldier!" In May 1890 Prince George was given a gunboat, H.M.S. *Thrush*; he traveled in it to the West Indies and North America during the rest of this year and the first half of 1891. On taking command of the *Thrush* he found waiting for him "an enormous sackful of official papers and correspondence," he recalled later. "I fished out the ship's log and one or two other things. All the rest I threw overboard." He was also seasick in the *Thrush*. It was during this period of his life, while his mother was writing letters to him full of praise for having "resisted all temptations so far," that the Prince acquired his first (so far as we know) mistress, a girl at Southsea whom he visited and, in the phrase of the day, kept; and there was now another young lady, this one in St. John's Wood, whom he may have shared with Prince Eddy: "She is a ripper," Prince George wrote.

While sailing abroad he also continued to receive mail from his grandmother, who urged him to consider marriage. "I think marrying too young is a bad thing," replied Prince George, now twenty-six. "The one thing I never could do is to marry a person that didn't care for me. I should be miserable for the rest of my life." He returned to England in July 1891 and in August was promoted to commander. This was the period of the infamous Baccarat Scandal, when a member of the Prince of Wales's circle was accused of cheating at cards at a house in Tranby Croft, in Yorkshire; and also of Lady Brooke, the future Countess of Warwick, to whom the Prince of Wales was openly attached. The papers and the prelates gave the heir to the throne a hard time. His younger son, despite the embarrassment to his mother, remained loyal to his father. "What a lot of rot the papers say," Prince George remarked.

In the autumn he fought off a potentially serious case of typhoid. And in December came the news that Prince Eddy had become engaged to Princess Mary of Teck. Generally known as Princess May, her mother was the daughter of the late Duke of Cambridge, a son of George III, and her father was Duke of Teck. Princess May was born in Kensington Palace in 1867 and had lived in Britain for most of her life. Despite her poverty, she was Queen Victoria's choice; and it was considered by the Prince and Princess of Wales a great boon that Prince Albert Victor should become engaged to a steady woman—not only because of the succession, but also because of his chronically weak nature. Though without money, the Tecks were known to be a family of character.

Prince Eddy had not improved with age. He rarely attended lectures at Cambridge and seemed to derive little from his matriculation there. "He hardly knows the meaning of the words *to read*," one of his tutors reported. He wrote ungrammatically, was a poor conversationalist, and generally struck his father as an alarmingly disappointing young man. Prince Eddy's greatest enthusiasm—inherited, perhaps, from the Prince of Wales—was reserved for his wardrobe. In the Hussars, in which he had a commission, he was found by his cousin, the present Duke of Cambridge, the commander-in-chief, to be "an inveterate and incurable dawdler, never ready, never there." The Duke was shocked to discover, Kenneth Rose tells us in his superb biography, *King George V,* that the heir presumptive knew nothing of the Crimean campaign and was unable to perform the most elementary drill movements on the parade ground. Rumors reached the Prince of Wales that his elder son visited the notorious homosexual brothel in Cleveland Street. He wrote to the Queen: "His remaining in the Army is simply a waste of time . . . the difficulty of rousing him is very great. A good sensible wife with some considerable character is what he needs most, but where is she to be found?" And so Queen Victoria, with the approval of the Prince and Princess of Wales, decided the time had come for an arranged marriage. She looked over the field. After a ten-day command inspection and grilling at Balmoral the Queen chose Princess May, said to be an exemplary and intelligent young lady—and above all, steady. Here was character. She and Prince Eddy were cousins but hardly knew each other; still, they could not resist the Queen and the Prince and the Princess of Wales even had they wished to, of which there is no evidence. And so the engagement was announced in December 1891, as we have seen, with the wedding planned for February 1982. The Waleses were taking no chances.

Princess May along with her parents arrived at Sandringham on 8 January 1892, Prince Albert Victor's twenty-eighth birthday. He had gone hunting the day before and caught a chill, quickly diagnosed as influenza. By the ninth he had developed double pneumonia. Five days later, murmuring over and over again "Who is that?" he died. The funeral was at St. George's Chapel, Windsor. On his coffin Princess May placed a replica of her unused bridal wreath of orange blossoms. On what would have been her wedding day she received from the Prince and Princess of Wales their intended present—diamonds—and a dressing case that the late Prince had ordered for his intended bride.

A last word here about the short life of poor Prince Eddy, whose fate was such a pathetic one. In recent years a great deal of wild speculation has swirled about his memory in a spate of books. Was he Jack the Ripper? Was he flagrantly homosexual? Did he suffer from syphilis? Was he feeble-minded? Was he assassinated by his own family to make way for his brother? Was he hidden away alive in a Scottish dungeon for forty years? This is the stuff of best-sellers, but the truth was less spectacular and more prosaic. Undoubtedly Prince Albert Victor was bisexual; so were dozens of his royal ancestors. He was probably a frequenter of the famous male brothel in Cleveland Street, a fact effectively buried by Lord Salisbury's government in 1889-90 to save the reputation of the royal family. Prince Eddy suffered briefly from gonorrhea but died of pneumonia in January 1892. He was a dreamy, kindly, sweet-tempered, and sensitive young man but also a languid, lazy, sometimes irresponsible one; he sought pleasure wherever it was to be found but at the same time inspired in his friends and most of his family a fierce protectiveness. He was not Jack the Ripper. He would have made a miserable king; but unlike his nephew Edward VIII he would have performed his constitutional duties, no doubt badly. He was no worse, in biographer Theo Aronson's phrase, than "a dissipated simpleton," and often much better. His family and friends loved him for his gentle, considerate, unpretentious, benign, generous spirit, which still comes through to us even in the most unflattering biographies of this most unfortunate prince.

III

Prince George, suddenly the heir presumptive to the throne in place of his brother, was shocked. "I am sure no two brothers could have loved each other more deeply than we did," he wrote to the Queen. "Alas! it is only now that I have found out how deeply I did love him." His brother's death gave the twenty-six-year-old Prince nightmares. Ever since he could remember, his brother had been his most ubiquitous and intimate companion—and the only companion, as Harold Nicolson reminds us, with whom his relations had been those of absolute equality. Now, stunningly, he was asked to take over his brother's role, to become his brother. Of course Prince George saw Prince Eddy as a beloved sibling rather than as a lackluster Prince without energy, ambition, or indeed much aptitude for anything except dress and dissipation. It would never have occurred to Prince George that the future of the monarchy and perhaps the country too was strengthened by this pathetic accident of history. But that was an undeniable result of this royal demise.

His late brother having been Duke of Clarence, Prince George was now given the title Duke of York; with it came a seat in the House of Lords. He wrote to thank his grandmother for the new honors and received a startling reply. "I am glad that you like the title of Duke of York," said the Queen. "I am afraid I do not, and wish you had remained as you are. A Prince *no one* else can be, whereas a Duke any nobleman can be, and many are! I am not very fond of . . . York, which has not very agreeable associations"—a reference to her disreputable Hanoverian uncle, the second son of George III, who, as Duke of York and Commander-in-Chief of the Army, was disgraced by his mistress's illicit sale of commissions. The Queen also asked her grandson, now that Prince Albert Victor was no more, to use the last of his official names, Albert. Prince George refused. "Like his father before him and his second son after him," Kenneth Rose writes, "he well knew the importance of not being Albert." To put it another way: he preferred pleasing his father to pleasing his grandmother.

As the new heir, Prince George was given a small personal staff, a suite of apartments at St. James's Palace, and the Bachelors Cottage at Sandringham as a country residence. In 1889 the Prince of Wales had managed to secure from Parliament an annual grant of £36,000 for his children. Prince George would now have the use of the largest part of this sum, which proved adequate to meet his expenses: he was not extravagant. (In terms of today's buying power, £20,000 in 1890 would be the equivalent of approximately $1.75 million.)

During the summer of 1892 Prince George fulfilled his naval commitments, commanding H.M.S. *Melampus* for several months and suffering as usual from seasickness. "I hope I shall not be in any other manoeuvres," the Prince noted. "Hate the whole thing." He would not be disappointed to give up his sailing career. During the fall he spent some time in Germany, attempting fruitlessly to improve his German. Upon his return to England he decided (or someone did) that the time had come for him to increase his grasp of domestic politics; the Prince devoted part of the winter of 1892-93 to attending parliamentary debates. In February he heard Gladstone introduce to the House of Commons his doomed Irish Home Rule bill. "He made a beautiful speech and spoke for 2 and a quarter hours, which is wonderful for a man of 83," Prince George wrote in his diary. "The House was crammed." The next day he heard Randolph Churchill speak against Gladstone's bill. "He was very nervous at first," the Prince noted. He spent much of the rest of that winter doing what he would do at almost every available opportunity for the rest of his life: shooting birds at Sandringham and anywhere else there was sport. He went to a production of *King Lear,* "but did not care about it." He read Thackeray and preferred him to Shakespeare—a good Victorian response.

Meanwhile the Queen was "in a terrible fuss about your marrying," the Prince of Wales told the Duke of York. In 1893 he would be twenty-eight; as the new heir presumptive, it was expected that he should be settled and start a family. The Queen wrote pointedly to her grandson: "Have you seen May and have you thought more about the *possibility* or *found out* what her feelings might be?" For the Queen's choice was, once again, Princess Mary of Teck—not only chronically impoverished but also, now, maritally stranded. The Prince of Wales agreed with his mother: if she was the right choice for the previous heir, why not also for the present one? British frugality spoke: why waste all that research and grilling—and those presents? Queen Victoria shrugged off the idea that such a quick re-engagement might suggest to a cynical world that the late Prince and his intended bride had not loved each other. It was more important to her to maintain continuity and stability. The unhappy precedent of Henry VIII, his unfortunate elder brother Arthur and the cruel fate of Catherine of Aragon, was sufficiently remote to be entirely ignored. So Prince George was encouraged all around to conduct a brief courtship of his late brother's fiancée. Courtship, it turned out, was not one of his strong suits. A surviving letter of this period to Princess May hopes that it "won't bore you too much, when you are finished stop and throw it away." The Princess's grandmother noted in her diary: "It is clear that there is not even a pretence at love-making. May is ... placid and cold as always, the Duke of York apparently nonchalant and indifferent." At this early stage of their relationship some of the undemonstrativeness was undoubtedly due to embarrassment on both sides.

In May 1893 the engagement was announced. "There is . . . ground for hoping that a union rooted in painful memories may prove happy beyond the common lot," pontificated *The Times*. Oddly enough, out of "private grief and dynastic need," as Rose puts it, came a truly happy union. The Queen was delighted with the engagement; even Princess Alexandra was pleased. The participants themselves, after they got over their initial shyness with each other, also came to like the idea. "I am indeed lucky to have got such a darling and charming wife," Prince George noted in his diary. Princess May wrote to him: "I am sorry that I am still so shy with you, I tried not to be. . . . It is so stupid to be so stiff together and really there is nothing I would not tell you, except that I *love* you more than anybody in the world, and this I cannot tell you myself as I wrote it to relieve my feelings." It was expected that they should love each other, and they were doing their best to meet the expectations. In response to Princess May's letter, Prince George wrote, with powerful feeling (and less powerful syntax): "Thank God we both understand each other, and I think it really unnecessary for me to tell you how deep my love for you my darling is and I feel it growing stronger and stronger every time I see you; although I may appear shy and cold." Their relationship and their position brought into the limelight two persons who preferred privacy; as time went by they took refuge increasingly in one another.

The wedding took place in the Chapel Royal, St. James's Palace, in July 1893. Queen Victoria violated protocol by appearing not last but rather first so that she could watch the guests arrive. She refused to shake hands with Gladstone, whom she detested; the octogenarian Prime Minister nonetheless sat down near her, much to her indignation. Among the many distinguished guests was the Tsarevitch of Russia, the future Nicholas II, whose extraordinary resemblance to Prince George was widely noticed. The Duke of York was married in the naval uniform of a captain. The newlyweds appeared with the Queen on the balcony of Buckingham Palace and later were driven through the crowded streets of London to catch their train for Sandringham. "Most enormous crowds I ever saw, magnificent reception the whole way, it quite took one's breath away," the Prince wrote in his diary.

He never considered going anywhere else but Sandringham after his marriage. Here, where all the recollections of his happy boyhood were still fresh, and here only, he felt at home: "the place I love better than anywhere in the world," he called it. Here he lived most of his life, and here he died. As Nicolson has observed, Prince George then and later "was a man who preferred recognition to surprise, the familiar to the strange." At Sandringham he could be what made him most happy: a country gentleman, a sportsman, a farmer—everything the reverse of a public figure. He disliked London, disliked going out, disliked society. He liked his home, his wife and later on his family, and shooting—and little else. He relished the fact that the Bachelors Cottage at Sandringham was too small to entertain anybody, and (probably) dreaded having to move into the main house there, as he would have to do eventually—where entertaining others could not possibly be avoided. He always favored the cottage at Sandringham over his more spacious quarters at St. James's Palace, where the royal couple would routinely spend part of the winter and where they were expected to, and did, entertain. The future George V always preferred the role of Norfolk squire to any other. Queen Victoria disapproved of Sandringham as the site of the royal couple's honeymoon, characterizing it in a letter as *"unlucky and sad."* Prince Eddy's room in the Cottage, in which he died, was left as it was. The rest of the place had been fitted and furnished by the Duke of York in an attempt to spare his young wife the trouble. She would have welcomed the challenge, since she enjoyed decorating—also because he ordered most of the furnishings from a large discount department store.

The new Duchess of York was less content, at least at first, with her unadorned rural existence. More culturally inquisitive and with greater intellectual curiosity than her husband's family, and living under the close observance of the Princess of Wales, the future Queen Mary felt wasted and stale in the early years at Sandringham, though later, perhaps through habit and usage, she also came to consider it their only home and continued to live there after her husband's death. But now, in 1893, she was not interested in shooting birds, Prince George's principal occupation at Sandringham, and she was not encouraged by her in-laws to put her own stamp on the Bachelors Cottage. One of her lifelong passions was collecting art, about which she was knowledgeable; over the years, provided with sufficient funds, she acquired a distinguished collection. She played cards with her husband in the Cottage, rearranged the discount furniture, and consented to have Greville's *Memoirs* read aloud to her by the Duke of York. Princess Alexandra came through and put the furniture back where it had been. Time passed; for the Duchess, one senses, it passed slowly. As George V's physician John Gore has written, "she came of a younger, more liberal generation, with far more serious notions of women's spheres of usefulness, and very strong ideas of the responsibilities demanded of the first ladies in the realm." A serious woman would have felt stifled and useless under the conditions of her early years at Sandringham. The Duchess of York, a quiet and intense person, was also disconcerted by the tendency of her husband's boisterous family to drop in on them unannounced. Prince George's parents and sisters had some difficulty just after the marriage disguising their jealousy of the intruder in their midst, resented her stiffness, which they took to be arrogance, and declared her dull. "All her thoughts, views and ideas appear to me to be rather banal, commonplace and conventional," said Queen Victoria's eldest daughter, the Empress Frederick. Such a serious person as the

Duchess of York was bound to be misunderstood by her husband's family, at least at first. One is reminded of what Elizabeth Bennet tells the diffident Darcy in *Pride and Prejudice*: "We neither of us perform to strangers." Undoubtedly this was true of the young Yorks. Perhaps understanding her position better than others, the Queen gave Princess May constant encouragement. "Each time I see you," she wrote, "I love and respect you more and am so truly thankful that Georgie has such a partner." Princess May fretted under all this scrutiny, but very soon was able to do something that calmed down the critical Waleses and their relations: she became pregnant.

The Duke of York, meanwhile, was given a crash course in constitutional history that included, much to his grandmother's indignation—she considered it an incendiary text—study of Walter Bagehot's *The English Constitution*.

The Duke's uxoriousness was demonstrated (for example) in a letter he wrote to his wife in 1894 while away from home: "I really believe I should get ill if I had to be away from you for a long time." He added: "When I asked you to marry me, I was very fond of you, but not very much in love with you, but I saw in *you* the person I was capable of loving most deeply, if you only returned that love. . . . I know now that I do *love* you . . . with all my heart, & am simply *devoted* to you. . . . *I adore you sweet May.*" The italics he learned from his grandmother, but the passion he learned at home. He wrote to a friend in the Royal Navy: "I am intensely happy, far happier than I ever thought I could be with anybody."

On 23 June 1894 Prince George wrote in his diary: "White Lodge, Richmond Park. At 10.0 a sweet little boy was born and weighed 8 lb. Mr. Asquith [Home Secretary] came to see him." The "sweet little boy" was the egregious future King, Edward VIII, with whom the future George V would have one of the stormiest relationships on record between a British monarch and his heir, stormier even than that between Queen Victoria and her eldest son.

Once again the Queen expressed herself vigorously on the question of names. "I am *most anxious naturally*," she wrote to the Duke of York, "that he should bear the name of his beloved Great Grandfather, a name which brought untold blessings to the whole Empire & that *Albert* should be his name." Prince George wrote back gently: "Long before our dear child was born, both May and I settled that if it was a boy we should call him Edward after darling *Eddy. This is the dearest wish of our hearts,* dearest Grandmama, for Edward is indeed a *sacred* name to us . . . of course we intend that one of his names *shall* be *Albert.*" The Queen could not help reminding her grandson that Prince Eddy's "*real* name . . . was Albert Victor." The child was eventually christened Edward Albert Christian George Andrew Patrick David, and would generally be known to the family by the last of these names.

Eighteen months later, on 14 December 1895, the Duke of York made another diary entry. This was the day on which the future George VI was born—an inauspicious day, actually, as it was the anniversary of two deaths: that of Prince Albert in 1861 and Princess Louise (daughter of Queen Victoria) in 1878. In her journal the monarch wrote of this "terrible anniversary" and of Prince George's "regret that this dear child should be born on such a sad day. I have a feeling it may be a blessing for the dear little boy and may be looked upon as a gift from God!" The Prince of Wales suggested that the child be called Albert and that the Queen should be asked to become his godmother. The Duke of York duly made the suggestion to Queen Victoria, who was unambiguously delighted by it. "Most gladly do I accept being Godmother to this dear little boy, born on the day his beloved Great Grandfather entered an even greater life," she declared. "He will be specially dear to me." The second son of Prince George was christened Albert Frederick Arthur George and called by the family—like his grandfather—Bertie. George VI, the second son of a second son, would have significantly less time than his father to prepare himself to be king when his brother suddenly abdicated after just eleven months on the throne, in 1936. But in back-to-back second sons named George, England turned out to be lucky—and lucky again to be spared the unlucky Edwards.

The Duke and Duchess of York would have four more children: Princess Mary in 1897, Prince Henry in 1900, Prince George in 1902, and Prince John in 1905.

As the father of a growing family who was not required as yet to step into the limelight, the Duke of York led a quiet and often secluded life at Sandringham during the last years of his grandmother's reign. His father coached him a bit, Princess May helped him compose his speeches, and sometimes he would talk to leading politicians of the day, but he had few official duties and did not see official papers. (For years the Queen had kept the Prince of Wales entirely out of matters of state.) Prince George was primarily a landowning sportsman, a country squire—then and later his favorite role. As John Gore has written, "The Duke and Duchess were in a backwater by choice"—his choice, not hers. They could have lived in London and been prominent in society. Generally the Duchess of York was more active and visible than her husband in these years, engaged as she was in work on behalf of various hospitals.

In November 1894 Prince George accompanied his father to Russia to attend the funeral of Alexander III ("a terrible calamity for the whole world, a more honest, generous and kind-hearted man never lived," he wrote in his diary) and the marriage the following week of Nicholas II and Princess Alexandra of Hesse. In the summer of 1895, now thirty, he was shown the new steam flying-machine built by Hiram Maxim. "It made two runs for me to see," the Duke noted. "I was in it for one of them: it did lift off the ground part of the time." The next summer brought a demonstration, in a tent, of Bert Acres's cinematoscope, constructed for "photo-electric reproductions of real life." He went to Ireland in August 1897, the year in which Queen Victoria's Diamond Jubilee was celebrated. In London, Prince George rode in the great Jubilee procession to St. Paul's. "The most wonderful crowd I ever saw . . . never heard anything like the cheering," he wrote. When Gladstone died in May 1898 the Duke of York and his father were among the pallbearers at the Westminster Abbey funeral. During that summer he served in a ship for the last time—bidding, in his diary, a brief and unemotional farewell to the Royal Navy. He preferred his life at home, where he was never seasick. June 1900: "Went in papa's new motor car. . . . The man managed it extraordinarily well."

Meanwhile the Boer War had begun late in 1899 when the two Boer republics, the Transvaal and the Orange Free State, declared war on Britain, invaded Natal, and, with only 45,000 (largely amateur) soldiers, inflicted a series of embarrassing defeats on the British Army. The government in London, led by Lord Salisbury, felt that British supremacy in southern Africa had to be reestablished and that the lucrative gold-mine industry of the Rand in the Transvaal had to be protected from the aspirations of the Afrikaners. With the help of 450,000 British troops, Lord Roberts and General French began to turn the tide against them in 1900, but the conflict remained ugly and inglorious, dragging on into 1902, inflicting 20,000 British casualties, shattering British complacency about the far-flung Empire, infuriating the British public, and provoking in Europe, which generally sided with the insurgents, a great deal of animosity against British interests around the world. Indeed, while in Brussels the Prince and Princess of Wales were shot at by a demented Belgian youth, who narrowly missed them. The last years of the nineteenth century provided a number of hints that Victorian Britain's industrial, commercial, and military supremacy were under threat, perhaps even beginning to decline. The British watched suspiciously as Germany, under the direction of Queen Victoria's grandson, built a navy to rival their own.

"Good bye Nineteenth Century," the Duke of York scribbled in his diary on 31 December 1900. Seventeen days later Queen Victoria suffered a stroke. The royal family, including the Kaiser, was called *en masse* to Osborne, on the Isle of Wight, where the Queen lay dying. On 22 January the Duke of York wrote in his diary: "our beloved Queen and Grandmama, one of the greatest women that ever lived, passed peacefully away, surrounded by her sorrowing children and grandchildren. She. . . called each of us by name and we took leave of her and kissed her hand, it was terribly distressing . . . I shall never forget the scene in her room with all of us sobbing and heartbroken around her bed." A few hours after the Queen's demise the family was once again summoned to the death chamber. "And there she lay," says Prince George's diary, "covered with flowers." At the very end the Queen extracted a promise from the Prince of Wales that he would never, in any way, change Osborne House, which had been designed by Prince Albert for his family. The first order given by the new King outlined a series of alterations to be made to Osborne House. Immediately upon his mother's death he dropped his first name (Albert) and announced he would be called King Edward VII. He was fifty-nine, tired of waiting, tired of all the criticism and notoriety, embittered and depressed. Suddenly the Duke of York was no longer heir presumptive to the British throne: he was next in line.

IV

On the day after the old Queen's death, the Duke of York became the first Briton to swear allegiance to the new monarch. "Papa made a beautiful speech in which he said that he wished to be called Edward VII," Prince George noted. For the next ten months he himself would be called Duke of York and Cornwall—and after that, Prince of Wales. Two days after Victoria's death, still at Osborne, "we all received Holy Communion in darling Grandmama's room, with Her lying in our midst," the Prince recorded in his diary. With increased responsibilities, his staff was now expanded to include a private secretary. It was a fortunate appointment. Sir Arthur Bigge was an experienced hand who had served the late Queen in a similar capacity for some years. He would remain in the service of George V until his death in 1931.

The Duke and Duchess of York had for some time been scheduled to undertake an arduous, eight-month journey to Australia, commencing in the spring of 1901. They were to open the first Commonwealth Parliament in Melbourne and deliver in person the thanks of the Empire to its dominions and colonies for their support of the British cause in the ongoing South African war. Prince George did not want to leave England, and his father did not want him to go; but Lord Salisbury insisted that the visit go forward, and go forward it did. Prince George preferred not to part from his parents, his children, and his cottage; the government's decision devastated him. On the day of departure in March, he noted in his diary: "I was very much affected and could hardly speak. The leave-taking was terrible . . . when I said goodbye [to his parents] broke down quite."

During this trip the Duke and Duchess visited not only Australia but also New Zealand, Tasmania, Gibraltar, Malta, Aden, Ceylon, Singapore, and Mauritius. On the voyage home the royal party stopped in South Africa, where the war dragged on, and were met by Lord Kitchener. They returned to England in November, via Canada and Newfoundland. Prince George was thus seen by a great many whose ruler, at least in title, he would become just nine years later. His favorite new acquaintance turned out to be the Prime Minister of New Zealand, Mr. Seddon, whose speech and tastes were as homely as the Duke of York's and who, it was said, had never read a book in his life. They must have had a lot in common. New Zealand had early on become a sort of socialist welfare state. The heir to the throne found this introduction to his future realm generally informative and enlightening. In a speech in December at the Guildhall, the Prince of Wales—as he had become in November, on his father's sixtieth birthday—attracted much press attention when he declared that "the Old Country must wake up if she intends to maintain her old position of pre-eminence in her Colonial trade against foreign competitors." "Wake up, England!" proclaimed the next day's newspapers.

The new King decided not to repeat his mother's policy of keeping her successor ignorant of and detached from all possible matters of state. On the contrary, as historian Denis Judd has said, Edward VII opened all official secrets to his son and heir, striving to instill in him a measure of self-confidence in the exercise of statecraft and to give, with the help of Sir Arthur Bigge, some much-needed coaching to a temperament by nature unimaginative, cautious, conventional, and potentially rigid.

As Prince of Wales, Prince George now had the use of Marlborough House in London and Osborne House on the Isle of Wight as city and country residences; he preferred, however, to go on living at his Sandringham cottage, a preview of his quiet habits as king. He "disliked large houses, and the hospitality required of their owner," as Rose has said. Several times King Edward would come across some quietly decaying country house that he would pronounce just right for the Prince of Wales and his family, only to be told by his son that he preferred to go on living at Sandringham. The only house in the country the Prince and Princess of Wales both liked and visited regularly was Frogmore, near Windsor, where the Queen and the Prince Consort were finally reunited in death. When Princess May wished to redecorate Marlborough House, which had been Edward's chief residence for forty years, the monarch was annoyed. Wasn't his taste acceptable? His taste, remarked the Princess of Wales, was not the point: "Surely he must know we really cannot go into a filthy dirty house, not even to oblige him." She restored the place to its eighteenth-century elegance and stripped away its Victorian accretions. It is possible that the King and Queen never quite forgave her for this—though they themselves were busily removing all traces of the previous occupant from Buckingham Palace and putting their own stamp upon it.

The next significant undertaking of the Prince of Wales was a good-will trip to Berlin in January 1902, ostensibly to help his cousin, the Kaiser, celebrate a birthday but in fact an attempt to keep relations cordial between an increasingly bellicose Germany and an increasingly resentful Britain. The visit went well—as far as it went; and the Prince of Wales, now thirty-six, was pronounced by his hosts to be genial and pleasant. The German

Chancellor, Prince Bülow, described him as "clear-headed, sensible and manly." Diplomacy and international affairs were never the strong suits of Prince George, but he could play the role he was assigned by the government of the day. Unlike his eldest son, he did what he was asked to do. He did not, for example, inquire about the wisdom of the British alliances made in these years with Russia and France; that was the government's business, and his father's. He would trust them.

After the coronation of Edward VII in the summer of 1902—"He is able to see everything that goes on with glasses," noted the Prince of Wales—Prince George inherited some of his father's old duties and titles and revenues, and his official activities were expanded again. These included additional travel, which the future George V always abhorred. He would have liked to stay at home. Nonetheless did he pay a state visit to the Emperor of Austria in the spring of 1904. "My goodness," his diary complains, "this Court is stiff!" There were also visits to provincial British cities, the conferring and receiving of university degrees, the opening of hospitals and bridges and docks, the reception of important visitors. He continued to prefer his country cottage to any other place and escaped to it as often as he could. While in Norfolk he tried to muffle himself away from the country's affairs. This was not always possible, of course. One morning in October 1904 he opened his newspaper to discover that Russia, which was at war with Japan, had ordered its Baltic fleet to fire upon some British fishing craft in the North Sea, near Hull; they were mistakenly thought to be Japanese warships. "It seems impossible that individuals who call themselves sailors should do such a thing," the Prince wrote to his father. "They must have been drunk." Fair play and the sailor's profession had been violated as well as England's territorial waters, and this roused the marine Prince from his rural torpor.

During his years as Prince of Wales, his family and the King's would spend Christmas and New Year's together at Sandringham. In April the court moved to Windsor and then to Buckingham Palace until June. Ascot, the Goodwood races, and sailing at Cowes were annual summer events. In late summer and early autumn they all went to Balmoral for the shooting. There was more shooting at Sandringham later in the autumn, the entertainment of foreign dignitaries largely at Windsor, occasional visits to private houses. At Windsor the Prince of Wales was given a desk next to the monarch's; this had not happened in the previous reign. The King obviously doted on his son, hated to be separated from him, and rejoiced each time they were rejoined after an absence. Different as they were, there was perfect confidence between them and a great deal of affection. The Prince could not tolerate criticism of his father. The only known complaint he addressed to the King, typically, was that the bowling alley at Sandringham had been turned into a library. Prince George found this inexplicable.

Through it all he thought of his cottage. Sandringham, the future Edward VIII would write later, "possessed most of the ingredients for a boyhood idyll." In this, at least, he agreed with his father, though in later years George's son was prone to collect country houses and live away from Sandringham. At Sandringham Prince George's family, detached from public scrutiny, could ride bicycles, play golf, learn to shoot (of course), and behave unroyally. Choosing to spend so much of their time in the small house at Sandringham, the Prince and Princess saw a good deal more of their children than did many of their well-heeled contemporaries. As Rose has said, Prince George "was a watchful and exacting father who let nothing go by default. His early years in the navy had trained him to instant submission and he saw no reason why his own sons should not benefit from the same discipline." The future George VI received from his father the following birthday letter: "Now that you are five years old, I hope you will always try and be obedient and do at once what you are told, as you will find it will come much easier to you the sooner you begin." As for the eldest son and heir: "The Navy will teach David all that he needs to know." Though the Navy certainly had not taught Prince George all that he needed to know—indeed, only the tiniest fraction of it—he saw no reason to tamper with the plan chosen by his father for him. And so he decided to keep his sons at home until they were old enough to become naval cadets. They had private tutors; by their own accounts they learned, like their father, practically nothing as boys. Typically, the future George V discovered the mathematical shortcomings of his heir only when the latter, at Balmoral, proved unable to calculate the average weight of the stags shot during the season.

The available evidence suggests that Princess May—the future Queen Mary—whatever her other admirable qualities, and though interested in the abstract in the treatment of children, particularly at schools and hospitals, took no interest at all in her own children when they were very young. As they grew up, however, she regretted the shortcomings of their education and tried to do something about it. "See how George has suffered from not knowing French and German," she said of her husband. "The other day in Paris *I* enjoyed everything. But *he* was not really amused. He knows nothing about pictures or history. He is told something about Francis I, and it conveys nothing to him. He could not follow the plays easily, and it is a great pity." Princess May was always an enthusiastic linguist—years later, listening to a broadcast by Hitler, she was struck by his dreadful German— and she wanted her sons as adolescents to learn languages and history. She was particularly impatient with the careless way in which Prince Albert's education was being supervised: "Look at William IV—he was a long way from the throne, yet he succeeded." In later years, at his wife's urging, Prince George relented and allowed his sons to attend public schools and universities. The twelve-year-old Prince Henry, at school, received the following rebuke from his mother: "Do for goodness sake wake up and work harder and use the brains God has given you. . . . All you write about is your everlasting football of which I am heartily sick."

Between October 1905 and May 1906 the Prince and Princess of Wales visited India and Burma. They drew huge and respectful but largely silent crowds wherever they went. The Viceroy's private secretary wrote of the royal visitor: "he has distinct ability, great shrewdness and a wonderful memory." It could have been worse. When asked about it, the Prince said he did not think Indians should play a larger role in the country's administration. Publicly he pooh-poohed the embryonic Indian nationalism and the leadership of Gandhi: "loyalty to the Throne" was what the people everywhere demonstrated, he wrote to his father. Still, he perceived that opinions and customs were slowly changing—how could he fail to?—and noted in his diary that "we are too much inclined to look upon them as a conquered & down-trodden race & the Native, who is becoming more and more educated, realizes this." He also thought the "natives" were treated rudely and unsympathetically by the resident British, and said so. Like his grandmother and his father, he seems to have harbored no color prejudices, which could not be said of the vast majority of his future subjects. When he got back to England and made a speech on India, Prince George appealed for "a wider sympathy" on the part of administrators for their subjects. He emphasized how important it was for Britons in India "to break down prejudice, to dispel misapprehension and to foster sympathy and brotherhood." These were progressive, nearly radical sentiments in 1906. Indeed, the Prince's private sentiments were even more startling. "Personally I think we have now come to the parting of the ways," he wrote of India to a private friend. "We cannot let things rest as they are. We must . . . trust the Natives more and give them a greater share in the Government or anyhow allow them to express their views."

The extent of the Prince's comparatively progressive views were now to be tested in another arena. In January 1906 the Liberal party, pledged to social reform, won its famous landslide (and last) election victory and ejected the Tories from Whitehall after two decades in office. It was the end of Balfour and the advent of Campbell-Bannerman and Asquith and Lloyd George and Winston Churchill (then a Liberal, afterward to lose his Manchester seat) and Sir Edward Grey and John Morley. These new ministers were not all to Prince George's taste. He pronounced Asquith to be "not quite a gentleman," a remark for which he later had to apologize, and referred to Lloyd George as "that damned fellow." And there was more. In the general election of 1906 the Labour party had won fifty-three seats: for the first time it was a political power in the land. Prince George called this development "a dangerous sign"; publicly he remarked of the new Labour members, "I hope they are not all Socialists." Social welfare, women's suffrage, industrial conflict, and Ireland (as always) were among the chief issues of the day: "The revolt of the internal and external proletariat had begun," as Nicolson puts it. "We are face to face," said the defeated Balfour, "with the Socialist difficulties which loom so large on the Continent. Unless I am greatly mistaken the election of 1906 inaugurates a new era." He was not greatly mistaken. Indeed, the issues and controversies of 1906 were to persist into the reign of George V, in the first years of which an unprecedented constitutional crisis arose. But not yet.

That a new era had begun was brought home to Prince George in a different context in May 1906. He and Princess May escaped an anarchist's bomb thrown at King Alfonso XIII of Spain and his bride, yet another cousin of the British royal family, just after their marriage; the Prince and Princess of Wales were representing Edward VII in Madrid. Twenty people were killed, but the royals escaped injury. The Prince's verdict on the affair: "Of course the bomb was thrown by an anarchist, supposed to be a Spaniard and of course they let him escape. I believe the Spanish police and detectives are about the worst in the world. No precaution whatever had been taken." Less than two years later the King and Crown Prince of Portugal would be assassinated by rifle bullets as they were driving in an open carriage in Lisbon: a new era indeed. While in Madrid, Prince George celebrated his forty-first birthday. Upon his return to England he was delighted, though he could hardly have been surprised, to learn that his eldest son had won a nomination for the Royal Navy and, following his father's path, was about to become a cadet. In the next year Bertie joined David, replicating the experience of Prince George and his brother Eddy three decades earlier.

During the last few years of King Edward's reign his heir interested himself more comprehensively in military matters. Beginning with the Anglo-German naval rivalry, the arms race accelerated all over Europe and tensions mounted. If his German cousin invaded Britain, Prince George wondered, could he be resisted? He argued for a stronger Home Guard and a better-trained army. Cabinet ministers were struck by "the sober and thoughtful manner in which the Prince expressed . . . carefully considered opinions" and his "sound common sense, coupled with . . . shrewd appreciation of the various problems, both naval and military." During one of his inspection tours the Prince, considered an expert on naval matters, was taken on board a submarine at Portsmouth, much to the dismay of his wife, who remained on the dock. "I shall be very disappointed if George doesn't come up again," she was heard to murmur.

In the summer of 1908 the Prince of Wales visited Canada again, on his way home helping to stoke the engines of the steamship H.M.S. *Indomitable,* of the new cruiser class of ships being built to keep pace with the German navy. He emerged black with coal dust and was cheered by the crew. Returning home, he found the country embroiled in a controversy that was to spill over into the next reign and present him, as king, with one of his greatest challenges. The House of Lords, with its Conservative majority, was exercising its veto power over almost every piece of progressive legislation emerging out of the Liberal House of Commons. In 1909 the Commons assented to Lloyd George's "People's Budget," which raised taxes on the wealthy in order to pay for old-age pensions and improvements in the Royal Navy; a new land tax was imposed as part of the package. Traditionally the Lords was not supposed to reject, or even amend, the Budget. But this time it did so, and the stage was set for the debate the times demanded: Was the Lords' veto a threat to or a guarantee of constitutional government? The issue was debated on into 1910, with a much reduced Liberal majority in the Commons after the general election of that year. Indeed, so thin was the new majority that the Liberals found themselves having to depend on the support of the Labour and Irish members in order to survive. This did not diminish the controversy. The Asquith government promised now, in the face of a threatened stalemate, to "define the relations between the Houses of Parliament, so as to secure the undivided authority of the House of Commons over finance and its predominance in legislation." It brought in a Parliament Bill that deleted the Lords' veto over money bills and guaranteed that bills passed by the Commons in three successive sessions should become law without the assent of the Lords. Asquith warned the Lords not to reject his bill. If they did, he said, he would flood the Lords with enough Liberal peers to create a new majority. The Conservative majority in the Lords condemned the Parliament Bill and the People's Budget as pieces of confiscatory socialism, threatened to reject them despite the warnings of the Prime Minister, and accused Asquith of conducting a war on property. At this interesting moment, however, parliamentary politics was unexpectedly thrust out of the spotlight.

After being out on the Sandringham estate in cold weather on 1 May 1910, King Edward developed a bad cold and then acute bronchitis. The Prince of Wales went to Buckingham Palace to see him. "His colour was bad & his breathing fast . . . talking makes him cough," he noted in his diary. The King characteristically refused to modify his rigorous schedule, and the doctors feared heart failure. Queen Alexandra was summoned from Greece, where she was visiting. The monarch continued to ignore all medical advice. "I shall work to the end," he remarked fatalistically. And so he did, continuing to smoke cigars one after another in the teeth, as it were, of his bronchitis. During the next two days the sixty-nine-year-old Edward VII grew much worse, and then suffered a series of heart attacks. He died just before midnight on 6 May, having done a great deal to increase the popularity of the monarchy during his short reign.

Prince George wrote in his diary: "I have lost my best friend & the best of fathers. I never had a word with him in his life. I am heartbroken & overwhelmed with grief, but God will help me in my great responsibilities &

darling May will be my comfort as she always has been. May God give me strength & guidance in the heavy task which has fallen on me." He had been lucky to have a father who was also a friend—a piece of luck his father had not had. A few weeks shy of his forty-fifth birthday, George Frederick Ernest Albert had inherited what his grandmother was fond of calling "the greatest position there is."

V

And so the second Georgian age began in the midst of violent and bitter party warfare in Parliament, with desperate problems in Ireland and in the trade unions requiring solution, at a moment in history when the poor in England were perhaps never so poor and the rich never so rich, and with the country having to face for the first time in many years a hungry and powerful and aggressive military power on the seas it once easily dominated. The Prime Minister was not particularly sanguine about the political future. "I felt bewildered and indeed stunned," Asquith recalled, when he heard of the death of Edward VII. "At a most anxious moment in the fortunes of the State, we had lost, without warning or preparation, the Sovereign whose ripe experience, trained sagacity, equitable judgment and unvarying consideration, counted for so much. . . . Now he had gone. His successor, with all his fine and engaging qualities, was without political experience. We were nearing the verge of a crisis almost without example in our constitutional history."

It has been said that during his reign King George V established a new meaning for the term constitutional monarchy. There can be little doubt that he strengthened the throne in terms of its place in the hearts of his people, both by the role he played in the political affairs of the nation and the affection he commanded and held among his subjects in the Empire. One could argue that, for the British monarchy, his reign was the most salutary in three centuries. During the twenty-six years George V sat on the throne, five empires, eight monarchies, and eighteen minor dynasties went out of existence, as Nicolson reminds us, but the British monarchy was stronger in 1936 than it was in 1910. Though it may have appeared in 1910 that the new King was badly prepared by education and temperament to grapple with and respond to a constitutional crisis, a world war, economic depression, labor strikes, and the end of empire, the fact is that he turned out to be, for England, the right man in the right place at the right time. Short (five foot six) and slim (147 pounds), he did not favor the raised heels used by his father to increase his height. Never a flashy personality—to put it mildly— in many ways conventional and even stodgy, almost entirely uncultured (Henry James called him at his accession "an arch-vulgarian"), this man found within himself the nerve and the sense to help lead his nation through a series of dire crises, the first two of which—a constitutional impasse and a war—had to be faced at the beginning of his reign. Britons saw his steadiness, his honesty, his desire to act strictly in accordance with the oath he took as a constitutional monarch, and applauded him. They also enjoyed his sense of humor. "Mind you give me a good big V," Rose reports he told the sculptor responsible for designing the first coinage of the new reign. "I don't want to be mistaken for any of the other Georges." Surely one reason the nation grew so impatient so quickly with the next monarch, Edward VIII, was that the differences in quality and character were so immediately apparent between the new King and his predecessor.

Thick volumes are routinely written about just a few years of the history of a nation and its leaders. George V was to reign until 1936 and participate in some of the most crucial and influential events of the twentieth century. Here, however, little more than the most cursory summary of the reign's significant moments can be considered, for George V is just one of the "Georgians" under our scrutiny.

In May 1910 the remains of Edward VII were buried at Windsor after a service attended by, among others, the Kaiser, the kings of Denmark, Portugal, Spain, Norway, Belgium, Greece, and Bulgaria, the Dowager Empress of Russia (Queen Alexandra's sister), Archduke Franz Ferdinand of Austria, former President Theodore Roosevelt, and assorted heads of state and royal heirs apparent. The late King's pet terrier, Rose tells us, was given a place in the funeral procession directly behind the coffin, causing the Kaiser to observe that he had never before been obliged to yield precedence to a dog. Well: the British love dogs more than kaisers.

Ten days after his accession the King complained that he could not sleep. "He wakes about five and finds himself making notes of things which lie before him in his day's work," a courtier wrote in his diary. Lloyd George, who saw the new monarch in his first days as King George V, reported that he "talked a good deal about his father of whom he was evidently very fond . . . his eyes suffused with tears." Queen Mary, as she was now addressed, wrote to a friend: "I regret the quieter, easier time we had, everything will be more difficult now and more ceremonious."

A few days into his reign the new King met with the Prime Minister. Asquith asked him to agree to the swamping of the House of Lords with enough new Liberal peers—he wanted to create five-hundred—to pass the Parliament Bill in the upper house; he would, he said, resign if he was refused. So immediately upon his accession George V was faced with what Nicolson calls "an unprecedented constitutional problem of which he had little previous knowledge and in which he was accorded no consistent guidance."

The King's advisors were divided in their counsels; and there were few if any historical models to follow in this crisis. Yet the monarch must come to a timely decision as to what his constitutional duty was. After much thought King George replied that if another election was called, and if the results of it gave a clear mandate for Asquith's position, he himself would act constitutionally—that is, on the advice of the Prime Minister. He asked that this guarantee be kept secret until after the election. "I disliked having to do this very much," read the stark but characteristically understated diary note. "I have never been accustomed to conceal things." Still, the verdict of history is that his decision was inspired. It was his own and, like the man, simple and sensible and not terribly sophisticated. Indeed, the King chose the only course open to him that led eventually to a satisfactory solution of the problem rather than exacerbation of it. It also should be noted that when he agreed to the creation of the peers if necessary, he suggested that they be life peers rather than hereditary ones, an idea whose time was to come half a century later. Late in the year (1910) another general election was held, and Asquith's Liberal government returned with a clear majority—including, once again, Labour and Irish members. The Parliament Bill would be brought up in the next session of Parliament in 1911.

That first autumn of the new reign, spent largely at Balmoral, witnessed a number of changes. Whereas King Edward's court had been lively and without a great deal of attention paid to virtue, King George's was dull, domestically oriented, and respectable—in a word, Victorian; so said the courtiers and hangers-on, anyway. One wrote: "It is altogether different here from former years. There is no longer the old atmosphere around the house—that curious electric element which pervaded the surroundings of King Edward. Yet everything is very charming and wholesome and sweet. The house is a home for children—six of them at luncheon—the youngest running round the table all the while. The Queen knits of an evening. Not a sign of 'bridge'." Remarked another witness: "How times change. A small party. Very peaceful life, enormously punctual in contrast to former years. Everything very orderly. . . . Not even bridge, so that the evenings are rather tedious." Bridge was called up whenever Asquith—an addict of the game, and a sometime partner of Henry James—was in the house; otherwise the court was organized around the children and the obsession with punctuality and order of the new royal couple. From Balmoral, Lloyd George wrote to his wife during that first autumn: "The King is a very jolly chap but thank God there's not much in his head. They're simple, very, very ordinary people, and perhaps . . . that's how it should be." Of the royal couple's politics, Lloyd George's is perhaps not an objective or even an accurate account, but here is part of it: "The King is hostile to the bone to all who are working to lift the workmen out of the mire. So is the Queen. They talk exactly as the late King and Kaiser talked. . . . 'What do they want striking?' 'They are well paid', etc."

At Balmoral the King and his family enjoyed the simple and healthy life of the country. Churchill, who often used his room at Balmoral as a studio for painting, "took particular care"—he said—"to leave no spots on the Victorian tartans." Queen Mary never liked Balmoral, whose weather brought on her neuritis; she called living there "sitting on a mountain." And she detested the tartan decor. Because it was rural and relatively small, King George enjoyed the place. He hated Buckingham Palace; it was not for him, he said. Indeed, he proposed pulling it down, turning its gardens into a public park, and when in London living in the more modest Kensington Palace instead. Nothing came of this. Windsor was less offensive to him, being more countrified than Buckingham Palace: he could be informal there. At Windsor he could ride, play golf, and walk around the gardens with his children; all of this was more difficult and complicated to arrange at Buckingham Palace. One guest compared staying at Windsor when the King was there to visiting a quiet vicarage: "The evenings were tedious." In his "Ballade Tragique à Double Refrain," Max Beerbohm referred to the fashionable world's abhorrence of the new régime in an imaginary exchange between two courtiers:

HE:
> Last evening
> I found him with a rural dean
> Talking of District Visiting. . . .
> The King is duller than the Queen.

SHE:
> At any rate he doesn't sew;
> You don't see him embellishing
> Yard after yard of calico. . . .
> The Queen is duller than the King.
> Oh, to have been an underling
> To [say] the Empress Josephine.

Society was disappointed in George V. He did not like parties, he did not like visiting fashionable houses, he did not drink very much, he did not chase after ladies: "I'm not interested in any wife except my own," he remarked. All of this of course was a huge departure from his father's habits. What fashionable people hoped would turn out to be the new monarch's strong Toryism was instead revealed to be a tenacious and independent will altogether unsusceptible to fashionable influences.

For King George and Queen Mary, Sandringham was still home, and the King always looked forward to returning to the cottage there. (In the early years of his reign, until her death in 1925, Queen Alexandra continued to occupy the main house.) "A glum little villa" the cottage might well seem to Harold Nicolson, but for George V it was home. Yes, it was furnished largely with things bought retail in Tottenham Court Road; yes, on the walls hung mostly reproductions. The new King did not care. Here he could be himself; and anyway he hated change, especially of the domestic variety. Queen Mary, who as always put up cheerfully with her husband's foibles, called the cottage at Sandringham "a doll's house," but made few objections to living there whenever they were able to do so. There was no study; the King conducted business in his bedroom, and anyone waiting to see him sat on a chair in the hall outside it. The drawing-room was tiny; the odor of whatever was being cooked in the kitchen pervaded the place at all times. The servants had to board out; the King admitted he had no idea where they went at night. He hated ostentation—almost as much as he hated entertaining. At the cottage he could be unostentatious and avoid parties or guests. Here too he could indulge in his favorite pastime of shooting birds—thousands every week, as many as a thousand a day. And yet, oddly, King George loved animals; a visitor to Windsor noted that when the King saw a dead bird in the garden there, tears came to his eyes. One less bird for him to shoot? No. There was sport, and there was life, and for the King these were, simply, different worlds. He would have been horrified had anyone accused him of cruelty to animals. Nor did he forget the more humble humans around him. Almost immediately upon his accession he raised the wages of his servants and laborers. This caused a strike: they wanted more. The King's Norfolk neighbors considered him a destabilizing local influence.

"The most terrible ordeal I have ever got through," said George V after he opened Parliament for the first time in February 1911. In June came the coronation: 50,000 troops under the command of Kitchener lined the streets, crowded with hundreds of thousands of would-be spectators. "I nearly broke down when dear David came to do homage to me, as it reminded me so much of when I did the same thing to beloved Papa, he did it so well," the new monarch wrote in his diary. For others the coronation was merely an inconvenience. "No more London for me till the timber is gone, & the huge disfigurements are a little obliterated," Thomas Hardy wrote to a friend; he was annoyed by the decorations and viewing stands placed all over the capital.

During the hot summer of 1911 the battle between the two houses of Parliament was rejoined and reached its final phase. The King's promise of the previous year to authorize the creation of additional Liberal peers if Asquith retained his majority was attacked by the Conservatives when it was revealed after the election. They argued that the Prime Minister had wrongfully and unconstitutionally forced King George to give promises that aided one political party: the Liberals and their allies. The crown, its prestige and its prerogative, was being systematically humiliated by the Liberals, they said. Should the monarch, the Tories asked, be coerced by the threat of a government's resignation into being the administration's puppet? King George's diary reveals that he was "greatly distressed and worried" by the controversy. The Prime Minister could not speak in the Commons without being howled down. During a particularly acrimonious debate, Lloyd George described the House of Lords as "Mr. Balfour's poodle"— Balfour was still the Conservative leader: "It fetches and carries for him. It barks for him. It bites anybody that he sets it on to." It was true that the Conservatives had nothing to fear from the Lords, since the upper house in this period always had a Conservative majority. But the Liberals, as Rose says, "lived in the shadow of the veto; holding office by the expressed will of the people, they governed only by the consent of a few hundred Tory landowners." The Liberals argued, accurately, that the Tory majority in the Lords was thwarting the wishes of the electorate. Between 1906 and 1911 the Lords rejected outright all of the government's proposed measures of reform—in education, in the church, in tax policy, in attempts to deal with social problems caused by alcoholism.

We have seen how the rejection of the People's Budget occasioned two general elections, leaving the Liberals in power after them. The voters wanted these measures passed, and the King understood this. He now went to work persuading the Conservatives in the upper house to assent to the Parliament Bill. Don't force me, he said in effect, to create five-hundred Liberal peers; but I will if I have to. When the Lords finally took up the bill, the King's promise that he would do what the government asked to assure the bill's passage if it was defeated in the Lords brought about its reluctant acceptance in the upper house, aided by the last-minute support of a group of Conservative peers. The King was delighted—and relieved that he would not, after all, have to create all those new peerages. At any rate, he had done his constitutional duty as he saw it, and helped Asquith and Lloyd George force the House of Lords to vote away its own veto.

In the resolution of the crisis, what Nicolson calls King George's "remarkable gift for conciliation" played an important role. It is also clear that George V understood quite well the nature of a constitutional monarchy. "A constitutional monarch," as Rose observes, "rejects ministerial advice at his peril, however unreasonable or distasteful it seems to him." Had the King refused to accept Asquith's advice, the government would have resigned and the crown itself would have become an issue in the ensuing election. The actions of the King in this crisis, because they were inspired and correct, and despite much criticism, were protective of the crown itself. Had the King, like the House of Lords, attempted to defy the House of Commons and its elected leaders, it might have meant the end of the royal prerogative—and, for better or worse, perhaps of royalty itself in England.

One last point here. Had the Conservatives driven the Liberals from office in the elections of 1910, inevitably they would have held the King to the promise they said he had no right to make (that is, to create the new peers only if the Liberals won), and the question of the new Liberal peers would have become moot. So the Torys' quarrel in fact was not with the King's conduct but rather with the sentiments of the voters.

The last months of 1911 and the early months of 1912 witnessed a series of devastating labor strikes, chief among them work stoppages by railroad workers and coal miners. In these strikes, the first of a sort that were to become all too familiar to the British over the next seven decades, the sympathies of the monarch, surprisingly enough, and despite Lloyd George's (largely inaccurate) estimate of the King's politics, were almost always with the workers. This could not have been the case in any previous reign. King George worried about the hardships suffered by the workers' families, about animosity between the classes and the wide economic gulf between them. During his reign he frequently visited industrial centers and even working-class families; he seemed to feel more at home with them than in the grand country houses of his aristocratic neighbors. By the time of his death the average British laborer undoubtedly felt a greater solidarity with the crown than with any recent government. "No British Monarch before his time," says Nicolson of George V, "had manifested so constant, or so obviously sincere, a liking for his poorer subjects." And the affection would be reciprocated.

VI

The brief visit of the King and Queen to India in 1911-12 was motivated primarily by the desire of George V, at a time of international tensions growing at least in part out of the expanding and sometimes conflicting appetites of European powers for overseas colonies, to underscore his interest in the British Empire and its subjects. He resolved, after his coronation in London, to go to Delhi and be crowned Emperor there. The government hesitated; its enthusiasm for the venture was not enhanced by the King's insistence, in the face of widespread terrorist attacks upon crowned heads, that "all classes should have a chance of seeing him at close hand." But it gave way at last, subject to the ancient rule that no one, not even a king, was allowed to take the crown out of the kingdom. So a new, imperial crown had to be manufactured expressly for this journey and this event. It was paid for, but not owned or retained by, the people of India; the imperial diadem accompanied the King back to England and ended its days on a shelf in the Tower.

The royal couple departed in November 1911, the Queen industriously reading Kipling, and returned to England in February 1912. On the day of the imperial coronation the King appeared on a small brown horse and wearing the uniform of a field marshal and an immense white sun-helmet. He rode with a large suite of gentlemen similarly attired. Mystified by this parade of identical personages, the Indian spectators failed to recognize the Emperor altogether—though George V had come among them expressly to be seen. Subsequently in the tour more care was taken, and wherever the King and Queen went thousands prostrated themselves on the ground. That was more like it. "It is a matter of intense gratification to me," said King George, "to realize how all classes and creeds have joined together in . . . welcome." This unique event seems to have had no impact whatsoever on the history of India, except perhaps to remind one and all that the Empire had an administration. A week after the royal couple's departure a bomb was thrown at the Viceroy, killing one of his servants. The King spent his last few weeks in India shooting at tigers and rhinos from the top of an elephant.

One of his first duties upon his return to England was to entertain at Buckingham Palace the Austrian Archduke Franz Ferdinand and his wife the Duchess of Hohenberg. "They are both charming & made themselves very pleasant," the King wrote blandly in his diary. A series of labor disputes and strikes punctuated the rest of 1912. "Really we have no luck, one tiresome thing after another," wrote Queen Mary. The Prince of Wales, meanwhile, went off to Magdalen College, Oxford.

The King of Greece was assassinated in March 1913. This did not prevent King George and Queen Mary from journeying to Berlin in May to be present at the marriage of the Kaiser's only daughter to a Brunswick duke. The Russian Tsar was also there, and the Kaiser spent much of the time attempting to insure that his British and Russian kinsmen, allied by treaties against him, were never alone together to discuss the present state of Europe. He complained publicly that the British should not be "making alliances with a decadent nation like France and a semi-barbarous nation like Russia and opposing us, the true upholders of progress and liberty." He was reminding one and all that England and Germany were protestant powers and that the others were not. The Kaiser also announced that as a grandson of Queen Victoria he would never allow Britain to be attacked at sea. "I am a man of peace, but . . . whoever falls on me I can crush," he said. The King wrote in a private letter: "The Germans suspect that there are English spies everywhere. Yet we have no secret service funds, or at least they are much smaller than those of any other State, and our spies are the worst and clumsiest in the world"—an early but not inappropriate characterization of the British espionage establishment in the twentieth century.

In England, meanwhile, feminist militancy was on the rise. At the Derby in 1913 a suffragette threw herself under the King's horse and was killed. The extent of the Queen's sympathy for the women's movement may be gauged by her concern for the jockey: "poor Jones . . . was much knocked about." In 1913-14 King George was also preoccupied with the latest Home Rule crisis in Ireland. Civil war there seemed a distinct possibility; Protestant Ulster refused to accept rule by any Dublin parliament, raised a large army, and solicited (and received) the support of some influential Englishmen, including sections of the Tory party—Kipling, Lord Roberts, and Edward Elgar among others. The government wrestled with the question, which persisted into the 1920s, of whether to exclude Ulster from Home

Rule. In July 1914 a conference at Buckingham Palace failed to resolve the Irish crisis, just as all other such conferences had failed. Now, however, other events intruded, and the current showdown over Irish Home Rule was postponed once again. For in June occurred the assassination at Sarajevo of the King's recent houseguests, the Austrian Archduke and his wife. While attending the Buckingham Palace conference in July, the Speaker of the House of Commons, Mr. James William Lowther (later Lord Ullswater), picked up a copy of the evening paper and to his horror read of the Austrian ultimatum to Serbia. Russia declared that it would defend the Serbs against the Austrians; Germany announced it would support its ally, Austria; France sided with its ally, Russia. Britain was allied with France; by a treaty of 1830 it was also a guarantor of Belgian neutrality.

The violent death of Franz Ferdinand did not immediately strike King George as politically significant: used to news of assassinations by now, the sovereign's only comment in his diary lamented the "terrible shock for the dear old Emperor" of Austria. By the end of July the King had been enlightened by the Foreign Secretary, Sir Edward Grey. "It looks," the monarch wrote in his diary, "as if we were on the verge of a European War caused by sending an ultimatum to Serbia by Austria." His diary entries for the next few crucial days in the world's history (July 29-August 4) speak for themselves:

Austria has declared war on Servia. Where will it end? Winston Churchill came to see me, the Navy is all ready for War, but please God it will not come. These are very anxious days. . . . Saw Sir Edward Grey. Germany declared War on Russia. . . . Whether we shall be dragged into it God only knows . . . I think it will be impossible to keep out of it as we cannot allow France to be smashed. We issued orders to mobilise the Fleet. . . . Saw Winston Churchill who told me the Navy was absolutely ready for war & all the ships mobilised. . . . We were forced to go & show ourselves on the balcony [at Buckingham Palace] three different times . . . tremendous cheering. . . . Public opinion . . . that we should not allow Germany to pass through English Channel & that we should not allow her troops to pass through Belgium . . . now everyone is for war & our helping our friends. Orders for mobilisation of the army will be issued at once. . . . Winston Churchill came to report . . . that . . . we had sent an ultimatum to Germany that if by midnight tonight [August 4] she did not give a satisfactory answer about her troops passing through Belgium . . . [we would] declare War with Germany, it is a terrible catastrophe but it is not our fault. . . . When they heard that War had been declared the excitement increased & it was a never to be forgotten sight when May & I with David went on the balcony, the cheering was terrific. Please God it may soon be over & that He will protect dear Bertie's life.

The future George VI was now serving in the Royal Navy.

So Russia mobilized to defend Serbia against Austria, and Germany declared war on Russia and its ally France. The British government announced that it would keep its word: that is, it would abide by its French treaty and by the older one that guaranteed Belgian neutrality. In a poignant moment Sir Edward Grey, who in the midst of all the uncertainty had made a speech that convinced his reluctant colleagues in the House of Commons that British neutrality in the present crisis would not be possible, looked out the window of his Whitehall office on the evening of that fateful August 4 as the gas lamps were dimmed. "The lights are going out all over Europe," he said. "We shall not see them lit again in our lifetime." And so it began.

The King could not, of course, help conduct the war itself, but he could influence events and people, and so he did during the four difficult years that followed the outbreak of hostilities in August 1914. Some of his activities were routine for royalty in such circumstances; some were not. Nicolson reports that while the war lasted, King George paid seven visits to the fleet, made five trips to the entrenched army in France, held 450 military inspections, toured 300 hospitals, and personally conferred 50,000 decorations. He visited industrial areas and factories and chatted with civilians injured by bombs. Both of George V's sons served on active duty. While in the Navy, Prince Albert (Bertie) participated in the Battle of Jutland. The Prince of Wales served as an army staff officer in France and Italy; it was said of him that he liked to take risks.

A detailed account of the Great War cannot be given here, but we may get a flavoring of these years from the King's perspective. This was perhaps his most testing time. When the war began, as Gore has written, King George's "qualities of kingship and leadership were still but half proved. When it ended, the Empire over which he ruled had acclaimed him a great leader and a great king." There is some exaggeration here, but Gore is largely right. He is also right to portray George V as hard hit and embittered by the outbreak of war: "He loathed war. . . . He had none of his grandmother's robust Victorian outlook on war. He was a man of peace, a very sensitive, highly strung nature"—subject not only to seasickness but to chronic indigestion, dyspepsia, and even melancholy. He was depressed by suffering, upset by every casualty list, haunted, until 1917, by the possibility that England and its allies could lose the war, and always concerned for the safety of his sons. From 1914 to 1918 he worried.

Some glimpses of the King, 1914 to 1916. He admired the stolid and notoriously silent Lord Kitchener enormously, but whenever they were together he complained that Kitchener would not stop talking and that he (King George) could not get in a word. In 1915, worried about alcoholism among munitions factory workers as well as in the general population and egged on by Lloyd George, the King pledged publicly that he and all members of his

1.2 King George V (second from left), with the Prince of Wales (the future Edward VIII; far left) as a young staff officer, behind the lines on the Western Front; by permission of the Imperial War Museum.

Y Y Y

court would "become teetotallers until the end of the war. I have done it as an example." There was almost no response to this—in the country, in the Commons, or in the government. As Lady Astor would discover, England hated teetotalism. Asquith, who was known to like brandy, continued to drink in public; and even the King, toward the end of the war, would retire discreetly in the evening for what he called "a little after-dinner business." George V ordered no new clothes for the duration of the war, stopped dining out, stopped going to the theater, stopped visiting his various residences (the royal family lived at Buckingham Palace during the war), ordered that vegetables be grown in the gardens at Frogmore, and ate frugally. (Macaroni, without meat or wine, was the fare at the Derby Day dinner in 1917.) War genuinely horrified the monarch, but one senses that the unadorned style of living it led him to impose upon himself and his household was not distasteful to the imperial palate.

Late in 1915, while King George was visiting the army in France, his horse reared after a sudden cheer for the monarch, slipped, and fell backward, fracturing the royal pelvis in two places as well as three ribs. The King, now fifty, was in agony for weeks, and ever afterward walked stiffly and with some pain. It was his war wound. Also in 1915, his support was instrumental in enabling Asquith to secure the resignation of the incompetent army commander Sir John French. And the King helped the government in its efforts in 1916 to institute a military draft. He finally persuaded the military not to single out captured U-boat crews for particularly unpleasant treatment, arguing—correctly, as it turned out—that the Germans would only retaliate against captured British submarine crews.

The fiasco on the Somme—420,000 British casualties, 57,000 on the first day—and other reverses during 1916 brought about the fall of Asquith at the end of the year and his replacement by Lloyd George at the head of a coalition government that included Balfour as Foreign Secretary; thus fell the last Liberal government. The King, like most kings, was not pleased with the change; he liked the relaxed Asquith and distrusted the manic Lloyd George, who throughout his tenure in office ignored the monarch as completely as he could—sometimes, it appears, unconstitutionally. "His duty to the King he discharged only when it suited him," Rose has written. "A myopic radicalism blinded him to the virtues of an hereditary sovereign."

Glimpses of the King, 1917 to 1918. In March 1917 the Tsar was forced to abdicate. King George—without consulting the government, which wasn't pleased—telegraphed his cousin: "Events . . . have deeply distressed me. My thoughts are constantly with you and I shall always remain your true and devoted friend." As we shall see, this turned out to be a premature claim. The fall of the Tsar inspired H. G. Wells to write a letter to *The Times* declaring that the moment had come for Britain to rid itself forever of the

1.3 King George V surveys the devastation of war in France, 1917; by permission of the Imperial War Museum.

scourge of royalism. The King, so far paying little attention to these possible danger signals, noted laconically in his diary: "Six degrees of frost. . . . The United States . . . declared war on Germany yesterday."

During the war years there was a good deal of anti-German sentiment in England; there still is. The royal family, because of its German origins and names and titles, was sometimes suspected—without grounds, surely—of pro-German loyalties. Ridiculous as this may have been, by 1917 George V had had enough of it; he determined to rid the dynasty of its Germanic taint and give it instead a resoundingly British name. Saxe-Coburg and Hanover and Teck and Brunswick and Gotha and Battenberg would no longer do. The past association of the present court with German influences as well as the kinship of the British and German ruling families must now be forgotten; the royal family needed a new name. The King searched for one and asked for help. He got plenty of it, as might be expected. Names floated by: Plantagenet, York, Lancaster, Fitzroy, others. Finally, in July 1917, the following announcement was made over the signature of George V:

> We, of Our Royal Will and Authority, do hereby declare and announce that as from this date of this Our Royal Proclamation Our House and Family shall be styled and known as the House and Family of Windsor, and that all the descendants in the male line of Our said Grandmother Queen Victoria who are subjects of these Realms, other than female descendants who may marry or may have married, shall bear the said Name of Windsor:
>
> And do hereby further declare and announce that We for Ourselves and for and on behalf of Our descendants and all other descendants of Our said Grandmother Queen Victoria who are subjects of these Realms, relinquish and enjoin the discontinuance of the use of the degrees, styles, dignities, titles and honours of Dukes and Duchesses of Saxony and Princes and Princesses of Saxe-Coburg and Gotha, and all other German degrees, styles, dignitaries, titles, honours and appellations to Us or to them heretofore belonging or appertaining.

And so King George V, by changing his name, christened a dynasty and transformed his family from Hanovers into Windsors. (This provoked the Kaiser to announce that he would commission a new opera: "The Merry Wives of Saxe-Coburg-Gotha.") The proclamation asked members of the royal family residing in Britain who bore German titles to relinquish these titles and adopt British ones. Thus, for example, the King's cousins, Prince Louis of Battenberg—who had been forced in 1914 to resign as First Sea Lord because of his German birth and name—and Prince Alexander of Battenberg, became, respectively, Marquess of Milford Haven and Marquess of Carisbrooke, with the family name of Mountbatten. The Queen's brothers, the Tecks, turned into Cambridges and Athlones. The people loved it.

Never, perhaps, as at that moment in the summer of 1917 was the British royal family held in higher esteem by the British public.

In this year, in addition to Russia, Italy (on the Allied side) and Austria (allied to Germany) were driven out of the war; the Germans, now virtually alone except for tottering Turkey, had to face the combined forces of Britain, France, and the United States. The end could at least be hoped for, if not yet actually seen. When General Pershing and his staff arrived at Buckingham Palace, the King in an uncharacteristic bout of enthusiasm declared that "the two English-speaking nations . . . united in a great cause . . . must save civilisation." "We must be courageous & go on to the end, however long it may take," George V wrote to his mother. "I shall never submit to those brutal Germans & I am sure the British nation is of the same opinion." It was around this time that he turned over to the Treasury, for use in the war effort, his own personal savings of £100,000 (about $8 million today).

Early in 1918 the Prince of Wales incurred his father's wrath by going, while stationed in Italy, to see the Pope, against the King's advice; Balfour had sanctioned the visit. It was the first of many disputes between father and son and by no means the last time the future Edward VIII relied too heavily on his own terrible judgment. As Prince of Wales he offended his parents over and over again by his refusal to stay with them at Sandringham, which was too quiet and dull for his rarefied tastes.

King George found himself outraged again, in July 1918, by what he called "the vindictive and unnecessary murder of the poor Czar." "It was a foul murder," he wrote in his diary. "I was devoted to Nicky who was the kindest of men, a thorough gentleman, loved his country & his people." He added: "It's too horrible and shows what fiends these Bolshevists are." Lloyd George saw it differently: "The Revolution whereby the Russian people have placed their destinies on the sure foundation of freedom is the greatest service which they have yet made to the [Allied] cause," he said. Ironically, when Lloyd George's government suggested that the deposed Tsar and his family be given sanctuary and a place to live in England, George V, by now an astute student of public opinion, demurred. "From all he hears and reads in the press," the King's private secretary minuted the government, "the residence in this country of the ex-Emperor and Empress would be strongly resented by the public, and would undoubtedly compromise the position of the King and Queen." "Revolution" and "Bolshevism" created in this King a fright greater than his affection for his Russian cousins. Rose sums up: "The King feared for his popularity, even for his throne; the Government wished for a close understanding with Russia's new rulers. . . . Neither spared much thought for the deposed Tsar and his family." In the early days after the revolution the new Russian government wished to be rid of the Romanovs, who were an embarrassment, and would have shipped the former Tsar and his family almost anywhere; later, when feelings had hardened, this was no longer possible. So those who say that George V must share some of the blame for what happened to his beloved "Nicky" and the others are not wrong; the British monarch closed the door on the most promising avenue of escape his doomed cousins had. After all, as the fate of the Romanovs must have reminded him, the first obligation of a monarchy is to survive. He preserved his throne.

The ultimate failure, after some initial success, of General Ludendorff's offensives in the spring and summer of 1918, and the counterattacks by General Foch's Allied army—observed in person by King George—finally exhausted Germany. The war slowly wound down in the autumn, ending on November 11—which, said the King, was "the greatest [day] in the history of the Country." The Kaiser went into exile in Holland: Lloyd George wanted to extradite him and try him for war crimes. The King wrote in his diary: "'How are the mighty fallen.' He has been Emperor for just over 30 years, he did great things for his country but his ambition was so great that he wished to dominate the world. . . . No man can dominate the world, it has been tried before, & now he has utterly ruined his Country & himself. I look upon him as the greatest criminal known." And so another royal cousin bit the dust. George V, a survivor, spent the last hours of the war much as he had spent so many preceding ones: working. He was in France, talking to wounded men straight from the front lines. Wherever he went "his presence had an electrifying effect on the troops who saw him. . . . It is a memory of the War still vivid with many who were in France at that time," says John Gore, writing in 1941.

The population of London streamed onto the streets after the armistice was announced; night after night huge crowds gathered in front of Buckingham Palace, demanding the presence on the balcony of the King and Queen so they could be cheered. By surviving, George V had become the symbol of victory. For months afterward, well into 1919, he was asked to review groups of veterans of the Great War, and did so—always with special emotion when the veterans were disabled. "There can be no question," said Lloyd George, usually a harsh critic of the King, "that one outstanding reason for the high level of loyalty and patriotic effort which the people of this country maintained [during the war] was the attitude and conduct of King George." Says Gore: "With a stern and calm courage and an infinite compassion he saw the dreadful business through to the end."

VII

By the end, however, Britain was not quite the same. About three quarters of a million men had lost their lives in the war and another million and a half were crippled by wounds, gas, or shell shock. There was a terrible housing shortage. On the other hand, wages were high and unemployment was negligible. In the general election held just after the war ended, Lloyd George's coalition—its slogan was "Let Germany Pay"—won a majority in the

1.4 King George V and a young "war worker" in Sunderland in 1918; by permission of the National Portrait Gallery.

House of Commons, though his Liberal party fared poorly. (Even Asquith lost his seat.) Labour won a new high of sixty-three seats. Women over thirty-five, but not younger women, got the vote, as did all adult men.

After the war in Europe ended, republics—as King George foresaw— became fashionable, and monarchies tended to disappear. In addition to Russia, Austria, Germany, Spain, Greece, Poland, and Turkey rid themselves of autocracies, though in some cases only briefly. Presidents were in vogue, and one of them, Woodrow Wilson, visited England at the end of 1918. In his speeches he forgot to mention the sacrifices of the British in the late war, and everyone was offended. "I could not bear him," said George V. "An odious man." After Wilson left, the King and Queen retreated gratefully to Sandringham for a much-anticipated holiday early in 1919.

In the first months of the new year there were riots due to discontent over the slow rate of demobilization—a foretaste, perhaps, of the bitter industrial strife and class warfare that were to overtake Britain in the 1920s. Churchill was quickly installed at the War Office, and in a few weeks 50,000 men per day were being demobilized. Meanwhile the former German Empire was dismembered and Germany loaded down with reparations at the Paris peace conference and the resulting Treaty of Versailles. "Vengeance was in the air," Gore reminds us. "It was breathed in and out in high places, and required no fanning from mean streets or public hustings to give it a place in political policy." Germany had put everyone through the wringer, and now it was its turn, and that of its late allies, to pay.

In November 1919, a year after hostilities ended, the King found courage to speak out on behalf of the defeated, declaring that he was "shocked at the condition of things in Vienna" and asking the peace commissioners to adopt "some measures for the provision of those necessaries of life which, owing to the conditions of the Peace Treaty, seem to be withheld from the people." It was always "the people" he worried about most, even when they were Austrian and recently his enemies. Throughout the next year, 1920, unemployment in England rose and strikes increased in length and intensity. King George blamed "extremists" and "bolsheviks." Nor did the imminent publication of Mrs. Asquith's memoirs sit well with him: "What on earth does this mean? People who write books ought to be shut up." Presumably he meant Mrs. Asquith rather than all authors, but this is not clear. On 11 November 1920, the second anniversary of the armistice, he unveiled the Cenotaph and walked behind the gun carriage carrying the coffin of the unknown soldier to Westminster Abbey. He was now fifty-five, his beard was white, and he limped.

Peace in Europe was made, however impermanently; but peace in Ireland, to which the King and his government had now to turn their attention, seemed more permanently elusive. The nationalists, in the person of Eamon de Valera and his Sinn Fein party—referred to by English politicians as the "murder gang"—had cemented their hold on the Irish Republic in the elections of 1918. The Irish Republican Army now commenced its murderous campaign to drive all British troops in Ireland (50,000 at this time) out of the country and unite it under its own rule—without, of course, the consent of the protestant minority, living chiefly in the north and still loyal to England. Instead of withdrawing its troops, the British government dispatched to Ireland additional auxiliary troops, most of them hardened veterans of the world war; these were the infamous "Black and Tans," after the colors of their uniform, whose unceremonious brutality struck terror into the hearts of the law-abiding Irish. (How the Anglo-Irish of the southern counties regarded the advent of the Black and Tans may be seen clearly enough in Elizabeth Bowen's novel of 1929, *The Last September.*) King George complained to his ministers about the harshness with which some of his Irish subjects—the "unoffending people in Ireland," as he called them—were being treated: "This cannot go on. I cannot have my people killed in this manner," the monarch is said to have told Lloyd George. It was again the fate of the "people" that provoked him. The King went on to demand that the Black and Tans be disbanded, but nothing came of this.

Despite threats of assassination, he agreed to go with the Queen to Belfast to give the speech opening the new Ulster Parliament in June 1921. In it he appealed for peace and declared that "the future lies in the hands of my Irish people themselves." In the spirit of compromise and truce, de Valera spent the autumn of this year in London negotiating a treaty with Lloyd George that, when completed, established the Irish Free State as a Dominion within the Commonwealth. "I trust that now after seven centuries there may be peace in Ireland," the King wrote in his diary. He was not the first to be disappointed. Nine years later he remarked to Ramsey MacDonald: "What fools we were not to have accepted Gladstone's Home Rule Bill. The Empire now would not have had the Irish Free State giving us so much trouble and pulling us to pieces." But this was a problem with no solution.

The years 1921 and 1922 were difficult ones for Lloyd George's coalition. The huge war debt inhibited public spending. There were continuous strikes: a general strike on behalf of higher wages was threatened. Salaries started to fall; unemployment started to rise. The Prime Minister tactlessly frightened war-weary Britons with talk of defending Greece against Turkey. He was frequently absent from the House of Commons. He shamelessly sold honors, much to the King's horror and remonstrance, to replenish party funds. The Conservatives, led by Bonar Law, Lord Curzon, and Stanley Baldwin, abruptly withdrew from the coalition, and the Prime Minister was compelled to resign. "I am sorry he is going," King George wrote in his diary, "but he will be P.M. again." In fact he wouldn't. Bonar Law became the new premier.

There were other novelties. More people than before the war smoked cigarettes in public, wore lounge-suits and soft hats, and listened to BBC radio broadcasts. The new leading literary figures appeared to be T. S. Eliot, D. H.

Lawrence, James Joyce, and Aldous Huxley, though Edgar Wallace remained a best-seller. The cinema introduced Charlie Chaplin to the public. The Prince of Wales, now twenty-eight, prided himself on being in tune with everything new; his father disapproved of his informality, his flippancy, his frivolousness, his frequent neglect of family duty, his failure to marry. Indeed, when the King's second son, the more retiring Duke of York, married Lady Elizabeth Bowes-Lyon, George V wrote to the future George VI: "I trust . . . that you will be as happy as Mama & I am after you have been married 30 years. . . . You have always been so sensible & easy to work with & you have always been ready to listen to any advice & agree with my opinions about people & things that I feel we have always got on very well together. Very different to dear David [the Prince of Wales]." "What a pity such a distinguished man should be so difficult," Queen Mary said of her eldest son.

In 1923 Bonar Law was found to have advanced cancer of the throat. He resigned; and the King, after a celebrated hesitation, and convinced that the Prime Minister should sit in the Commons rather than the Lords, chose Stanley Baldwin over Lord Curzon to replace him. In those days the sovereign was expected to make such choices; nowadays the constituent parties elect their leaders and make these royal decisions unnecessary. In any case, Baldwin and Curzon were never quite able to sustain a friendship after this brief passage of political history. "I met Curzon in Downing Street," Baldwin wrote later, "from whom I got a very chilly nod and the sort of greeting a corpse would give to an undertaker."

The new Prime Minister immediately called a general election—and was defeated. And so in January 1924 in came the first-ever Labour government, led by Ramsey MacDonald. "I wonder what . . . dear Grandmama would have thought of a Labour Government," the King mused in his diary. Some years earlier he had declared that "the Order of Merit should not be given to Socialists," no matter what their distinction. He now had to preserve at least the facade of impartiality; as a fair-minded man he was apparently successful in doing so. He was helped by having met the Labour leaders informally over dinner at Lady Astor's table—and by the instant liking he took to Ramsey MacDonald, whom he found to be a kindred soul. King George was heard to remark soon after Labour's advent that MacDonald kept him better informed than any of his previous premiers. He wrote to his mother, Queen Alexandra, about the new Labour ministers: "they all seem to be very intelligent & they take things very seriously. They have different ideas to ours as they are all socialists, but they ought to be given a chance & ought to be treated fairly." MacDonald later commented on how gently and kindly he was treated by the King, who wanted to do whatever he could to assist his new government, socialist or not. There survives a long protocol written out for MacDonald by one of King George's private secretaries, instructing the new premier when to write to the sovereign, what (and what not) to tell him, which papers required his signature, and so on—a sort of crammer for How to Be Prime Minister.

Labour's thin majority rested on the sufferance of the Liberals, and in the autumn of 1924 another general election was held; Labour hoped to tighten its grip. The Conservatives campaigned against the government's desire to recognize and lend money to Soviet Russia, and this issue, plus some others, returned the Tories to power with a large majority. And so the callow, shallow, slothful, indolent, ignorant Baldwin, who believed and said—in reference to Lloyd George—that "A dynamic force is a very terrible thing," moved once again into No. 10, this time for a long stay (1924 to 1929). He was, as Lord Curzon correctly described him, "a man of the utmost insignificance." The Liberals, meanwhile, had nearly ceased to exist, with only forty seats in the new Parliament: it was the left versus the right now, with the usually well-trampled middle ground of British politics for once unoccupied. Labour assumed for the first time its familiar twentieth-century posture as the principal opposition party.

The King could not help feeling sorry for his new friend, the late socialist Prime Minister. "I like him," he wrote in his diary of Ramsey MacDonald, "and have always found him quite straight." At the end of this year (1924) King George opened the new Parliament. "The crown gave me an awful headache," he noted afterward. "I could not have borne it much longer." He was fifty-nine.

The new Conservative government may be characterized in terms of Harold Nicolson's masterful assessment of its leaders:

> Mr. Baldwin was an indolent and therefore unassuming man. Sharing as he did the solid, sentimental virtues of the English bourgeoisie, he also possessed an intuitive understanding of the thoughts and feelings of the proletariat. In that he never strove to be clever, he conveyed the impression that he never sought to outwit . . . He was not a man addicted to intellectual analysis: he regarded logical processes as un-English: he preferred to rely upon instinct, and would sniff and snuff at problems like an elderly spaniel. Even when sitting at question time in the House of Commons, he would sniff frequently at the order-paper in his hand. Unlike most Prime Ministers, he had no desire at all to display or vaunt his prowess, charm and power upon the European scene. He was only too glad to entrust the direction of Foreign Policy to the Foreign Minister and his staff.
>
> Mr. Austen Chamberlain was well prepared to profit by this free opportunity. In him the administrative capacity of the Chamberlain family was lightened by imaginative sentiment. He envisaged international problems as floating shapes: coloured pink, or blue, or mauve: whereas his brother, Mr. Neville Chamberlain, was inclined to interpret affairs in terms of typewritten maxims, absorbed during his early

Birmingham manhood and thus only rarely applicable to continental temperaments or an altering age.

"What do you do with a leader . . . who sits in the smoking room reading the *Strand Magazine*?" complained one parliamentary member of Baldwin's party. The Prime Minister tended, on those rare occasions when he found himself unable to avoid the front bench of the Commons, to bury himself in *Dod's Parliamentary Companion,* which helped make him an adroit party manager. Indeed, his own perpetuation in office was the only thing that animated him. As Kenneth Rose has noted, he "preferred crosswords to Cabinet papers, and the King more than once expressed concern that Baldwin should spend the summer ruminating at some French spa while the red boxes piled up at No. 10." According to Denis Judd, Leopold Amery, the Colonial Secretary, remarked that Baldwin's usual response to the nation's affairs was to puff his pipe and, like Brer Rabbit, "lie low and say nuffin'." He had no interest in foreign affairs. Whenever foreign policy was discussed in Cabinet he would close his eyes and ask to be awakened "when you have finished with that."

Churchill now reentered the government, this time as Chancellor of the Exchequer, which effectively separated him from the Liberals and Lloyd George. The Foreign Secretary, Sir Austen Chamberlain, who never approved of Lord Curzon's pugnaciousness in foreign affairs, determined to befriend foreign leaders—to embark upon what Nicolson calls "a policy of general appeasement." Broadened and exaggerated to the point of irresponsibility, this was the policy for which Baldwin and later Neville Chamberlain would be chiefly remembered, a policy that by the late 1930s had become—there is no other word for it—treasonous. In deliberately leaving Britain defenseless against the growing might of his friend Hitler, Baldwin behaved like a traitor. No one, not even a British prime minister, could be as stupid as he later claimed to have been. Fortunately, Baldwin lived just long enough to understand how despised he would be by history. The fact is that he and influential members of his government in the 1930s found fascism very much to their taste and acted accordingly, always against the best interests of the people they purported to represent. What is this but treason?

Baldwin's longevity in office resulted from his ability to maintain, for an astonishingly long time, both in the country and in himself, the fantasy that he both understood and could assuage the needs of the nation; this ability in turn grew out of his capacity to inspire in others, perhaps as a result of his so-called ordinariness, the illusion that, in Nicolson's terms once again, he "was a man immune to partisan prejudice or rancour, whose central purpose was to serve the Nation as a whole." Nothing could be less true. He believed that the highest patriotism consisted in keeping himself and his friends in office; this depended on not rousing the country to discuss anything, and that in turn depended on not telling the voters the truth about foreign or any other affairs. "Never get people steamed up. They start doing things," says the big boss in the film *noir* classic *The Big Heat* (1953). He knew. The proofs of Baldwin's perfidy came out later, after the death of George V and the rise of Churchill; but we are getting ahead of ourselves.

Austen Chamberlain got off to a good start, helping, in the autumn of 1925, to negotiate the Locarno treaties, which aimed at establishing a lasting European peace—or, as others have put it, at the pacification of Europe. The agreement's chief features were the fixing of Germany's eastern and western boundaries; it also "outlawed" war, endorsed the principle of arbitration in case of difficulties, and guaranteed the status quo of the Treaty of Versailles, leaving the enforcement of its clauses, fatefully, to the League of Nations. Essentially it was a nonaggression pact among France, Germany, and Belgium, guaranteed by Britain and Italy. At the time the treaty was considered significant, since it seemed to bring Germany back into concert with its European neighbors, signaling (supposedly) the dawn of a new era in European relations.

During the Locarno negotiations the King was an enthusiastic cheerleader. "This morning the Locarno Pact was signed at the Foreign Office," he wrote in his diary on 1 December. "I pray this may mean peace for many years. Why not for ever?" He had had a bereaved autumn. His mother, eighty, utterly deaf and often forgetful, died on 20 November after suffering a heart attack the day before. Queen Alexandra was interred beside Edward VII in St. George's Chapel, Windsor. King George V buried himself in Sir Sidney Lee's biography of his father. "Very interesting & well written but not always quite accurate," was the royal verdict. E. F. Benson on Edward VII received even less favor: "amusing writer, but I didn't find that a very nice book."

With the death of his mother, the King moved his Sandringham household from the cottage to the house. And he gave over Marlborough House, the usual abode of the Prince of Wales, to his eldest son and heir. On 21 April 1926, while at Windsor, King George was informed by the Duke and Duchess of York of the birth of their first child, Princess Elizabeth; the King and Queen Mary rushed up to London to view this fateful infant—who, as Elizabeth II, would succeed her father, George VI, as the British sovereign a quarter-century later.

VIII

The mid-1920s witnessed a brief but spectacular domestic dislocation of British life.

The General Strike of 1926 grew out of a work stoppage by coal miners in 1925, which the King predicted "will play the devil in the country." A Royal

Commission recommended that British coal, which was being undersold, could become competitive in world markets only through a reduction of wages and increased working hours. The union's reply was succinct: "Not a penny off the pay, not a minute on the day." The mine owners locked out their workers. On 3 May 1926 the miners were joined by other big unions: transport workers, railwaymen, construction workers, printers, and employees of utilities, to name just a few—all in all, about 80 percent of the union work force. Churchill, describing strikers as "the enemy," used armored cars to send supplies through the streets.

George V, as Judd has pointed out, advised the government in the strongest possible terms not to introduce emergency measures, especially measures aimed at reducing the financial stability of the unions. It would be "a grave mistake," the King argued, "to do anything which might be interpreted as confiscation, or to provoke the strikers, who until now have been remarkably quiet." This monarch always saw himself as King of the poor as well as the rich. During a coal strike in 1912, as Rose reminds us, he had given 1,000 guineas (about $900,000 today) out of his own savings to distressed miners' families. In 1921 he complained that unemployment benefits were too meager. During the coal strike that had precipitated the crisis of 1926, King George asked the government to address more comprehensively than before the industry's root difficulties, declaring—to the astonishment of ministers—that no owner of or investor in coal should receive a dividend higher than 10 percent on his or her investment. When Lord Durham, a coal tycoon, told the King that the striking miners were "a damned lot of revolutionaries," George V snapped back: "Try living on their wages before you judge them." He was, in this emergency, a force for moderation and conciliation, deliberately damping down the more inflammatory and incendiary inclinations of some of his ministers. Generally he was opposed to anything that might push the strikers toward more desperate measures and sought to avoid any actions by the government that might damage the economic future of the workers.

Four million workers went on strike during the first week of May 1926; there were scattered incidents of violence, but on the whole both sides remained remarkably restrained. There was no doubt, however, that the middle classes and the working classes were facing off across a wide economic chasm. Ex-officers and students signed up to become special constables; radicals threatened revolution. Most people just wanted a compromise so the thing could be over and done with and their lives no longer disrupted. King George, like the rest of the country without coal, was cold. "The Palace is like an ice house," a courtier (but not the monarch) complained. The King felt that his benignity had its limits. "I hope they will be severely punished," he remarked of suffragettes who joined the union side and became engaged in the smashing of windows. At Sandringham he remarked at breakfast over the newspaper to an eminent visitor whose son had been arrested for riotous behavior: "I see that your son was also my guest last night."

Nine days after it began the General Strike collapsed, and though the miners refused to return to work for another six months, when near starvation drove them back to the pits, English life largely reverted to normal. Stanley Baldwin, of course, had done practically nothing during the General Strike, saw his indolence justified, and vowed to continue doing nothing in the future, a promise that he kept. George V wrote in his diary: "Our old country can well be proud of itself, as during the last nine days there has been a strike in which 4 million men have been affected; not a shot has been fired & no one killed; it shows what a wonderful people we are." The defeated strikers were less upbeat—their wages were cut and their working hours lengthened, as had been recommended in the first place—but everyone else shared the King's relief. The sovereign issued a public statement as soon as the strike ended. It said in part: "Let us forget whatever elements of bitterness the events of the past few days may have created, only remembering how steady and how orderly the country has remained, though severely tested, and forthwith address ourselves to the task of bringing into being a peace which will be lasting."

When the Duke and Duchess of York sailed for Australia in January 1927 they left their daughter, Princess Elizabeth, with her grandparents at Buckingham Palace. More, perhaps, than he had ever done with his own children, King George played with her the games of childhood. It was not uncommon during this period at the Palace to see the small girl leading the sixty-one-year-old monarch around by the beard, or riding on his back while he shuffled painfully along on all fours. In May the King received Charles Lindbergh after his famous solo flight across the Atlantic. "A very nice boy & quite modest," noted the sovereign. It is typical of George V that the only question he asked Lindbergh was probably the first question most of his subjects would have liked to ask: "How on earth did you *manage*?"

Baldwin managed the King the way he managed the voter: by not ruffling him. Typical of the soothing, smarmy, sleek sort of stuff he wrote to the monarch is this passage about the backbenchers of his own party: "During the Coalition Government there was an excessive element consisting of men who obviously bore recent traces of newly won and easily acquired prosperity. It is a source of satisfaction to all that this element has been largely diminished"—after the latest elections, he means.

Peace, both abroad and at home, seemed to be the order of the day in England in the late 1920s. Cowed by the quick disintegration of the General Strike, the Labour party reposed for the most part uncontentiously upon the opposition benches. The prosperous grew more prosperous than ever. When the voting age for women was lowered from thirty-five to twenty-one there was scarcely a ripple. An "updated" Church of England prayer book was proposed and rejected. When Gandhi visited London, George V, who simultaneously deprecated any challenge to law and order in India and desired a contented Indian people even if that meant accepting some advance toward self-government, could not help himself. After staring resentfully, so Rose tells us, at Gandhi's bare knees all during dinner, the King burst out as his guest was leaving: "Remember, Mr. Gandhi, I won't have any attacks on my Empire." The reply was grave, deferential, and tactful: "I must not be drawn into political argument in Your Majesty's Palace after receiving Your Majesty's hospitality." At the other end of Indian affairs in 1928 the architect Edwin Lutyens, with the backing and encouragement of King George, received the commission to build the Viceroy's House in New Delhi—actually a palace, and perhaps the last such grandiose building to be ordered up by the British government. As it turned out, the Viceroy's House, that vainest of erections, would only be occupied for two decades.

In November 1928 King George, now sixty-three, came down with what was thought at first to be a feverish cold with bronchial spasms; quickly the illness was identified instead as an acute septicemia, an infection of the blood due to a pleural abscess behind the diaphragm. The Prince of Wales was summoned back from an East African safari and told there was some "cause for anxiety." The doctors also feared heart failure. There were no sulpha drugs, antibiotics, or penicillin to fight the infection: this was 1928. Crowds assembled regularly outside Buckingham Palace in bitter cold weather to await and read bulletins on the King's health. The public donated nearly £700,000 (about $60 million nowadays) to the Thanksgiving Fund for his recovery—by any reckoning an enormous sum. A Council of State was appointed to act for the sovereign. George V's greatest fear, meanwhile, was that he might go mad like his unfortunate antecedent George III. On 12 December, nearly comatose, the King underwent surgery to drain the abscess; a rib was removed. The Prince of Wales had by this time returned from Africa, assuming with his usual charm that if he had not done so the throne might be bagged by his younger brother, the Duke of York—a bashful, retiring man who did not want to be King. In Africa, hearing of his father's illness, the Prince's response was characteristically selfish: "Imagine," he told a friend, "I could be King of England tomorrow." There is a story, probably apocryphal, that the period of George V's recovery commenced at the moment he first spied his awful son—whom he hadn't seen recently—hovering hopefully over his bedside.

The King convalesced through the winter at Aldwick, near Bognor, in a private house overlooking the Channel. In March 1929 he was again able to receive visitors; in April he resumed writing in the diary he had put aside five months earlier. As the royal party made preparations to leave Bognor, a deputation of its leading citizens, so Rose tells us, came to ask permission to rename their town Bognor Regis. In another room, away from the delegation, George V was asked for his consent. In his mind and experience Bognor was associated with the twin horrors of illness and boredom. The moment elicited the most famous remark of the reign: "Bugger Bognor!" In the other room the delegation of local citizens was informed that the monarch was delighted to grant its request.

In May 1929 the King traveled to Windsor and there suffered a relapse due to the formation of another abscess at the site of the surgery—and perhaps due as well to the fact that he had resumed smoking cigarettes, though this never occurred to his physicians. In June he was again convalescent; but in July, shortly after returning home to Buckingham Palace from a Thanksgiving service at St. Paul's and receiving a tremendous public welcome in the streets along the way, the sovereign suffered yet another relapse. A second operation was performed, in the course of which another rib was removed. And so the royal convalescence stretched itself into August, with the King at last back at his beloved Sandringham. It was not until September, ten months after the monarch's initial illness, that he was said to be fully recovered: "in a good mood and cursed as in earlier days," noted a courtier. King George was thought by those who saw him now to be frail and weak compared to his old self, though he quickly resumed his daily habit at Sandringham of shooting.

Ramsey MacDonald described the King at Windsor in June 1929 as arrayed "in Chinese dressing gown with pink edges and ground of yellow with patterns blue and green. Face seemed longer and easily excited. Spoke at times rather loudly." Here is part of Harold Nicolson's account of George V's near-fatal illness and its effect upon his subjects.

The King was not by temperament an equable man. Even before his illness, there had come moments when [those around him] had been startled to recognise in those blue eyes a fixity of expression that recalled ... Queen Victoria's sharp indignation. The King was a bad patient and an even worse convalescent. Like all men who possess few internal resources and whose greatest pleasures are associated with outdoor life, the King became restless and irritable when his physical liberties were circumscribed. The chaff in which he indulged so gaily sometimes assumed during those weary months an irascible tone. He was often querulous; he frequently indulged in moods of self-pity; and he was terribly difficult to persuade.... One of the most dangerous of enemies was the demon boredom. Fortunately, the King had a liking for the cinema and much of his tedium could thereby be relieved. He was fond, moreover, of young children, and the constant presence of Princess Elizabeth ... acted as a useful emollient to jaded nerves.... The people of Great Britain, faced with the possibility of the King's death, were startled by the realisation of how much each one of them really cared. Men and women were surprised, not only by the intensity of their own feelings, but also by the reflection of that intensity in others. It came as

a revelation to many that here was no transitory wave of mass sentiment but a personal anxiety shared by all. Rarely has an emotion been
both so intimate and so diffused. For all his diffidence, the King could
not fail to be encouraged by this national tribute to his personality.

Asked what he had read during his illness when he was well enough to
read, George V said he had read the Bible. "A wonderful book," he
observed, "but there are some very queer things in it." Sailing on one Sunday during his convalescence aboard the royal yacht *Victoria and Albert*,
the King, who had always enjoyed singing hymns since his youthful days as
a sailor, discovered that a new hymn book had been introduced in place of
the old one so familiar to him. "I'll have all the bloody books burned," the
sovereign shouted at the yacht's unfortunate captain. "I'm not the Defender
of the Faith for nothing."

While King George had been ill the second Baldwin government had run
its course. There was a general election in May 1929. The Tories displayed
large photographs of the Prime Minister ("looking his most sedative,"
Nicolson reports), whose slogan for this contest, not uncharacteristically,
was "Safety First." However, Labour turned up first in the returns, and in
June Ramsey MacDonald became Prime Minister for the second time.
Labour had won a plurality of seats in the Commons but needed support
from the Liberal rump to form a government. In any case, Baldwin was out.
"The umpire has given me out and I do not protest," declared that sporting
gentleman. MacDonald, along with the rest of the new Cabinet, waited
upon King George at Windsor, where the Prime Minister was spotted hiding a half-smoked cigar in a flower pot; the fragile monarch was arrayed in
his Chinese dressing gown. At this meeting the King went out of his way to
welcome the first female Cabinet minister, Margaret Bondfield.

By the start of 1930 George V had returned to a more normal work
schedule, though he did not resume riding until April. He opened conferences, met diplomats (as few from the Soviet Union as possible—this government, after all, had murdered his cousin the Tsar and all his family; the
sovereign often pleaded illness whenever asked to meet Soviet visitors), and
resumed his heavy round of shooting expeditions, complaining only of
arthritic pain in the region affected by his old riding accident in France.

The effects of America's sudden financial collapse in October 1929 took
some time to be felt across the Atlantic, but by 1931 the end of American
loans and investments in Europe had caused severe and continuing unemployment, and nowhere more acutely than in Britain. By the close of 1930,
2.5 million were unemployed, and a year later the number had reached 3
million. There was a disastrous run on sterling during the summer of 1931,
and a panic; Britain's gold reserves were being depleted quickly. The Cabinet considered resignation, leaving the current social upheaval in the hands
of the Tories. MacDonald during this time was variously described by

observers as looking exhausted, frightened, and even unbalanced. "It is doubtful," writes Kenneth Rose, "whether any Government could have surmounted the world slump in trade and the financial crisis of 1931; but MacDonald's was memorably inept." In mid-August King George noted in his diary, after a meeting with the Prime Minister: "The Cabinet is divided and he fears he will have to resign." Declaring to a colleague that he was "off to the Palace to throw in my hand," MacDonald wrote in his diary an account of what happened next: "I advised [the King] to send for the leaders of the other two parties and have them report position from their point of view. He said he would and would advise them strongly to support me. I explained my hopeless parliamentary position if there were any number of resignations. He said that he believed I was the only person who could carry the country through." The new Liberal leader, Sir Herbert Samuel, discussed with the monarch the need in the present emergency for a unified National Government, a nonparty government constituted for the sole purpose of overcoming the financial crisis, and composed of all three parties. As soon as the immediate crisis—the run on the pound and the depletion of the gold reserves—was over, a general election would be held, but there was not time for one now. Baldwin, who had to be summoned back from rustication in Aix-les-Bains, agreed. MacDonald, says Judd, rather harshly, "wished . . . to be the saviour of his country, even at the expense of temporarily ruining his party." His agreement to head a National Government provoked the resignations of many of his Labour colleagues and destroyed his own standing in the party; indeed, shortly thereafter another Labour leader was elected, and it was Labour that formed the principal opposition to the National Government during its life, MacDonald being seen by his own party as having gone over to the political enemy out of personal ambition. "I commit political suicide to save the crisis," he predicted, and to a large extent he was right.

In any case, a National Government was duly sworn in late in August 1931, a government that would outlive George V; indeed (in name at least) it lasted for fourteen years, keeping the Labour party in opposition until the end of the war. The National Government was in part the creation of the King, who had been convinced of its necessity and then pursued its accomplishment with the political leaders of the day. For most of the British public the formation of a non-partisan National Government at this low ebb of the country's fortunes seemed fortuitous and at least temporarily reassuring. This was what King George had in mind. As Rose puts it, "He induced MacDonald to lead the new ministry and so proclaim to the world that Britain spoke with a united and resolute voice in her determination to remain solvent." For the moment the run on the pound stopped.

This is another example of George V as an active rather than a passive sovereign, concerned with the state of mind as well as the physical welfare of his subjects. For this skillful exercise of his constitutional powers in a great crisis, the King once again deserves high praise—and surely Ramsey MacDonald deserves less contempt than he has met with at the hands of socialist historians such as Harold Laski. MacDonald knew he was committing political suicide and did it anyway. Merely out of ambition to retain power? The impulse to commit political suicide is not the stock-in-trade of those in MacDonald's profession, most of whom have a more pragmatic perspective upon the future and their own place in it. Surely MacDonald's Labour colleagues (with only a few exceptions) acted more cynically than he did.

The drain on British gold abated briefly. In a letter to him, the King praised the Prime Minister's "courage" in standing "by the country in this grave national crisis. By this proof of strength of character & devotion to duty," the sovereign concluded, "your name will always hold an honoured place among British Statesmen." MacDonald's Labour colleagues turned their backs on him and strolled into the political wilderness.

The run on sterling recommenced in the autumn. Disagreements among the three political parties over economic policy produced a deadlock, which in turn forced a general election in October 1931. "I want the National Government to get every vote possible," George V, unconstitutionally un-neutral, commented. At the conclusion of this campaign the National Government and Ramsey MacDonald secured a huge mandate to govern— indeed, the most sweeping victory in British election history (a majority of 502; hordes of Labour M.P.s lost their seats). "Thank God, I am an optimist & I believe in the common sense of the people of this country, if only the situation is properly explained," said the King. Neville Chamberlain became Chancellor of the Exchequer in the new administration when Stanley Baldwin made it clear that the job was too strenuous for him.

As time passed, MacDonald's government, abandoned by Labour and supported loyally by the Tory plurality in the House of Commons, became both more conservative and more Conservative, and power gradually gravitated away from MacDonald and back toward the indolent Baldwin. Mac-Donald himself noted at the time, quite accurately: "a Prime Minister who does not belong to the Party in power will become more and more an anomaly, and . . . his position will become more and more degrading." He remained premier for another three years, ultimately yielding power once again to Baldwin in 1935.

The King, in 1932, was reading a book he found fascinating, a life of Al Capone. Another item on his reading list he deplored: Lloyd George's best-selling *War Memoirs*. George V, who in any case always disliked contentious "insider" books, had asked an intermediary to try to persuade the former Prime Minister not to publish his memoirs. "He can go to hell," Lloyd George is said to have replied. "I owe him nothing. He owes his throne to me." When the draft chapter on the King duly arrived on the sovereign's desk, George V merely made one grammatical change—one serves "in" a ship, not "on" a ship—and returned the manuscript without comment to its vain, pugnacious author.

IX

From 1933 on Baldwin's was the guiding hand of the National Government; MacDonald was the weaker partner. Under Baldwin's brand of "deft quietism," as Nicolson terms it, Britain "settled down to a period of illusive calm." Illusive indeed: in this year Hitler became the German chancellor, the Reichstag burned, Japan and Germany withdrew from the League of Nations, a world disarmament conference dissolved in failure. Despite the steady rise of fascism in Europe and Asia, the governments of the leading powers did not seem, in 1933, to be bent on war. As Judd reminds us, rearmament was not a popular cause in the Western democracies in these days; those who, like Winston Churchill, advocated and harped on it were considered dangerous. Typically, Baldwin counseled passive calm. "The bomber," he told the House of Commons, "will always get through."

George V had no interest in air power: on the contrary, he had a horror of flying and in fact never did fly. As the dictators rose, however, he spotted the looming dangers long before Baldwin woke up to them. "I am an old man," the monarch remarked to one of his ministers. "I have been through one world war. How can I go through another? If I am to go on, [the government] must keep us out of one." He was at the same time both pacifist and suspicious. As early as 1923 he had characterized Mussolini as "a *mad dog* which must bite somebody." But it did not seem to him, in 1933 and 1934, that another war would inevitably be required to contain the dictators. And in his rabid isolationism he reflected a horror of war understandably shared by many of his subjects: "I will not have another war. *I will not.* The last one was none of my doing and if there is another one and we are threatened with being brought into it, I will go to Trafalgar Square and wave a red flag myself sooner than allow this country to be brought in." He was spared that annoyance.

Rose reminds us how unwelcome to the British the prospect was of having to rearm, especially in a country so recently escaped from bankruptcy—not to mention the extinction, in the Great War, of one-third of the male population. "What tarnishes the memory of the so-called appeasers," Rose writes, "is not that they were deterred from robustness by the strategic and economic realities of a defence policy; it is the sycophancy with which they embraced an evil regime, the callous indifference with which they witnessed the creeping enslavement of Europe." George V, let it quickly be said, though he hated the idea of another war, was never one of these people. We know his opinion of Mussolini. He refused, as early as 1932, to let the

Nazi-loving Prince of Wales attend the marriage of one of Hitler's hench-
men; he referred contemptuously to "those horrid fellows Göring and
Goebbels"; he spoke out against Nazi attacks on the Jews and the violence
by which Hitler's party consolidated its power. The King on several occasions during 1934 took it upon himself to warn the German ambassador in
London that the vast scale of German rearmament was gratuitously
provocative; no one in the government did this. "Germany [is] the peril of
the world," he is supposed to have told the ambassador on one occasion.
Early in 1935 King George warned his sleepy government "that we must
not be blinded by the apparent sweet reasonableness of the Germans, but be
wary and not taken unawares."

In May 1935 Hitler proposed, in a letter to George V, that "the two Germanic nations" cooperate together on land and sea to secure world peace.
The King scoffed. "The French are not mentioned," he noted; "it seems to
me, reading between the lines, that Hitler's object is to form a block against
the French and other countries in Europe." The monarch was continuously
upset by reports of Germany's rearming and let his ministers know it. The
Tory admirers of Hitler were unmoved. The point is that the King spoke
more harshly to and of the Germans during these years, and understood
them better, than did any member of his despicable government. Churchill,
who was in the political wilderness in these days primarily because of his
pugnacious views, saw what the sovereign saw and said many of the same
things.

George V always liked Churchill, who was frequently invited to visit the
royal household. From Balmoral in 1928 Churchill wrote to his wife:
"There is no one here at all except the family, the household and Princess
Elizabeth—aged 2. The latter is a character. She has an air of authority and
reflectiveness worthy of an infant." One morning at Windsor, according to
Rose, the officer commanding the guard strode across to where a pram
stood, containing the future Elizabeth II. "'Permission to march off, please,
Ma'am.' There was an inclination of a small bonneted head and a wave of a
tiny paw."

During the summer of 1934, now sixty-nine, the King went yachting,
using Cowes as his headquarters, and recalling that 55 years earlier he and
Prince Eddy had joined the *Bacchante* from there. In September he and the
Queen traveled to Clydebank to dedicate a great new vessel, named the
Queen Mary. It was in this year also that the King and Queen visited the
National Gallery: no reigning monarch had ever been there before. Their
guide was its director, Kenneth Clark. As reported by Meryle Secrest, in the
course of his visit George V dismissed Turner as a madman and threatened
to attack the paintings of Cézanne with his cane. "He cheered up notably,
however, before *Derby Day,* by William Powell Frith, the famous Victorian
painting of the races which attracted such crowds when it first went on view

at the Royal Academy that barriers had to be erected. The King remarked appreciatively on the numerous incidents depicted and regretted only that there had been no room to show the race itself." Clark is on record as having said that George V "was perfectly ignorant about art, although he liked to take complacent tours of the royal collections."

The last months of the reign, though they heard the distant rumble of approaching war, had their lighter moments too. When Anthony Eden replaced Sir Samuel Hoare as foreign secretary, he went to Buckingham Palace to kiss hands and pick up the seals of office while on his way to a conference in Geneva. He was received by the sovereign in a much disused room situated just above the bandstand in the forecourt of the palace. The King apologized for receiving the new Foreign Secretary here—his private rooms were then under repair—but added that Mr. Eden need not worry: "I have told the band not to play till I give the word." King George proceeded to lecture his new minister on what should come up at the conference he was going to attend and how each item should be resolved. He concluded. Eden had just begun to reply when George V rang a small gold hand-bell at his side. A page appeared. "Tell the bandmaster that he can start playing now," said the King. And to Mr. Eden: "You were saying?"

In 1935 the irresponsible and reactionary heir to the throne was forty-one. All accounts agree that in this last year of his father's life the Prince of Wales, in Rose's words, "showed no readiness either to marry or prepare himself for the restraints of a constitutional monarch . . . neither his political judgement nor his private life inspired confidence among those who knew him best." The future Edward VIII was an unrepentant cheerleader for the Nazis; he was fond of declaring that in the next war England and Germany would fight on the same side—though against whom he was unable to say. His view of a constitutional monarchy also was unusual. He does not "hold his father's view that the King must . . . accept the Cabinet's decisions," the German ambassador in Washington told his masters. "On the contrary, he felt it to be his duty to intervene if the Cabinet were to plan a policy which in his view was detrimental to British interests." The Prince of Wales knew nothing, and refused to learn anything, about constitutional government. On several occasions the King was forced to rebuke him for expressing in public his private political opinions without consulting anybody about what he was going to say. The Prince in public was especially prone to utter his preposterous pro-German sentiments. He routinely greeted with defiance the fatherly rebukes he received; and the King worried, presciently, that such terrible judgment at such a mature age was a terrible omen. The Prince's frivolity was as worrying as his character. During the years 1934 and 1935 the Prince of Wales had been living openly with Wallis Simpson, a divorced and remarried American woman with two husbands still very much alive. The King thought her, as indeed she was, an unsuitable and disreputable companion, and of course unimaginable as a queen of England.

George V and Mrs. Simpson met once, at a Buckingham Palace party. Of this encounter the lady wrote: "David led me over to where they were standing and introduced me. It was the briefest of encounters—a few words of perfunctory greeting, an exchange of meaningless pleasantries, and we moved away. But I was impressed with Their Majesties' great gift for making everyone they met, however casually, feel at ease in their presence." The King's reaction to Mrs. Simpson was not quite so sunny. He complained that the lady had been smuggled into the palace without his knowledge and against his will: "That woman in my house!" And of the Prince of Wales: "He has not a single friend who is a gentleman. He does not see any decent society. And he is forty-one." King George V in his last year of life became convinced that his heir would never succeed to the throne, that he would betray his trust when the time came. His prognostications were chillingly lucid. "I pray to God that my eldest son will never marry and have children, and that nothing will come between Bertie [George VI] and Lillibet [Elizabeth II] and the throne," he told Baldwin. "After I am dead the boy will ruin himself in twelve months." Actually, it took eleven. When these sentiments were expressed they were put down to low spirits in the fading old King, but in fact he understood his egregious son perfectly. Apologists for Edward VIII have sometimes tried to lay the blame for his enormous deficiencies on the shoulders of his father, but in fact George V set his heir a magnificently salubrious example that was simply ignored, scorned, and defied by the younger man, all of whose passions were thoroughly selfish. The old King was patently the least selfish of men; and surely one explanation of the British public's willingness to see Edward VIII off the throne so quickly lay in its instinctive understanding that a dedicated and compassionate public servant had been succeeded by a monster of pomposity, self-importance, and self-indulgence.

By 1935 George V had sat on the throne of England for twenty-five years. The people revered him: he had been there for most of their lives, he had somehow gotten them through the Great War and the Depression, he had always done his duty and seemed to have few if any defects, he was still a Victorian gentleman in an age of increasing unmannerliness, and above all he seemed to care what happened to his people. King George did not understand the depth or the cause of this reverence, but he felt it, and it moved him. He had not, as Rose points out, sought popularity; he never smiled into cameras, and he disliked reporters. He read only *The Times*. But from 1924 he was persuaded by John Reith, the general manager of the newly organized BBC, to speak occasionally over the radio to the inhabitants of his Empire. This he did with increasing frequency during the last decade of his life; indeed, his annual Christmas broadcasts were eagerly anticipated, and heard, by millions. He had, A. C. Benson wrote in his diary, "an odd, hoarse voice, as if roughened by weather." He spoke with the accent, it was said, of an Edwardian country gentleman, which is what he was. The King always dreaded these broadcasts and had to be dragged back to the radio microphone each time. The Christmas broadcasts in particular made him nervous and, he complained, spoiled his Christmases. But typically he kept on giving them because he was asked to. Ramsey MacDonald was an especial fan of the radio. "How interesting it would be," he remarked to the monarch, "if we had a talkie of Queen Elizabeth." "Damn Queen Elizabeth," was the reply. Appreciative letters kept pouring in, and each year King George went reluctantly back to the microphone. When he spoke he seemed to people to be their friend, as indeed he was. This was a tone his unfortunate son was never able to catch; but then he was not, after all, anyone's friend.

The National Government, against the sovereign's advice—"All this fuss and expense. . . . What will people think of it, in these hard and anxious times?"—decided to proclaim and celebrate formally the Silver Jubilee of George V. The monarch told a friend:

> In looking back during these last 25 years, I am indeed thankful for all that has been done for me. I have passed through some very difficult times, with a ghastly war which lasted over four years, thrown in. I do indeed appreciate all the love and affection which my people are expressing, from all over the world. The festivities will entail a lot of extra work, and I shall be pleased when they are all over. I hope I shall survive them. I remember so well both Queen Victoria's Jubilees and can't yet realize that I am having one now.

On 6 May 1935, the twenty-fifth anniversary of his accession, the King and Queen Mary attended a Thanksgiving service at St. Paul's. Afterward the sovereign addressed his subjects over the radio, saying in part: "How can I express what is in my heart? . . . I can only say to you, my very, very dear people, that the Queen and I thank you from the depths of our hearts for all the loyalty—and may I say so?—the love, with which this day and always you have surrounded us." He added: "I am speaking to the children above all. Remember children, the King is speaking to *you*." George V wrote in his diary that evening:

> A never to be forgotten day, when we celebrated our Silver Jubilee. It was a glorious summer's day, 75 degrees in the shade. The greatest number of people in the streets that I have ever seen in my life, the enthusiasm was indeed most touching. May & I drove alone with six greys. . . . The Thanksgiving Service in St Paul's Cathedral was very fine. 4,406 people present. . . . On our return we went out on the centre balcony & were cheered by an enormous crowd. . . . By one post in the morning, I received 610 letters.

The King had only one complaint, which did not find its way into his diary. "A wonderful service," he told the Dean of St. Paul's that morning, "just one thing wrong with it—too many parsons getting in the way. I didn't know there were so many damn parsons in England."

For the next month, in the course of which George V turned seventy, the King and Queen attended an exhausting number of celebrations and received an undiminishing flow of official visitors. The monarch made dozens of speeches; on some days he had over a thousand letters to contend with. Later it was said by some that all of this sudden and unchecked exertion helped to hasten his demise seven months later. True or not, he received incontrovertible proof during this time of the reverence in which he was held throughout the Empire. It is typical of the man that he was astonished; never for a moment did he feel that, after all, he was only getting his due. "I'd no idea they felt like that about me," he said after a tumultuous progress through the East End. "I am beginning to think they must really like me for myself." Routinely the King would make a brief speech thanking those who cheered him, and routinely he would break down whenever he mentioned his wife. "I can't trust myself to speak of the Queen when I think of all I owe her," he told a secretary. "When he came to references and reminiscences personal to himself and the Queen," noted Ramsey Mac-Donald on one such occasion, "his voice broke and tears stood in his eyes. Everyone deeply moved." A socialist newspaper, Rose recounts, lost so many readers when it ceased to publish news of the royal family that it was forced to resume its coverage.

What was the source of all this affection for apparently so ordinary a man? Why was George V, whose chief occupation in life after the monarchy, it could be argued, was shooting birds—why was George V so revered by the British in the spring of 1935? What does so "Georgian" an occasion as his Silver Jubilee reveal about the position of the King and the views of his people on the monarchy?

For John Gore, one of the King's physicians, George V's great appeal lay in his unfailing dignity on all occasions, and in his humanity: the British people, Gore believed, saw the King as a real person rather than as an exalted symbol of something. "He was a simple, shy man who disliked ceremony, and the dignity and grace with which he played his part . . . had their source in his wholly impersonal consciousness of his great office and in the simplicity of his nature," which his subjects understood, Gore says. Indeed, "impersonal consciousness of his great office" seems to be just right. Denis Judd's analysis, composed three decades after Gore's, is remarkably similar in sentiment. Says Judd: "King George had clearly established an enviable rapport with his people which owed nothing to artifice or deep calculation. The British public were responding to the unpretentious, trustworthy, ordinary man who was their monarch." The emphasis is again on unpretentiousness, ordinariness; the people saw him as one of themselves, or perhaps rather as someone who was not pretending not to be one of themselves. "But with it all," observed Ramsey Mac-Donald, "he retains the demeanour and status of a King"—only, in Harold Nicolson's phrase, "devoid of all condescension, artifice or pose. The effect was wide and deep," Nicolson declares, and he goes on to focus on the King's "probity" as a source of general respect. During the reign of George V, Nicolson says, his subjects came to recognize that the monarch "represented and enhanced those domestic and public virtues that they regarded as specifically British virtues. In him they saw, reflected and magnified, what they cherished as their own individual ideals—faith, duty, honesty, courage, common sense, tolerance, decency, and truth." In him they saw themselves, a compliment that would not be paid to the next sovereign. Reverence for royalty coexisted with a love of the ordinary—a kind of mirror image of some of the contrasting strains of Georgian life, simultaneously reactionary and progressive, traditional and "modern," conventional and daring.

X

In June 1935 MacDonald resigned as Prime Minister, due to failing health, and was again succeeded by Baldwin. The King noted that MacDonald had been premier during seven of his twenty-five years on the throne and told him in a farewell letter: "I gratefully recognise the sacrifice of old associations and friendships which you faced in 1931 to form a National administration. During the succeeding four years the National Government, with you at the helm, has been successful in steering the Ship of State into smoother waters. It has been a relief to me to feel that I had a stable Government under your leadership, and that in times of anxiety I could turn to you with confidence." MacDonald relates that in a private audience with the King before his final departure from the government, George V said to him: "I hoped you might have seen me through, but I now know it is impossible. But I do not think it will be very long. I wonder how you have stood it—especially the loss of your friends and their beastly behaviour. . . . You have been the Prime Minister I have liked best; you have so many qualities, you have kept up the dignity of the office without using it to give you dignity." So one unpretentious man addressed another.

The last months of King George's life were plagued by disaster and uncertainty as order, humanity, and hope decayed in a Europe discernibly staggering toward another convulsive conflict. In October 1935 Mussolini invaded Abyssinia. The resultant League of Nations sanctions "were sufficiently irritating to drive Signor Mussolini and the Italian people into a state of frenzy: they were not sufficiently compulsive to impede him seriously in the conduct of the campaign," as Nicolson puts it. The fact that the League could neither prevent war nor stop it—nor bring to book those who violated its charter—was interesting to some other heads of state with plans for national expansion. Typically, the Prince of Wales chose this moment to propose a yachting trip to the Mediterranean.

On 14 November the King went out shooting for what proved to be the last time. This was also the day of a general election. The National Government was returned with a reduced but still substantial majority, and Baldwin remained Prime Minister. Ramsey MacDonald was unseated by Labour in his County Durham constituency.

It seemed to Baldwin that George V was "packing up his luggage and getting ready to depart" for another place. The King himself predicted on several occasions that he had only a short time to live. Still recovering from the exhaustion of the Jubilee celebrations and continually plagued by his old bronchial problems, King George now uncharacteristically tended to fall asleep during the day and complained of sleeplessness at night. Six weeks after Mussolini's invasion, Abyssinia was the cause of the royal insomnia, so the sovereign said. His rest was further disturbed by the tragic antics of the newly elected government. It turned out that Baldwin had come to a private arrangement with the French—behind the back of the League of Nations, the violation of whose principles the Prime Minister had pledged himself to resist to the death—whereby peace was to be established between Italy and Abyssinia so long as Abyssinia agreed to surrender vast stretches of its territory (60,000 square miles). Not only was this further evidence of Baldwin's penchant for the most ignominious brand of craven appeasement; it also demonstrated, in the blow it dealt the already weakened League of Nations, that, in Nicolson's words, "the theory of Collective Security had been proved fallacious." France and Britain, it was now clear, would have to rely upon their own resources when that day dawned on which Germany had to be faced down. And yet the Baldwin government took no steps to prepare for that day—claimed, rather, that that day was never going to dawn. Was this incompetence, or was it treason? The number of Nazi-lovers in the Tory government makes this a valid question.

Dismayed and worried, the King asked for and received some private advice from a friend in the Foreign Office. He was discouraged and perplexed to be told that Britain was woefully unequipped militarily and generally unprepared to confront the resurgent Germany, and that any British government which favored a free hand for German expansionism was bound to cover itself in further ignominy. It was of course the path of ignominy that Baldwin and his successor Neville Chamberlain were determined to tread throughout the rest of the 1930s. But it is a matter of record that George V, no lover of Nazis, felt strongly that his government was on a disastrous course—that is, that the expansionist fantasies of European powers must always be opposed, and that if Britain needed to rearm itself in order to mount that opposition then it should do so, and quickly.

On 3 December 1935 the King learned that his favorite sister, Princess Victoria, had died. It was a physical blow as well as an emotional one. "How I shall miss her & our daily talks on the telephone," he wrote. (Her typical greeting to him each morning had been "Hello, you old fool.") "No one had a sister like her." In despair he canceled the state opening of Parliament scheduled for that afternoon; it was rare indeed for this monarch not to keep a scheduled public date. But he couldn't do it. In fact, George V never appeared in public again. His sister's funeral at Windsor affected him deeply. Gore notes that from the day of her death his handwriting underwent an obvious change for the worse. When Baldwin saw the sovereign on 20 December, "The King appeared to him like a man who had seen the end of his life's work for better or worse," Gore reports.

King George went as always to Sandringham for Christmas, arriving in icy weather. He gave his Christmas broadcast as usual, though in a voice noticeably weaker than before. "I suppose it does give pleasure, but it is rather an effort for me," the monarch wrote after this latest and last broadcast. "No doubt it brings me into close touch with my peoples all over the world, & that of course I am very keen about." He went about his familiar duties as squire of Sandringham, though complaining now of breathlessness. He tended to fall asleep at meals and at the movies shown in the evenings. Feeling unwell, he nonetheless rode his pony about the park on 15 January, but his shooting days were over. On the sixteenth he went to his room and stayed there. And on the next day, the seventeenth, he made the last, almost illegible, entry in the diary he had faithfully kept since 1880: "A little snow & wind ... I ... feel rotten." He was distressed by his own poor handwriting and asked the Queen to write in his diary for him, but there were no further entries.

The King's physician now arrived and saw that the monarch had no energy: "felt life on top of him and . . . said so." The doctors said later that the sovereign's heart had been damaged from his long illness in 1928 and that the failure to recover fully left him especially susceptible to bronchial attacks. The Prince of Wales was summoned to Sandringham by the Queen and arrived from Windsor, typically, in an airplane—another generation indeed. The heir to the throne found his father, Rose reports, "sitting sleepily before a fire in his bedroom. There was a flicker of recognition before he relapsed into a twilight world."

As he lay dying, as in life, George V remained close to his people. Bulletins to the nation mentioned "cardiac weakness." The monarch drifted in and out of consciousness, sometimes lucid, sometimes not. His famous deathbed query, "How is the Empire?" might have been uttered in either state. The celebrated question was answered by the King's secretary: "It is all absolutely right, Sir." As in 1928, a Council of State was appointed to act for the sovereign; the problem was that King George had to sign the warrant for the Council and he was too weak to hold a pen. He was now confined to his bedroom at Sandringham, a room described by Gore as "small, cheerful and as simply furnished as a cabin in a big yacht . . . containing the fittings specially built for his father's voyage in the *Serapis* and . . . filled with memorials of his travels in many lands, pictures of ships he had sailed in and of scenes he had loved." On the morning of 20 January 1936 the King, propped up in an armchair in front of a roaring fire in his bedroom at Sandringham and wearing a brightly flowered Tibetan dressing gown, verbally approved the warrant but had to have his hand guided over the paper in order to initial it. "I feel very tired," said George V when the signing was over. "I am unable to concentrate." Typically, he apologized to the Privy Councilors, some of them in tears, for keeping them waiting while he attempted to sign the document.

The monarch slept through the rest of the day as the end of his reign was tolled in medical bulletins. On the afternoon of the twentieth the chief royal physician announced that "The King's life is moving peacefully towards its close." "The message," Gore says, "was heard at regular intervals during that dark and bitter night all over Britain and the Empire, solemn, inexorable, peaceful." The family gathered around the bedside; the deathwatch began. But the usually punctual George V kept no one waiting and died at midnight. He was seventy.

"*Am heartbroken,*" Queen Mary wrote in her diary. She graciously kissed the hand of the new King, who instantly absorbed himself in little acts of petty revenge against his late father. Edward VIII's first order was given to the staff at Sandringham: they were to put the clocks, which his father had set to run half an hour ahead to avoid being late for anything, back to the correct time. The omens for the new reign were not good. The imperial crown, which had been secured to the late King's coffin for the trip to Westminster, fell off as the cortège entered New Palace Yard and lay in a gutter until retrieved.

The body of King George lay in state in Westminster Hall for four days; nearly a million mourners filed past. The King had expressed a wish that no religious service of any kind be held at his funeral. In fact just one hymn was sung over his body. Then, in a gun carriage manned by sailors, the last voyage of George V commenced, this time to the chapel at Windsor for burial. He would not have approved of his own late arrival, due largely to the vast crowds of people on the streets blocking the way. Typically, Lloyd George had agreed to cover the funeral for one of the newspapers, and ostentatiously took notes during the service. "As the triumphant litany of death unfolded," Rose writes, "all marvelled at the dignity and fortitude of the widowed Queen: but no less at the new King, who in his forty-second year seemed still to have the promise of youth before him. His father's coffin sank slowly to the vault below, and he sprinkled symbolic earth from a silver bowl; a last salute. . . . And so King George V went to join his ancestors."

Mourners emerging from the chapel at Windsor found the lawn blanketed with wreaths sent by the late King's subjects both high and low. This was symbolic. He was not an especially cultured or deep man, but that gave him a touch of commonness appreciated by his subjects. He did not solicit their veneration, as we have seen, nor did he try to lead them morally or teach them anything. But he was, in John Gore's phrase, "sentient and sympathetic," and this his subjects seemed to understand instinctively and respond to. He tended to be nostalgic and sentimental, conventional, even old-fashioned—and these things too suited the British people. Unlike the next king, he maintained respect for the throne without ever seeming to condescend to anybody.

"The flower of our modern ideal of constitutional monarchy bears the name of George V," Gore has written. "No sovereign in our history had proved himself more honourable, more selfless, more approachable. None had ever gained a greater knowledge of the Empire and of the lives of all sorts and conditions of men within it." Here is Denis Judd's final assessment of George V:

> The worth of a constitutional monarch is not measured by the sophistication of his intellectual pursuits but by the way in which he performs his constitutional functions. In this respect, King George stands head-and-shoulders above his predecessors. He had none of Queen Victoria's awkward partiality, and little inclination to force his views on his ministers, like Edward VII. The constitutional improprieties of his great-great-uncles George IV and William IV would have been unthinkable to him. Yet, at certain crucial times during his reign, his firm but discreet touch on the constitutional tiller helped to put events on their proper course.

This last is surely the most important point to be made about George V, who has had an unfortunate reputation in the late twentieth century as an intellectual midget, a neglectful father, and a knee-jerk reactionary, among other things. This reputation is both unfair and inaccurate. An examination of his reign shows that it was, politically and constitutionally speaking, remarkably successful, progressive, and enlightened. Like his own second son, he came to the throne unexpectedly and as it were accidentally. He embarked upon his reign in the shadow of two particularly illustrious predecessors, Victoria and Edward VII. But at the first sign of trouble—the constitutional crisis over the House of Lords' veto power, which engulfed his reign just as he entered upon it—he gave instant evidence of being a lucid, sensible, fair, and intelligent man, and thanks to his leadership the crisis was resolved quickly and satisfactorily. Almost immediately afterward he had to become, most reluctantly, a leader of his country in the midst of a devastating and protracted world war. During the war years he worked as hard as any soldier; and he emerged from these years, like so many of his countrymen, with a severe physical disability, the result of that fall under his horse in France. During the General Strike he made sure that class hostilities did as little damage as possible and that the damage they did do stood a chance, at least, of being repaired. At another great moment of crisis, when Britain was plunged in a great Depression and seemed on the brink of bankruptcy, he concocted a means of providing a unified political approach to the country's problems that ruled out, for the time being, the destructiveness of narrow partisanship. And as the next great world conflict loomed, a conflict he could see coming when many others were unable or unwilling to do so, he did what he could to urge on an inert government some measures of preparation and self-protection, and condemned the rising new world powers so appealing to so many upper-class Englishmen of the day. He did his duty, took his job seriously, and worked hard at it. And so perhaps it was truer of King George than of any other modern monarch that he stood, in Gore's words, "as the sole link which bound together the commonwealth of nations called the British Empire by a personal tie of which the strength was nothing but the character and integrity of one man." After all it is character not cleverness that counts.

As the coffin of George V descended into the vault of the chapel at Windsor, placing his remains next to those of his parents, the country he left behind was in great danger simply because of the fact of his absence—an absence articulated memorably by John Betjeman:

> *Spirits of well-shot woodcock, partridge, snipe*
> *Flutter and bear him up the Norfolk sky:*
> *In that red house in a red mahogany book-case*
> *The stamp collection waits with mounts long dry.*
> *The big blue eyes are shut which saw wrong clothing*
> *And favourite fields and coverts from a horse;*
> *Old men in country houses hear clocks ticking*
> *Over thick carpets with a deadened force;*
> *Old men who never cheated, never doubted,*
> *Communicated monthly, sit and stare*
> *At a red suburb ruled by Mrs. Simpson,*
> *Where a young man lands hatless from the air.*

2

THE GOOD TIGER:
ELIZABETH BOWEN

I

IN THE 1940s Elizabeth Bowen had occasion to wonder if her prose style was beginning to resemble Henry James's. Her editors complained that sections of *The Heat of the Day* (1949) were "more Jacobean than James." Asked in 1959 about his influence upon her work, she replied: "You can't say it's like catching measles, because it's a splendid style, but it's a dangerous style." She disliked, she said, the very late James: "I really belong to *The Portrait of A Lady*" (early–middle James). Her friend Virginia Woolf had warned her to beware the influence of James, Bowen reported: "She foresaw him as a danger to me." From this time on Bowen asked her editors to scrutinize her manuscripts carefully and watch out for double negatives, for sentences that placed the adverb before the verb ("To whom do you beautifully belong?"), for grammatical inversions and stylistic tricks in general. She was very much aware of the Jamesian "measles" and somewhat apprehensive about catching them.

Despite her vigilance, Elizabeth Bowen's style resembles James's in many particulars, and of course she could have done worse. Harrison says to Stella in *The Heat of the Day*: "You, I mean to say, have got along on the assumption that things don't happen; I, on the other hand, have taken it that things happen rather than not. Therefore, what you see is what I've seen all along." "You're great; it's that that I've felt in you," one character tells another in the story "Aunt Tatty." In "The Inherited Clock" Clara says to Paul: "Have you *no* idea that I've no idea what you mean?"

But there is much more here than merely a stylistic resemblance. The two novelists shared many assumptions about what fiction should do and how it should do it. The echoes of James one hears everywhere in Bowen's work, from her first novel to her last, over five decades and all through her many stories, are the products more of the temperamental affinity of artists than of conscious or unconscious mimicry. Though the death of the Master occurred when Bowen was only seventeen, they shared as writers a strikingly similar community of interests—in, for example, the shocking moment of psychological insight, of sudden and total vision. Both deal in their fiction with people highly intelligent, if not always highly perceptive; on the one occasion when Bowen departed from this practice she self-consciously made fun of herself and her subject by calling the story "The Dolt's Tale." Her dialogue, like James's, is less naturalistic than expressive. Uninterested in politics, and believing in any case that art and politics do not mix, like James she was so certain of the value of civilized behavior that to articulate this belief directly in her work would have seemed to her inept. An instinctive artist with an instinctive sense of form, she shared James's interest in what she called "the art of exclusion" in her writing; "shape is possibly *the* important thing" in fiction, she said. Like James, she was fond of declaring that the French novelists had influenced her more than the British. She said of herself: "I am fully intelligent only when I write." "Art is the only thing that can go on mattering," one of her novels observes. She often says things that sound like James—that sound, that is, as if they should have been said by him. "My writing, I am prepared to think," Bowen declared, "may be a substitute for something I have been born without—a so-called normal relation to society. My books *are* my relation to society."

In the works of both novelists the tiny gesture may be all-expressive, with apparently small actions carefully discriminated and people's motives minutely scrutinized. In *The Last September* (1929) Lady Naylor remarks of Lois and Gerald, who seem to be too innocent to know that they are in love: "Of course, naturally, *they* haven't thought of it—if they had, don't you see, they'd be much more careful to make it appear they hadn't." Subsequently, going to a meeting with her niece's fiancé, Lady Naylor has an unpleasant surprise of the sort that may be epoch-making in a James story: "Lady Naylor, coming into Fogarty's soon after four, was annoyed to find Gerald there before her. She had now, instead of being discovered, to manoeuvre more or less openly for position."

There is a great deal more than this. Bowen was a writer, as her biographer Victoria Glendinning has observed, whose atmospheric descriptions of place and other-worldly perceptions, hyperaesthetic responses to shifts of mood, light, pace, and mass, may allow one to characterize her as a literary impressionist—very much an artist, that is, of the school of James and his disciple Joseph Conrad. "It seems to me," Bowen said of herself, "that often when I write I am trying to make words do the work of line and colour. I have the painter's sensitivity to light. Much (and perhaps the best) of my writing is verbal painting." James was fond of making analogies like this between the writer's craft and the painter's. The language of sensory perception is everywhere in the work of each. Like James, Bowen often took as her subject something only momentarily glimpsed or half understood and thus suggestive.

A watcher, a dedicated recorder of what she saw, Bowen also described her fiction as "transformed biography," feeling that the novelist should tell stories that are "true." James often said that fiction was greatest when it most closely resembled biography in its revelation of the "real" lives of its personages. Like James, Elizabeth Bowen thought of her characters as persons in "real" life and of the novelist as the historian and chronicler of that life. The underpinnings of her realism cannot be separated from the importance to her of "things"—"things are what we mean when we speak of civilization," she declares in *The Death of the Heart* (1938). Sounding like Madame Merle in her favorite novel by James, or any one of several characters in *The Spoils of Poynton,* Bowen writes in *The Death of the Heart,* her finest novel, of the "solicitude for *things.* One's relation to them, the daily seeing or touching, begins to become love, and to lay one open to pain." Her interest in "things," especially English "things," must have been generated in part by their romantic strangeness to her, for England was no more her native land than it was Henry James's. Perhaps because both were expatriates, both pay great attention to place and the atmosphere it generates. "Am I not manifestly a writer for whom places loom large?" Bowen asked rhetorically in a posthumous volume of recollections called *Pictures and Conversations* (1974). Place, for her, is what "gives fiction its verisimilitude . . . Nothing can happen nowhere." Four decades earlier, in 1935 and at the height of her powers as a novelist, Elizabeth Bowen wrote to Virginia Woolf: "Places are so exciting, the only proper experiences one has. I believe I may only write novels for the pleasure of saying where people are." She called the settings of her stories "Bowen terrain"—a landscape as distinct as James's, as her readers know. The importance of place may also be seen, in the work of each, in the interest devoted to comparative manners: the international theme, for example, is at the heart of Bowen's first novel *The Hotel* (1927). Non-natives writing (often about the English, both were extremely sensitive to national differences and similarities—but mostly the differences.

Many of Bowen's shorter tales are ghost stories in which the ghosts seem more real to the characters than "real" people do. Like James yet again, Bowen felt the thinness of the barrier between the living and the dead. One example is the volume of stories she wrote during World War II, *The Demon Lover* (1945), ghostly tales produced at least in part to demonstrate, according to Bowen, that the "wall between the living and the dead thinned" during the war, as she puts it in *The Heat of the Day.* And speaking of the living and the dead: what has been called James's "vampire" theme—the preponderance in his fiction of people living emotionally and financially off of others, and (metaphorically) drawing sustenance and the life-blood out of their victims in the process—may be found everywhere in Bowen's work, in which human relationships are always unbalanced or unsatisfying. Nowhere in James's vast *oeuvre* can one find any relationship between adults that is equally and reciprocally satisfying or fruitful for both partners. (He is in good company. The only happy couple in Shakespeare is the Macbeths.) Like James, Bowen fills her tales with frustrated and empty lives, needs unfulfilled, expectations dashed. Her story "The Secession" is a reworking of James's famous story on these themes, "The Beast in the Jungle." And there can be no doubt, though no one has noticed this, that Bowen's third novel, *Friends and Relations* (1931), is a revising and a reworking and nearly a rewriting of *The Golden Bowl*. Both novels examine carefully (among other things) the complications of relations among four adults who are intimately connected.

Living is a complicated business, and contented people are not always interesting subjects for the novelist. Bowen and James both believed, and show in their work, that tragic vision and tragic complexity can be more fruitful subjects for the novelist than, say, successful interpersonal relationships. In this they differ patently from many of their Victorian predecessors in the novel.

The equally sympathetic understanding of both sexes suggests a sort of androgyny in both James and Bowen: the gender of the author becomes irrelevant; other people's lives are viewed with the novelist's sexual antennae unplugged. Both write a good deal about love; the point is that desire, in their work, is not tied exclusively to gender. One result of this authorial androgyny is that children who have not yet reached sexual awareness play large parts in the fiction of each. Both novelists also like to use children as narrators, thus raising the question of *knowing*: how much do we, can we, should we know? Both were fascinated by human innocence and the havoc it could bring, by virtue of its ignorance, into the lives of the more worldly. In the stories of Bowen and of James, children are often palmed off on relatives or others, become extremely conscious of and sensitive to their unfamiliar surroundings—again, the expatriate view—and are plunged into the corrupting maelstrom of the dance of desire going on around them. Such prodigies tend to grow frighteningly observant. The tightrope between innocence and experience may be found hanging somewhere in all of Bowen's best books; the confrontation of innocence by evil is everywhere in her tales, as it is in James's.

But innocence can be inadvertently cruel in its blundering ignorance, and it is this understanding and this theme that tie Bowen and James most closely together. James's *What Maisie Knew* and "The Pupil" are just two of many examples. In Bowen's *Friends and Relations*, as in *The Golden Bowl*, knowledge is portrayed as impotent when confronted with impenetrable innocence. The murderousness of innocence is an important theme in another early Bowen novel, *To the North* (1932), and in her very last one,

Eva Trout (1969). And it is a central concern of *The Death of the Heart*, another tale with a child narrator. Bowen develops expansively here her theme of the cruelty of innocence. When innocents meet, she declares, "their victims lie strewn all round." More than anything else she wrote, critics are fond of quoting what she says on this subject in *Collected Impressions* (1950): "it is not only our fate but our business to lose innocence, and once we have lost that it is futile to attempt a picnic in Eden."

The need for illusion and ignorance as buffers against reality to preserve sanity—a radical theme in James's work (as, for example, *The Ambassadors*) as well as in one work after another by Joseph Conrad—is articulated succinctly in *The Death of the Heart* when the writer St. Quentin tells the child-narrator Portia: "if one didn't let oneself swallow some few lies, I don't know how one would ever carry the past." Portia wonders if perhaps "it's better . . . to know." "No, truly it is not," replies St. Quentin, who clearly would not mind a few more picnics in Eden. His final words to her express most eloquently Elizabeth Bowen's great debt to Henry James. After all, says St. Quentin, "society" is "people making little signs to each other."

What Bowen means by "people making little signs to each other" is *manners*, and this is where a great deal of her interest lies. Manners form the texture by which society is bound together, if at all. Like James, Bowen is fascinated by what underlies social behavior, what constitutes it.

And so Elizabeth Bowen may be seen as the spiritual daughter of Henry James—indeed at times, perhaps, more Jacobean than James himself. In this sense her work is traditional. At the same time she was doing new things in the novel, as we shall see. Simultaneously an innovator and a conservative, she resembles her age; she is both "modern" and old-fashioned. The best place to see this, perhaps, is in her first novel, *The Hotel*, where she takes the international theme and reworks it so completely that the critics howled. Their chief complaint—resembling, incidentally, early criticism of the work of Bowen's contemporary Mary Renault, another expatriate—was that the women in *The Hotel* were too intimate, too close. Bound by traditional models of gender, such criticism finds itself antagonized by expanding categories of desire, which it wishes to shrink back into conventionally tidy compartments.

What made Elizabeth Bowen decide to revise her favorite literary models? How did she become a traditionalist addicted to iconoclasm? Why were *The Hotel* and its successors written at all?

II

The woman her friends remember as tall, gaunt, and handsome, elegant, acerbic, and witty, an aristocratic respecter of conventions but not, somehow, a conventional person, was formed as an artist, she wrote later, by

2.1 Elizabeth Bowen, ca.1929, aged about thirty; by kind permission of Elizabeth Jenkins.

Y Y Y

being "motherless since I was thirteen" and "in and out of the homes of my different relatives—and, as constantly, shuttling between two countries: Ireland and England." Her rootlessness, which was to reappear in later life, instilled in her, she said, "a submerged fear that I might fail to establish grown-up status. That fear, it may be, egged me on to writing: an author, a grown-up, must they not be synonymous? As far as I now can see," she declared in 1948—sounding, and not for the only time, like her fellow expatriate Edith Wharton—"I must have been anxious to approximate to my elders, yet to demolish them." It is for these reasons, no doubt, that Elizabeth Bowen, for so many years without what she calls a "normal relation to society," saw her books as her connection to it.

An only child, she was born on 7 June 1899 in Dublin, the daughter of Anglo-Irish Protestants. Her father was a barrister, and the family traditionally divided its time between Dublin and an eighteenth-century country house in County Cork called Bowen's Court. The Bowens were Unionist, prosperous, and socially prominent; theirs had been a well-known family in Ireland for two and a half centuries. Elizabeth's mother's family had resided in Ireland since the sixteenth century. Historically, the Bowens and Anglo-Irish families like them, the critic Edwin J. Kenney has written, lived as a part of Ireland but separate from the native Catholic Irish, who remained distinct from them due to nationality, religion, position, and various protective walls, some symbolic and some, like those of Bowen's Court, very real indeed. The country house in a sense personified Bowen's emotional and imaginative connection to Ireland and to the aristocracy; she loved living at Bowen's Court, was always closely identified with it, and in her sixties was devastated upon hearing that its new owners had pulled it down. It and its milieu represented what she knew and treasured; her greatest novels are pre–World War II tales in which country houses remain an important part of the social landscape. When, after 1945, such houses could no longer be kept up except by the very rich, her fiction crumbled along with them: she was never the same. Probably she had no real sense of belonging to a minority culture. Bowen knew few Roman Catholics; the society she grew up in, like that of Edith Wharton four decades earlier in America, was sophisticated, wealthy, sure of itself: an autonomous entity in the midst of a diversity that was only rarely glimpsed and difficult to understand.

As a child Elizabeth divided her year between the houses in Dublin and Cork. Early on she became used to parties, regarding them as usual rather than unusual. Her social circle tended to be English rather than Irish; she was so insulated from contemporary Irish culture that she did not hear of the Irish Literary Revival until she was seventeen.

When Elizabeth was five her father, probably as a result of overwork and stress, had what today we would call a nervous breakdown. (In those days it was called "anemia of the brain.") On one occasion he politely asked his colleagues to open a window and then tossed out of it the pile of papers in front of him. In subsequent years he would be treated for depression, not always successfully. When he grew violent his wife left him, taking their daughter with her. Elizabeth and her mother settled at Bowen's Court, leaving the house in Dublin and in fact never returning to it. Mrs. Bowen was not a good manager; severe financial troubles eventually would overtake Bowen's Court and its inhabitants (and not for the last time). Very early on, Glendinning has written, Elizabeth was taught "not to notice" things, starting with the anomalous household, apparently well-to-do but fatherless and often moneyless, of which she was now a part. That childish assessment of adult life that runs continuously through her fiction commenced in her own life when she was six, the beginning of what the novelist later described as "a career of withstood emotion," also a ubiquitous theme in her fiction. What Kenney has called "Anglo-Irish landowning Big House life" also entered her consciousness as a subject of interest in these early years; it was all she knew.

Isolated, insulated, inimical, independent, distant, precocious, secretive: Elizabeth Bowen as a child was enacting the role she would later give to a number of fictional but well-understood protagonists. That "something cool and plaintive and delicate and rather sharp" that her friend the novelist and critic Elizabeth Jenkins would later detect as a "flavour" in Bowen's life as well as her work, begins, no doubt, here—the early feelings of difference and deprivation creating a sense of spiritual distance or opposition. In her life, as later in her work, distance, alienation, and anomalousness were always radical themes. What some people detected as coldness in the mature woman was no doubt a defense mechanism, a deliberate shielding of the self from further disappointment and betrayal.

Elizabeth's father was institutionalized when she was seven, and Mrs. Bowen took her young daughter with her to England. Here the girl's education and welfare were looked after by a gaggle of Anglo-Irish relatives; the novelist in later years was prone to refer to them as the "committee of aunts." It would have been surprising if this sudden uprooting from the only world she knew had not engendered in her some feeling of betrayal— "betrayal by her father when she needed him most, betrayal by her mother for taking her away from her father, betrayal by the whole adult conspiracy of governesses, doctors, lawyers, and family advisors" in taking her away from Ireland, as Kenney suggests. Such feelings would be magnified because she was consistently misled or kept in ignorance of just about everything until it happened, and she came to understand this perfectly.

Out of these traumatic early events Elizabeth Bowen developed a stammer that she never entirely outgrew, though it was never seriously debilitating. Like Somerset Maugham's, her stammer was undoubtedly the result of early insecurities and tragedies and unarticulated terrors. The stammerer, modern psychologists and speech therapists tell us, is usually ambivalent about oral communication, wishing to communicate but not to reveal himself or herself in any way. Stammering is also a sort of appeal for sympathy and, sometimes, for attention. No one knows what actually causes a stammer to develop; modern medical science teaches that there is some connection between early grief and stammering, but it cannot tell us what it is. The relentless stammer that afflicted Maugham probably reflected the persistence and penetration of his dreadful early years into his mature, successful years. He was orphaned early and sent to live with unsympathetic relatives in a foreign country (England; he grew up in France). Something of the same thing was happening now to the young Elizabeth Bowen, though in her case the worst was yet to come.

Elizabeth and her mother settled at Folkestone and later near Hythe, both on the Kentish coast, an area that years later became the setting for sections of *The Death of the Heart* and a later novel, *The Little Girls* (1964). There they lived in a series of rented "villas" more or less continuously for the next five years, from 1907 to 1912, Elizabeth's eighth to thirteenth years. As a child she found England, as Glendinning puts it, "romantically different" from Ireland, and thrived intellectually on the differences, as her novels and stories would show. Years later she declared that England had made her a novelist by rendering her conscious of diversity, giving her an introduction to comparative cultures and lives—an instance of the international theme being interjected into one's own life without any possibility of choice in the matter. And she would refer to her early "Anglo-Irish ambivalence to all things English," a subject for thought and later for fiction.

Elizabeth as a child became addicted to English history—daydreaming, as she said later, inside a sort of continuous historical novel of the imagination. From these years onward she was the willing dreamer of imaginary games, situations, families, events—a habit of mind resembling that of the fiction-writer she would soon become. "Elizabeth and her mother," the late Rosamond Lehmann told me, "used to play a game of visiting houses to let or for sale in Hythe, and inventing stories about the families who might have lived there or would do so in the future. This imaginative game they played together seems to me to penetrate her novels and stories." It was around this time that Elizabeth wrote several chapters of a would-be novel about Bonnie Prince Charlie, her first "work" of fiction.

Her father was ill, she was told, rather than mad, which is what he had become, at least temporarily, back in Ireland. Later he recovered both his sanity and his practice, and in 1911 he visited his wife and daughter briefly in Hythe. Elizabeth at this time, if family accounts can be trusted, was an uproarious, daring, lively, imaginative child, always with something to say. The adventures she had with her friends in Hythe during these years, and later with school friends at Harpenden, would be recalled half a century later in *The Little Girls*. Her education, like that of most girls of the pre-war era, was haphazard, dependent more upon day schools and tutors and governesses than any sustained tuition or institution.

Elizabeth visited Bowen's Court for the last time in the company of her parents in the summer of 1912. In the autumn of that year, in the Kentish villa where Elizabeth and her mother were living at the time, Mrs. Bowen, who had become her daughter's last connection to "continuity and security in the midst of all this disruption and uncertainty," as Kenney says, died of cancer. Elizabeth was thirteen. In a sense she never recovered from the shock of her mother's death. (One of the words over which her stammer frequently stumbled in later years was "mother.") Elizabeth had been told that her mother was unwell, but little more. Mrs. Bowen's desperate passages with surgery had been concealed from her; her mother, she was told at these times, was "away." If Elizabeth Bowen's novelistic children tend to be suspicious of what adults do and say and mean, this may be one reason why. This early betrayal, this early shock, helped shape a fixed view of the adult world: that much is clear. "The imaginative writer was the imaginative child," Bowen said later, "who relied for life upon being lied to." Fiction, as she implies here, is another kind of lying; the novelist, after all, is someone who makes things up, who lies for a living. Kenney shrewdly points out in his excellent study of Elizabeth Bowen that the writing of fiction would allow her "to establish a kind of legitimate lying that in itself was not capable of betrayal; whatever happens in a book, however horrible it may be— and Dickens's novels of suffering children, especially *David Copperfield,* were among her favorites—it does not change radically and suddenly on one; it is and remains known, which life does not." To move from a reader's view of this imaginative world to a writer's view of it is logical and comprehensible. "To do so," says Kenney, "is to draw closer the connection of the self and the uncertain actualities of one's own life to the fuller more coherent world of fiction. The great difference . . . between being lied to and lying oneself is what constitutes the loss of innocence and the achievement of adulthood along with the creation of art." Bowen as a writer never forgot the spectacle, taken from her own early years, of adults lying to a child to hide unpleasant truths. Having no children of her own to lie to, she grew up to "lie" to the world as a writer. "Elizabeth Bowen the novelist was the only adult Elizabeth the . . . child could trust," Kenney suggests. "As an adult she knew she was lying, and as a child she knew she was being lied to, but the needs of both were fulfilled in the fiction." Is it any wonder that, in her stories, the problematical nature of innocence, especially in the person of a child, is so radical a theme?

Elizabeth Bowen would later confide to her friend May Sarton that the worst thing that could possibly happen to her (Bowen) happened when she was very young, and that she never got over it. She had begged her mother not to be sent away to school; her mother promised her that this would never happen. As soon as Mrs. Bowen had breathed her last, Elizabeth's aunts, turning her worst nightmare into reality, enrolled her at Harpenden

Hall, in Hertfordshire. Rosamond Lehmann on this: "I remember her telling me that the effect of her mother's death when she was [thirteen] was to last [and make her] become completely withdrawn. She never spoke of her mother, and was, according to herself, difficult and abrasive, refusing all offered sympathy. But every night [at Harpenden Hall], she told me, she fell into heavy dreamless sleep, and woke with her pillow drenched and soaked with tears. This, I thought, was an absolutely heartbreaking reaction of intense suffering."

Again like Somerset Maugham—the parallels are striking—Elizabeth Bowen was sent away to a school from the only home she had, and given over to unknown relatives. For Maugham it was a clergyman and his wife in Whitstable; the story, of course, is told in *Of Human Bondage*. For Bowen it was a clergyman uncle and his sister in Harpenden. Elizabeth was now entrusted, like the orphan in *To the North*, to "a committee of relatives." Elizabeth's father returned to his law practice in Dublin, content to leave his only child behind in England. Again like the young Maugham, Bowen had been, in addition to everything else, expatriated.

She was luckier than Maugham in one respect: the relatives in whose house she landed were not the inimical, harsh, humorless misers depicted in *Of Human Bondage*. But the Harpenden pair were no prizes either. The vicar was shy and passive; his sister, a sort of frantic do-gooder and religious zealot, became the disciplinarian of the household. Bowen said later that she began her schooling in Harpenden enmeshed in "a sense of disfigurement, mortification, disgrace." She had been palmed off on second-rate connections; no one wanted her. To be dispatched from a house of love and contentment at so early an age, and so suddenly, must give one an inalienable sense of loss, of paradise lost, and possibly of personal worthlessness.

Fortunately the school was not bad. It provided Elizabeth with a chance to shine socially in a new circle, though she did not distinguish herself academically then or later. The remaining summers of her childhood, war permitting, were spent with her father at Bowen's Court, though he showed no sign of wanting to see his daughter at other times of the year. During part of the summer of 1913, when Elizabeth was fourteen, her father took her with him on a sortie to Belgium, Germany, and Switzerland. This would be the last summer before the Great War, though of course Elizabeth could have had no sense that she was seeing out the end of an era. She was at Bowen's Court in August 1914 and was told there of the outbreak of war. "Then can't we go to the garden party?" she asked her father. But the party was over. As Ireland became engulfed in its own war, the garden parties ceased altogether; houses were burned and armed soldiers were seen on the roads. This passage of Elizabeth's life, extended into the early 1920s, the period of the Irish Civil War, would be mined some years later for the stirring background of her superb early novel of Ireland, *The Last September*.

Elizabeth Bowen discovered the pleasures of reading fiction during her fifteenth and sixteenth years; Rider Haggard, George Macdonald, Baroness Orczy, E. Nesbit, Jane Austen, and Dickens. In her book *English Novelists* (1945) she says of the latter: "He gives a child's value . . . to the enjoyment of sheer physical bliss. . . . At the same time, he keeps a child's apprehensiveness of the weird, the unknown, the unsubstantially threatening. He gives loneliness, sense of loss or sense of betrayal all the frightful force they have as a child." Dickens's understanding of some of childhood's bereavements, psychological as well as familial, obviously spoke directly to Elizabeth at fifteen; sometimes, in her adopted home, she must have found herself feeling like a Dickens child. Toward the end of her life she reread Dickens and was especially moved once again by *David Copperfield.*

In the autumn of 1914 Elizabeth was sent to Downe House, a girls' boarding school in Kent started in what had once been Charles Darwin's home. Here she would remain, during school days, for three years, and here, as she said later, she learned how not to write.

One interesting aspect of Elizabeth's education at Downe House was the cultivation of her conversational abilities, noted and admired by virtually all who met her—in spite of her stammer—after she became famous. The mistresses at the school, Glendinning tells us, expected to be continually entertained by the conversation of their pupils at mealtimes: "To be able to keep up a stream of amusing talk was a matter of prestige" for the girls there. Elizabeth's tendency to shine in this context gave her some small measure of adolescent self-confidence. The Downe House system worked, at least for her. Among those who have commented on her conversational brilliance in later years is her close friend Elizabeth Jenkins: "She was a delightful companion because, among other attractions, she was a brilliant listener as well as a brilliant talker; but if you encouraged her and she was in the mood, she could talk for an hour on end; it was riveting but so high-powered you were both limp at the end of it. One has heard people who were merely loquacious, but her talk on those occasions, had such drive, and impetus, one never heard anything like it, before or since." The mature Elizabeth Bowen liked to talk; and when there was no one around to talk to, such was her love of talking, she habitually talked to herself.

In games at Downe House Elizabeth did not shine, being shortsighted and eschewing glasses. Glendinning speculates that Bowen's poor vision "was partially responsible for the 'impressionistic' quality of her writing." Like Henry James, much of whose work could also be described as impressionistic, as we have seen, "what she saw and responded to," Glendinning surmises, "was the general effect of light, colour and form; and she fully focussed only on a nearby detail, which thus acquired a disproportionate significance." Whether her literary impressionism grew out of her poor eyesight is problematic; place, as we know, always fascinated her, and undoubtedly it would have continued to do so through a pair of spectacles.

Elizabeth felt challenged and happy at Downe House. Here she read poetry, the Bible, and the encyclopedia, among other things. It was at Downe that she encountered the Irish Literary Revival for the first time. She shows no signs of being influenced by any Irish writer, though she came to admire Swift and Sean O'Faoláin. Fond in later years of describing herself as an "Irish novelist," in fact she remained largely immune to the literary influences of her native land. All of her literary roots are English, perhaps because both her formative years and her education had an English rather than an Irish flavor. At Easter 1916, with the outbreak of civil war in Ireland, Elizabeth's father and one of her cousins went off to fight for the British (not the Irish) cause there. She was not immediately affected, except perhaps in the crystallization of her loyalties, which were her father's. The desire of Sinn Fein in those years and indeed until recently to make English rule in Ireland impossible would provoke Elizabeth Bowen some years later, in *The Last September*, to describe, as the critic Patricia Craig puts it, "a countervailing spirit, that of 'big house' civility and *savoir-vivre*" among those who thought little of Irish republicanism. Politically conservative, Bowen never embraced the Irish republican cause; indeed, as we shall see, during World War II she agreed to spy on Ireland for England, and did so with enough distinction to have her dispatches noted by Churchill and Halifax.

In the summer of 1917 Elizabeth left Downe House and returned to an edgy, tense Dublin. This is the Ireland of *The Last September*: British garrisons bristling, young officers moving between tennis parties and dances on the one hand and Sinn Fein bullets on the other. Now eighteen, she divided her time between work in a hospital for shell-shocked soldiers in Dublin and weekends at Bowen's Court, where her father, who remarried in 1918, was in residence with his new wife, a woman he had known for many years and whom Elizabeth, fortunately, always liked. The Great War came to an end in this year, though the war in Ireland was to go on, and on.

Elizabeth returned to London to study painting at an art school in Southampton Row in 1919. Henry James also wanted to be a painter, and as a young man in Newport he worked hard at it for a while; in this too he and Elizabeth Bowen resemble one another. Both were, all of their lives, frustrated painters; the painter's sensibility is ubiquitous in their work, as is the painter's vocabulary in their commentaries on their work and the work of others. Elizabeth quickly recognized her limited abilities in this *genre*. In 1920 she briefly studied journalism, but this led nowhere. And in 1921, now twenty-two, she fell in love, apparently for the first time in earnest: a fairly straightforward account of this is given in *The Last September*, though most of Elizabeth Bowen's critics have unaccountably failed to see it. But there it is, plain as day, in the story of Lois and Gerald.

Elizabeth's infatuation was with a British army lieutenant garrisoned in Ireland, a solid and serious young man five years older than she and, it appears, rather unremarkable. In *The Last September* the lovers become engaged largely at the girl's insistence; having nothing much else to do at the time, Lois's life seems dull to her. In the novel Gerald is dragged into the engagement by one woman and chased out of it by another, a high-handed aunt of Lois, Lady Naylor. One of the "committee of aunts" quashed Elizabeth's brief engagement just as briskly in 1921, and that was that. In the novel what gives the Lois-Gerald relationship its special interest, as Patricia Craig points out, is the context of political tension surrounding it. *The Last September,* published in 1929, is set in Cork in 1920. British patrols are under attack, as they were in Cork in 1919; and in fact the killing of a British soldier there in that year undoubtedly was the model Bowen used for the end of Gerald, who is shot on a road while on patrol. Bowen's Court is brought to life in *The Last September* as Danielstown, a stronghold of Anglo-Irish sentiment and as a result constantly under threat of burning by the Irish republicans. In fact a number of houses in the neighborhood of Bowen's Court were burned by republican torches. In Bordighera on the Italian Riviera in 1921, in what would turn out to be the setting of her first novel, *The Hotel,* Elizabeth, who was there with an aunt to "recover" from her broken-off engagement, was told by her father to prepare for the worst: Bowen's Court, he wrote to her, would certainly be burned. It wasn't, of course; but the burning of Bowen's Court, as Craig suggests, was "antici-pated so intensely by Elizabeth that she must have written the ending of *The Last September* [Danielstown is burned] as a kind of exorcism." For many years afterward the specter of Bowen's Court in flames haunted Elizabeth Bowen's imagination—until, unable in later years to keep the place going, the conflagration began to take on the trappings in her mind of something approaching wish-fulfillment.

Elizabeth began writing for publication in 1918—poetry first, inevitably, and then, very quickly, fiction. She started composing short stories in 1919 (she was twenty) as she saw herself failing to become a painter. She scribbled away in various venues—at Bowen's Court; at her aunt's house in Harpen-den; at the home of a great-aunt, Lady Allandale, who lived at Queen's Gate, London. When in London she roamed the bookshops and the poetry salons; once at the Poetry Bookshop, "upstairs, after dark, in a barn-like room, I listened to Ezra Pound reading aloud what was hypnotically unin-telligible to me by the light of one candle." Lady Allandale, meanwhile, was trying to get her grand-niece suitably married off. But the old lady was not always au courant, as witness her attempt to promote an understanding between Elizabeth and Eddie Marsh, the famously handsome and flamboy-antly homosexual friend of the late Rupert Brooke, and of course an editor of *Georgian Poetry.*

Elizabeth Bowen's earliest stories, like those of most writers, were reject-ed by the magazines to which they were sent; and like all ultimately success-ful writers, she persevered. Her first published tale, "Breakfast," would open the collection that also became her first published volume, *Encounters* (1923), which appeared when its author was just twenty-four. At this time she was not yet, as Glendinning reminds us, the well-read author who could talk easily of Henry James, Maupassant, or other masters of the short story; she had read collections by E. M. Forster and Richard Middleton (*The Ghost-Ship*) and perhaps a few others. She would later describe these first stories of hers as "a mixture of precocity and naivety." Not surprisingly, they reflect the interests and concerns of the young Elizabeth Bowen as well as some of the characteristic themes of her subsequent work. The well-to-do and the mature, frequently women and frequently effusive, overly sensitive, pompous, narrow, confused, and underdeveloped emotionally, are often watched here by a passive or inarticulate young observer (as, for example, in "The Return"). In "The Shadowy Third" and "The Lover" the young author demonstrates her interest in the love story, an interest that would never flag. The title character in "Mrs. Windermere" is a sort of dry run for the character called Mrs. Kerr, whose vanity, heartlessness, and egotism are so memorably savaged in *The Hotel*. The story "Coming Home," as Glendinning points out, is the most autobiographical of this group, concentrating as it does on the writer's still-raw grief over the shocking loss of her mother. It is about a girl living with one parent after the death of the other, a death that provokes in her feelings of guilt. It can be said of these initial efforts that they introduce an author extremely sensitive to setting, to the physical surroundings of her characters—as well as an author for whom irony is never very far away. Also, as Kenney points out, these earliest tales, which must have been painful for Elizabeth to write, strike what would become a characteristic Bowenesque note about children, who are always seen as existing in a context of insecurity, loneliness, and deception.

Encounters, which was on the whole favorably reviewed upon its appearance in 1923—including a notice by L. P. Hartley in the *Spectator*—achieved publication by the firm of Sidgwick and Jackson largely through the intervention of the novelist Rose Macaulay, an old friend of Elizabeth's former headmistress at Downe House. Macaulay also got Elizabeth invited to some literary soirées; suddenly she found herself meeting the likes of Aldous Huxley, Walter de la Mare, and Edith Sitwell, among others. Rose Macaulay "lit up a confidence I never had," Bowen said later. She also remarked of *Encounters* that its composition was a "cry . . . for affirmation" and that she hoped to find, through its acceptance, a sign that she was "not mad." Thus were the trials of her youth still with her. Her profession, now that she had one, gave her life a new focus, a new center, a new point of reference to which, from now on, she could always return.

But this year, 1923, provided an even more tangible anchor to Elizabeth Bowen's life. For on 4 August (the date so beloved of Ford Madox Ford in *The Good Soldier*) she was married.

III

The bridegroom was Alan Charles Cameron. After the war ended Cameron took some time to recuperate, in Oxford, from a wound and gas poisoning, living there with an older male friend. By the time Elizabeth met him, while visiting friends in Oxford, he had become Assistant Secretary for Education for Northamptonshire. The two went off on long walks—Elizabeth Bowen was always a great walker—often chatting about literature. The wedding was at her uncle the vicar's church at Blisworth in Northamptonshire. Elizabeth was twenty-four, Alan Cameron, thirty. Their first home, determined by Alan's job, was in the town of Kingsthorpe, Northampton.

In time Alan Cameron would become an accomplished administrator in the Civil Service. And for a while, just after his marriage, he would remain, as Glendinning remarks, the dominant partner: "he had been to Oxford, he had been through the war, he had read a lot, he could talk about what he read." A handsome and well-turned-out man who grew obese and alcoholic in later years, he taught his wife in the 1920s how to dress both stylishly and smartly. She came to depend on him for virtually everything in her life, especially after she grew famous and more careful organization of her time became necessary. In return, according to those who knew them, he adored her, probably more than she adored him. She had no maternal desires, then or later, and he accepted that. He had few if any carnal desires, and she accepted that, perhaps even welcomed it. To some of those who met them later, when he seemed little more than a Blimp-ish appendage of the famous novelist, the liaison appeared incomprehensible. May Sarton told me: "I couldn't imagine why she married him." Her novel *A Shower of Summer Days,* published in 1952, "is about Bowen's Court . . . Violet [Gordon] is *not* Bowen but her husband [Charles Gordon] is an accurate portrait of Alan Cameron—and Bowen wrote me a fine letter about the book." Elizabeth could hardly complain about the portrait of Alan, if that is what it is, in *A Shower of Summer Days,* for in it he is painted as tactful and practical, unexciting but incisive, avuncular, and above all comfortable, soothing.

In the wake of her disappointment over her first disastrous engagement, recently ended, Elizabeth probably married him for safety, because she was lonely and adrift, and because he proposed. As the years went by she grew to depend on him, even through a series of love affairs of her own. But if she can be believed on the subject, she never considered leaving him, despite the radical bohemianism she cultivated in later years. "He is not a person that one could leave," she was quoted as saying, nor was she the leaving kind—though she was frequently absent. She would always come home to him when one of her affairs ended, and having him to come home to gave her life a steadiness and a center. He consistently gave her good advice, and consistently she took it. They traveled together a good deal and enjoyed each other's company for many years (nearly thirty). When he died she was genuinely devastated. Elizabeth Jenkins commented on the marriage in these terms: "Alan was immensely proud of her, and devoted to her; she had a deep-laid affection for him but her social and professional life were very high-powered, whereas he was quiet." It was a good fit, and in this way the marriage was successful for three decades—at any rate more successful than many marriages.

Over the years the balance of power shifted and Elizabeth became the dominant partner. May Sarton tells the story of going to a zoo with Alan one day when Elizabeth was elsewhere and watching him step in front of every cage holding a lion, a tiger, or a leopard. He gazed upon each animal for a while, speaking but a single word in front of each cage: "Elizabeth!" He seems not to have had affairs; she was always involved with somebody, and often her female friends were jealous both of her attractiveness to men and of the freedom she enjoyed to attract them. The Anglo-Irish novelist Molly Keane (M. J. Farrell) remarked: "When you went to a party, all the men you'd like to meet were standing in a ring around Elizabeth Bowen."

Elizabeth and Alan lived in Northamptonshire for two years before moving to Old Headington, Oxford, in 1925, when he was appointed Secretary for Education for the city of Oxford. Here they would live for the next ten years. And here Elizabeth would write all or most of *The Last September, Joining Charles* (1929; stories), *Friends and Relations, To the North, The Cat Jumps* (1934; stories), and *The House in Paris* (1935)—altogether the most productive period of her writing life, the period in which some of her greatest works were composed. But the two years at Kingsthorpe had also been productive: she was able to put together another volume of stories after *Encounters*, published as *Ann Lee's* in 1927, and her first novel, *The Hotel*, published in Britain in 1928 and the United States in 1929. In America it became an unlikely Book-of-the-Month Club selection and made its author famous overnight at the age of thirty. Virginia Woolf, reading *The Hotel* before becoming a friend of its author, wrote in her diary that "Eth Bowen . . . tries to write like me," one of her usual delusions about other authors, especially successful ones; in fact *The Hotel*, as we shall see, owes as much to Henry James as any book Elizabeth wrote. Though they were to become quite good friends, the literary influence of Virginia Woolf on Elizabeth Bowen was virtually nil.

In *Ann Lee's*, as Glendinning has noted, the "image of people leaving or having left, disappearing, ceasing to exist for each other" recurs again and again; Bowen in her late twenties still felt very close to the theme of loss, especially sudden or inexplicable loss. Clear echoes of autobiography abound in "The Visitor," for example, which is about a boy made to stay with some old maids while his mother is dying and no one will tell him anything about her. "Making Arrangements" is the story of a dull man nobody finds interesting married to a lively woman everyone finds amusing—a lucid but probably subconscious pre-vision, as it were, of the way many of the Camerons' friends would perceive and speak of them in later years. One is reminded too of the Quaynes in *The Death of the Heart*. Thomas hides in his study until his wife's clever guests leave the house. There is also the scent of Henry James here in the inequality of the relationship—one who is valued, one who is not, a social and spiritual disparity between them always perceived (real or not) by those they meet.

In Oxford the Camerons' social life blossomed. They grew particularly close to John Buchan and his family, the classicist C. M. Bowra, the poet Cecil Day Lewis, and the novelist L. P. Hartley. On one evening in the early 1930s John Buchan, Elizabeth Bowen, Virginia Woolf, and Rosamond Lehmann simultaneously inhabited the drawing-room of the Buchans' home.

Another of Elizabeth's new friends was Lord David Cecil, a young don at Wadham College. Bowen and Cecil were to become close friends, and their relationship would inspire one of her finest novels, *To the North,* which was dedicated to Cecil. Whether they were lovers has been a subject of some speculation and controversy over the years, but probably they were not. Glendinning declares: "they were not lovers." Elizabeth Jenkins, who knew Bowen as well as anybody, characterizes their relationship as an "undying amitié amoureuse." In *Glimpses of the Great* (1986) A. L. Rowse says that "though [it] was an emotional relationship, a love affair, it was platonic, apparently non-sexual." He adds: "Though I had a close friendship with [Cecil], neither of them betrayed anything to me, though I was a bit curious."

Lord David introduced the Camerons to his Oxford friends, and their social circle expanded again. At one gathering Bowen met the young Francis King, who, hearing only the name "Mrs. Cameron," proceeded to lecture her on his favorite subject, the modern novel. Harold Acton, Glendinning reports, "spent a whole evening trying to extract from 'Mrs. Cameron' who she was," and failed. She also met many of Bowra's circle, including Rex Warner, Cyril Connolly (who would become a friend), Kenneth Clark, Henry Green, John Betjeman, Evelyn Waugh, Anthony Powell, Isaiah Berlin (another future friend), and A. J. Ayer.

IV

In July 1926 Rose Macaulay wrote to another publisher friend of hers, Michael Sadleir at Constable. She recommended for publication a new novel, *The Hotel,* by Elizabeth Bowen. It appeared two years later. Elizabeth had worried that she lacked the concentration and the range to move from the short story to the novel until the idea of hotel life on the Italian Riviera, where she had spent the winter of 1921 after her first, broken engagement, struck her as a suitable subject, as Glendinning tells us. The novel's setting, as Patricia Craig has said, enabled its author "to poke fun at the social life of such places, full of potty English residents: the ecstasies of misunderstanding, the burning attachments" which so often burn down and go out. The central figure in the novel is a girl who forms an unsuitable attachment to an older man, recognizes her mistake, and regains her senses. The broken engagement and the setting point again toward autobiography. There is also in *The Hotel* what would turn out to be the usual Bowenesque element of what Craig calls "the *bois dormant* motif": "intelligence temporarily displaced by some kind of torpor seems to be associated by Elizabeth Bowen with late adolescence in interesting girls." Another autobiographical scent may be found, perhaps, in the searing account of the way the girl (Sydney Warren) might be dominated and influenced by a middle-aged woman (Mrs. Kerr): of course this was the sort of influence Bowen had had to deal with throughout much of her life.

Glendinning is one of the few readers of Elizabeth Bowen to recognize how funny *The Hotel* is. Virtually all of the characters are eccentric; the novel is composed of a series of scenes in which the hotel's residents are moved around and placed in counterpoint with their fellow guests to underline their ruling neuroses—food, landscape, bathrooms, foreigners, and on and on.

Once again here we come back to Bowen's great debt to Henry James. It is a large debt already in this first novel—which, unlike many first novels, is extraordinarily accomplished. Bowen, for example, has undoubtedly picked up from her reading of James—rather than from her own experience, which in the 1920s was still quite limited—the theme of the unequal relationship. We have seen that in James's fiction mutually satisfying relationships between men and women do not exist: there is always an imbalance of desire, of control, of contentment. One member of the partnership may be happy—even this is rare—but never both. James seemed to feel that humanity was foredoomed to unsatisfactory interpersonal relationships, and Bowen absorbed this lesson early on. So, for example, in *The Hotel* we encounter one character who "cannot believe . . . in any satisfactory *modus vivendi* between two people that's based on an attraction," and another who finds it "odd . . . that men and women should be expected to pair off for life." And there are passages that sound like James—two characters watching "from rise to fall the whole drama of lunch," for example; or this, which seems to catch the Jamesian tone and syntax:

He had been alarmed and impressed by the idea that she had not an inkling of his subtleties; or rather, would not exert herself to perceive them. But since his arrival at this hotel, he had been amazed by the fineness of her perceptions, not only from moment to moment but by a sudden vista of them along the past, perceptions so delicate, appreciations so faultless that it could only have been some lack of an equal fineness that had made him suffer an infinite deprivation.

The subtlety and complexity and precision of this language, its minute analysis of motives and feelings, as well as certain turns of phrase such as "an inkling of his subtleties," "the fineness of her perceptions," "sudden vista," "equal fineness," and "infinite deprivation" would lead almost any reader playing a game of Who Said That? to put Henry James's name under this passage.

Another obvious inheritance from James is the novel's international theme. The clash of cultures and the comparison of manners and mores between and among nationalities and classes is achieved by James in book after book by placing Americans abroad, often for many years, and writing about them there, surrounded by the inimical and sometimes impenetrable social perspectives of the natives. Just as all of the major characters in Bowen's favorite novel by James, *The Portrait of A Lady*, are Americans, though the novel is set in England and in Italy, so here, in *The Hotel*, also set in Italy, all of the chief characters are English. One of their constant topics is the level of civilization surrounding them. They are often amused, sometimes baffled; but we are invited, as in a novel by James, to see how very little moral advantage, if any, these visitors have over those whose culture they treat with such patronizing curiosity.

Equally to the point is that, in this first novel, we hear a voice that is authentically and, one may say from hindsight, unmistakably that of Elizabeth Bowen—a voice, that is, of her own: arch, ironic, full of humor, pathos, and a sad delight in the oddness of things. The subject matter may be drawn from James, but at times the sound is uniquely Bowen. Some examples of the characteristic Bowen sound:

- "How complete the Riviera was, thought Sidney, one could even die here."
- "Isn't it funny that for everybody there seems to be just one age at which they are really themselves?"
- "What people call life's larger experiences . . . are so very narrowing."
- "It was another of these idyllic evenings, agonizingly meaningless."
- "I suppose there is nothing like buying experience that somebody else pays for."

Witty, tart, cynical, aphoristic, subtle, complex: the Bowen sound. A reader familiar with her fiction would recognize her hand in these passages—and in a sentence like this one, with its unique, exact, sophisticated sentiment: "One cannot, however casually, present these native carnations to a friend and remain quite unaffected, while the pleasure with which carnations are received is intensified by some vague agitation." How utterly Bowenesque that is. What does it mean, exactly? It is probably indefinable, though Elizabeth Jenkins comes as close as anyone has to defining the unique Bowen style. What "I can connect with her writing," Jenkins has remarked, as we saw earlier, "is something which is the same in anything of hers I have ever read: something cool and plaintive and delicate and rather sharp, like a flavour or a scent." The Bowen reader understands this immediately.

Finally, there are some interesting echoes of Ibsen in *The Hotel*. In the following passage we hear them in the language and in the articulation of a realist's creed: "I have often thought it would be interesting," says Sydney Warren, "if the front of any house, but of an hotel especially, could be swung open on a hinge like the front of a doll's house. Imagine the hundreds of rooms with their walls lit up and the real-looking staircase and all the people surprised doing appropriate things in appropriate attitudes as though they had been put there to represent something and had never moved in their lives." Ibsen's idea of realistic drama as tantamount to removal of the "fourth wall," the "wall" facing the audience, seems to mesh with Bowen's desire to see into the private lives of ordinary people doing ordinary things. (The passage also may remind us, no doubt inadvertently, of Hawthorne's description of a novel by Trollope.) Interestingly enough, the final paragraph of *The Hotel* alludes once again to Ibsen: "The Hotel from up here was as small as a doll's house." Why Ibsen? Does Bowen want her reader to think of her as an Ibsen of the novel, unshrinking from the facts of "real" people's lives?

With the immediate and deserved success of *The Hotel*, Elizabeth Bowen became a literary lion, in demand both for her work and herself—especially the latter. Maurice Bowra has left an impression of her during her first years of celebrity:

> She was tall and well built and had the manner of someone who has lived in the country and knows its habits. She was handsome in an unusual way, with a face that indicated both mind and character. Unlike some Irish, she did not talk for effect but kept the conversation at a high level and gave her full attention to it. . . . She had the fine style of a great lady, who on rare occasions was not shy of slapping down impertinence . . . with all her sensibility and imagination, she had a masculine intelligence which was fully at home in large subjects and general ideas.

Bowra also remarked that Elizabeth Bowen had "a historical insight lacking in many historians" and resulting, he thought, from an extreme sensitivity to place and its past. And he added, according to Glendinning, that Bowen had "the gift of making everywhere visited in her company seem magical and mythical, and everyone . . . encountered with her more interesting than they really were; quite dull people, first met in her company, retained afterwards a spurious fascination." Perhaps without knowing it, what Bowra perceived were the attributes of a storyteller. For Elizabeth Bowen, after

The Hotel, there were no barriers to publishing her stories, and she was always looking for material, even, perhaps especially, among "quite dull people."

Another volume of stories, *Joining Charles,* and another novel, *The Last September,* appeared in 1929, when Elizabeth Bowen was thirty.

Joining Charles, her third collection of short stories, is one of her least distinguished productions, but the novel is one of her finest. Bowen's interest in Cork and in her old home never flagged; throughout the 1920s she and her husband continued to pay visits to Bowen's Court and to her father. She was both revisiting her girlhood and reseeing contemporary Ireland; out of this came *The Last September.* "Of all my books," Bowen would say later, not surprisingly, this one "is nearest my heart"; she added that it had a "deep, unclouded spontaneous source" in her own experience. As Craig points out, Bowen's youthful summers in Ireland are compressed, in this novel, into the summer of 1920. "With its romantic, elegiac feeling and its sharp social interludes," *The Last September* focuses on characters and settings, settings above all, closest to the novelist's own experience. A part of the autobiographical resonance here, as Kenney has observed, lies in the divisions between being, on the one hand, English or Irish, and, on the other, an adult or a child. With these divisions, especially when they overlapped, Elizabeth Bowen, of course, was amply familiar.

The aimlessness of the novel's nineteen-year-old protagonist, Lois Farquar, makes her long for form and pattern, as Bowen undoubtedly did before she found them in her work and in her life. "This was a creature still half-awake, the soul not yet open, nor yet the eyes," Bowen wrote in the preface to the American edition of *The Last September.* "And world war had shadowed her schooldays; *that* was enough—now she wanted order." The "pattern" that Lois finally perceives in her life is what Kenney calls "a pattern of tragedy"—that is, "that there is no security, that security and happiness are a game played by grown-ups." One cannot avoid life, its opportunities and pitfalls, by "not noticing" things: "things" will make themselves felt in your life whether you choose to notice them or not. Passion and terror are always near, acknowledged or not. These themes are ubiquitous in Bowen's work, though here once again we are at the edge of the Henry James country too.

In addition to Lois, there may be something of Elizabeth Bowen, as Glendinning suggests, in the elegant, detached character called Marda, who is older and more worldly and assured than Lois is. But certainly Lois is Elizabeth at nineteen. Lois falls in love with a soldier, as we have seen, and is talked out of it by an aunt, who wants to send her niece to an art school instead, though Lois can't draw. What could be clearer? There is a political resonance too. The Danielstown family, though thoroughly Anglo-Irish,

2.2 Meet of the Duhallow Hunt at Bowen's Court, County Cork, Ireland; by permission of Celia Lanyon and Victoria Glendinning.

with the emphasis on the Anglo, is caught between conflicting loyalties much as the Bowens were during the Troubles. That is, both families, the fictional Farquars and the real Bowens, could not help but become involved in the difficulties of their neighbors and of Cork generally during this period. Though the Bowens remained loyal to England, they lived in and among the Irish and could not pretend they did not. The difficulties of the Farquars— their own "troubles," mostly to do with individuals rather than causes— reflect those of the Bowens in the years following the Great War.

V

In the year after *The Last September* was published—that is, in 1930— Elizabeth's father died, and she became the sole owner of Bowen's Court. Throughout the 1930s, until the outbreak of war in Europe in 1939, the Camerons frequently stayed at the house in Ireland, though they continued to live primarily in Oxford, where Alan worked. Though Bowen would reside at Bowen's Court throughout much of the 1950s and almost entirely after Alan died in 1952, the 1930s were both the heyday and the last hurrah of Bowen's Court. Never again would it be so lively, so full of distinguished guests, so well maintained. Visitors arrived from Oxford, from London, from New York. Though the 1930s were, in Auden's indelible phrase, "a low, dishonest decade," this was also the last time, as Glendinning has observed, that one could speak of "society" under the old meaning of week-day London and country-house life during weekends—rural servants, din-ner-parties, weekend guests: "The big difference between then and now [1977] was that the upper-middle-class world of society and the world of the arts very largely coincided . . . Charm, wit, and cleverness were at a pre-mium and good manners and 'civilized' behaviour were not yet discredited among people whose values dominated even the depression years."

Then as now, literary London was small enough for writers to seek each other out, if they chose to do so, and live in each others' pockets. By the 1930s Elizabeth Bowen had become friendly with Virginia Woolf, Lady Ottoline Morrell, Rosamond Lehmann, Stephen Spender, Evelyn Waugh, L. P. Hartley, Graham Greene, Henry Green, A. E. Coppard, Ivy Comp-ton-Burnett, Humphry House, Raymond Mortimer, May Sarton, and Elizabeth Jenkins. She also met T. S. Eliot and his wife and left an account of an evening with them. She found their flat, Glendinning tells us, "sinister and depressing" due to "the atmosphere of two highly nervous people shut up together in grinding proximity." Of Eliot himself: "so very funny and charming and domestic and nice to be with, besides being so great. I love knowing him," she said. Eliot informed her that without alcohol he could not get into the writing mood.

May Sarton told me that when she stayed at Bowen's Court in the 1930s it was "very cold, there were no screens on the windows, moths came in, and

Elizabeth Bowen was terrified of moths." The cooks, Sarton recalls, were local girls from town, and the food was poor. There were no bathrooms at Bowen's Court. "You had to walk half a mile to a neighbor's house for a martini and a bath." Maids brought hot water up to houseguests in the morning for washing and shaving. There were enclosed gardens to walk in. "One ate in a great hall surrounded by portraits in red velvet but run down." In *A Shower of Summer Days* Sarton makes the local Irish cleaning lady of "Dene Court" reflect "how shabby everything was, how worn the carpets, how faded the curtains and walls."

Elizabeth Jenkins felt quite differently about Bowen's Court when she stayed there in the 1940s. The house, she said, was "large and gaunt. Its being very sparsely furnished was an advantage, it hadn't been de-natured by furnishing and decoration," though "there were some very interesting pieces in Bowen's Court. I slept in one of those Regency beds like a boat; Elizabeth had a four-poster with beautiful yellow curtains." Jenkins has a decidedly different recollection of meals at Bowen's Court: "The food she provided was wonderful: of unlimited, pure ingredients and tasting delicious. She had several at a time of little Irish girls to run Bowen's Court and she said how diligent the Catholic priest was in promoting innocent enjoyments for them so that they should be happy and kept out of mischief; he arranged such a social programme for them, she said it was sometimes quite inconvenient; you wanted one or the other of them but they were out at a dance or a whist drive or some expedition on pleasure bent." And Jenkins said this about Elizabeth Bowen and her Irish neighbors: "Her relations with the villagers were so completely cordial and unself-conscious: naturally enough as her family had been there for generations. When one went on a walk with her, one constantly met Irish inhabitants, so small and weazened-looking, like leprechauns but full of gaiety. She stopped to talk, and listen, to all of them, and was deep in their family affairs before you could say knife." Jenkins also felt, however, that keeping the place up imposed a severe strain, both financial and emotional, on Elizabeth Bowen, and that in later years she developed a somewhat ambivalent attitude toward Bowen's Court, dreaming on several occasions that it had burned to the ground—a dream initiated, as we know, by her father's warnings during the Troubles.

Victoria Glendinning in her biography and Patricia Craig in her critical study of Bowen both tell us that Elizabeth Bowen saw Virginia Woolf for the first time at tea in the garden of Lady Ottoline Morrell's house in Gower Street, Bloomsbury. But Bowen herself told Elizabeth Jenkins—so Jenkins told me—that she, Bowen, had first seen Mrs. Woolf at a Cambridge garden party; Woolf, Bowen told Jenkins, "was standing about with a parasol under her arm, so slender and so gauche, she looked like an undergraduate." Virginia Woolf was fifty at the time (1933); Bowen was thirty-four. Jenkins, who also knew Woolf, believes there was, personally, a vast gulf between the two novelists even as there were many similarities. "I think what [Elizabeth] was, was as remarkable as what she wrote," Jenkins told me. "She was the only person in literary society who could be regarded as the successor to Virginia Woolf; they were so different: Elizabeth being exquisitely kind, and Virginia Woolf, exquisitely unkind, but as regards eminence during their lifetimes I think they were on an equality. In that respect, they have no successor. I am speaking of course of their social influence."

VI

Elizabeth Bowen published four volumes of fiction during the early 1930s: *Friends and Relations* and *To the North*, two of her finest novels; *The Cat Jumps,* her fourth volume of stories; and *The House in Paris,* a novel controversial with the critics. We shall look briefly at each of these.

Friends and Relations (1931) demonstrates as forcefully as anything Elizabeth Bowen wrote the influence of Henry James upon her work. The general situation of the characters in her novel is nearly identical to that in *The Golden Bowl* (1904): two couples, each of the four connected in some way with a member of the other couple. In *Friends and Relations* we have two married sisters, one of whom is emotionally involved with her sister's husband. In James's novel it is likely, though never actually stated or shown, that adultery has taken place and has continued to do so over a significant period of time. In Bowen's novel it is more likely that it hasn't, but this very question of whether it has or has not, whether it will or will not, is at the center of the story, as it is in *The Golden Bowl.* Each novelist asks the story's characters, and through them us, to balance personal desire against family commitment. In both tales these claims clash continuously; and in both personal desire is stifled and defeated, supposedly for the general good. In *The Golden Bowl* this defeat is presented to us as tragic, a tragedy for the individuals in question; in *Friends and Relations* the defeat of desire is depicted as part of the social comedy. And herein lies the most important difference between the two books, as between the two authors. Bowen sees the tragedies of life but does not forget the social comedy; life goes on, and we must make the best of it, not always getting everything we want. For James the personal tragedy is the end toward which everything, and especially human relationships, moves; ultimately the social comedy is seen by him to be not so amusing after all.

James said of *The Golden Bowl* that, in it, he had gone as far as one could go in fiction in examining the psyches of a small number of characters; he focuses on nothing but those psyches for hundreds of rich pages in *The Golden Bowl,* describing the novel as "a real feat of engineering." In the novel's preface, written in 1909 for the New York Edition of his works, James says of the narrative system he adopted in *The Golden Bowl* that "the advantage" of it was that it could "display the sentient subjects themselves at the same time and by the same stroke with the nearest possible approach to a desirable vividness." Thus the "scheme" of the novel, James remarks here, is that although we "see" very few persons in *The Golden Bowl*—no more than six, and only four in detail—"we shall really see as much of them as a coherent literary form permits." The narrative angle of the novel, then, is designed to expose as fully as possible the minds of the four protagonists in counterpoint to one another. In *Friends and Relations* Elizabeth Bowen adopts the same narrative angle; she uses the same perspective for the same reasons; and she tells virtually the same story for some of the same thematic reasons. This is not to belittle her; what a great model she chose—and after all she does amend the story's focus and its lessons to suit her own ends.

As in most of his novels, James uses "scenes" sparingly in *The Golden Bowl*, drawing out the spaces between the confrontational dialogues his characters have with one another in order to make the reader look forward to them and to make them, when they come, as dramatic as possible. In *Friends and Relations*, similarly, Bowen uses "scenes" sparingly and creates dramatic interest in the same way. Though it has not been noticed, Bowen in *Friends and Relations* takes her method and her story from *The Golden Bowl*, and with great success. *Friends and Relations*, after all, is much shorter and in some ways more coherent than *The Golden Bowl*, though it is nowhere near as great a novel: it does not attempt as much. But it could be argued that *Friends and Relations*, a piece of perfection, is the less flawed of the two. Whatever the argument, the two novels taken together illustrate once again Elizabeth Bowen's bottomless debt to Henry James.

Both *Friends and Relations* and its successor, *To the North*, feature as observers of the action and of their elders precocious, self-conscious, rather unpleasant adolescent girls, a type repeated in Bowen's novels, as we know. Both also describe interfering and obnoxious older ladies, sort of generic Bowen aunts. Like *Friends and Relations*, *To the North* focuses on two women closely connected, in this case sisters-in-law rather than sisters; once again their relations with men, the same men, are under scrutiny. *To the North* embodies for the first time in Bowen's fiction, but not the last, what Sean O'Faoláin has called "the kid and the cad" syndrome—that is, the adolescent observer confronted with an older male immoralist. The confrontation is usually destructive in some way to each. In *To the North* the cad, Markie, is undoubtedly drawn from Bowen's friend Maurice Bowra.

The Jamesian aspect of *To the North* may be found chiefly in its theme of the confrontation of innocence with—well, if not evil, exactly, then let us call it experience, or perhaps sophistication. How much is it good for us to know? Is a little ignorance acceptable? Must one's moral education always be a tragic process? These questions, raised by James in virtually all of his major works, inform *To the North*, though not as powerfully as in *The Death of the Heart*. In these novels Bowen examines the "havoc" innocence can cause, its destructive power in a cynical world in which innocence is unexpected, unanticipated, misunderstood, and often misinterpreted.

Among her earlier works, *To the North* has the most somber ending; comedy for once is muted as the novelist examines the destructiveness, the "dire conjunction," in Craig's phrase, of interpersonal relationships—also the great theme, of course, of Henry James.

Unusually for a volume of stories, *The Cat Jumps* (1934) sold out its first printing immediately, a mark of the public following Bowen had acquired by this time. She wanted to call this book "Hard Fantasy": "One hears much of 'hard fact,'" she said. "Fantasy can, to my mind, be more of a tyrant."

The House in Paris (1935) draws at least in part on a love affair Elizabeth Bowen had in Oxford with the literary critic Humphry House—Bowen's biographer, Victoria Glendinning, goes through contortions to omit the name, but it was House—who was eight years her junior. A lecturer in English literature at Wadham College, House was engaged to another lady when Bowen met him, and he duly married his fiancée in 1933, though he and the novelist continued to meet with Madeleine House's knowledge. (Elizabeth sent her a tea service as a wedding present.) Mrs. House, in later years an editor of Dickens's letters, remarked afterward that in her opinion Elizabeth Bowen, "avid for experience," required this affair with her husband for her own growth and reach as a writer, that for her the affair was only part of her professional development. According to Glendinning, Bowen's unnamed lover told his wife "that he had taken Elizabeth's virginity," though she had been married to Alan Cameron since 1923. Alan is alleged never to have known of the affair with House, but that is unlikely. In a letter to House in 1934, Bowen acknowledged the "professional" relevance their affair had for her: "One spends one's life time objectifying one's inner life, and projecting one's thought and emotion into a form—a book . . . it is hard for me (being a writer before I am a woman) to realize that anything— friendship or love especially—in which I participate imaginatively isn't a book too. . . . I may easily forget that a relationship with a person isn't a book, created out of, projected by, one's own imagination and will." Being a writer before she was a woman may account for the late commencement of her sexual history, if the Houses can be believed on the subject of Bowen's virginity. Virginia Woolf's celebrated opinion that the sexual orgasm was greatly overrated may have been shared in her early years by her friend and contemporary Elizabeth Bowen; but in Elizabeth's life, unlike Virginia's, sexual liaisons with men tended to be frequent and thus, one assumes, not so overrated after all.

Elizabeth's affair with Humphry House went on for another three years and gradually cooled into friendship. Later she told Elizabeth Jenkins that at the worst moment of an emotional crisis she always found herself asking "What effect is this having on me *as a writer*?" A writer before a woman indeed. The affair limped to an end shortly after a stay by House at Bowen' Court in the course of which he was summoned home via telegram by th pregnant Madeleine when the roof blew off their Oxford house. According to May Sarton, Elizabeth found these grounds for departure too impossibly unromantic; the Houses' roof turned out to be the ceiling, as it were, of a faded intimacy.

Now back to *The House in Paris,* in which a woman gets pregnant by a friend's fiancé rather than her own. As Craig says, the novel then goes on "to subvert the idea of love as a rational passion," a feeling that Bowen apparently drew out of the torrid but ultimately aimless affair with House. The disorder and the pain of passion are stressed here. The three central characters of the novel are drawn from herself, House, and Madeleine, and the novel's central theme is articulated in its famous if cynical pronouncement that "nobody speaks the truth when there's something they must have." We remember Bowen's declaration in later years that "any fiction . . . is bound to be transposed autobiography"; this aspect of *The House in Paris* seems to be as good an example of that as anything in her many books. Indeed, she would say of this novel: "I don't feel I in any way invented or, as it were, devised 'The House in Paris.'"

The tale also has its Jamesian properties, chief among them the theme of the innocent woman who finds, when she opens herself to experience, that knowledge can be disastrous, even if inevitable: tragedy, thy name is understanding. The spiritual destructiveness of passion in *The House in Paris* may remind us once again of the later James, the James of *The Wings of the Dove.* Yet again too, in Bowen's novel, we encounter precocious children who observe the action and whose impressions of what the adults are doing form a significant part of the story's content.

VII

In 1935 the Camerons moved to London: Alan was appointed Secretary to the Central Council of School Broadcasting at the BBC. They found a house at 2 Clarence Terrace, Regent's Park, evoked in detail as the primary setting of *The Death of the Heart.* Elizabeth Jenkins told me: "The house, very clearly described, in which most of the story takes place, is an exact description of Elizabeth's house in Clarence Terrace overlooking Regent's Park. It had very large sash windows admitting oceans of light, and lovely pieces of Regency furniture." The Camerons had a boarder in a flat at the top of the house—John Buchan's son William, who worked for Alfred Hitchcock at Elstree Studios.

Though they lived in London now, Elizabeth and Alan continued to visit Bowen's Court whenever they could get away. Virginia and Leonard Woolf stayed a night with them there in 1936. Bowen's Court, it turned out, was not Mrs. Woolf's favorite country house. "To our horror," Virginia wrote, with her usual kindness, to her sister Vanessa Bell, "we found the [Cyril] Connollys—a less appetizing pair I have never seen out of the zoo." She described Bowen's Court as "a great barrack of grey stone," and commented, according to Craig, on "the cracks in the grand piano, the stains on the walls, and what she unfairly called 'the faked old portraits.'" The furniture also offended the fastidious Mrs. Woolf: "clumsy, solid, cut out of single wood." Horrors. Cyril Connolly's account of the meeting suggests that the Woolves were shocked by everything and preoccupied with minutiae. At dinner the conversation turned to homosexuality. "I mean what do they *do*?" Mrs. Woolf kept asking. Now fifty-two and a close friend of both Lytton Strachey and J. M. Keynes—not to mention Vita Sackville-West and Harold Nicolson—she must have known very well what they did. But she always enjoyed being annoying.

This was Woolf's only visit to Bowen's Court. Elizabeth said later of her famous friend: "Oh, she was awfully naughty. She was fiendish." She understood immediately Woolf's notorious professional jealousy, her legendary inability to tolerate praise of any writer other than herself. If you praised another, you were, by omission, criticizing her. Elizabeth Bowen called this "a side of her that one had to watch." At a tea-party at the Woolves the two novelists were observed by Hugh Walpole sitting together "like two goddesses from a frightfully intellectual Olympus." In later years Bowen used to complain that the tragic picture of Woolf that had come down to posterity was not altogether accurate because it omitted Virginia's wonderful humor, her irreverence, her sense of fun, her infectious laughter. On the other hand, shortly before her own death, reminiscing with Rosamond Lehmann about some of her Bloomsbury friends, Elizabeth admitted to darker feelings. "Noble though they all were, they were *smug*," she declared. "And their godlessness gives me—always did give me—a feeling of depression, and what else—claustrophobia?"

On the morning of George V's funeral in January 1936, Elizabeth got up at 4:00 A.M. to watch the procession go by in the Edgware Road: "I remember nothing else about the afternoon except being anaesthetized by tiredness, plus in vain looking for food for that night's dinner (to which I do remember ... Tom Eliot came) with all shops shut: a condition I'd forgotten to foresee." Her friend William Plomer says in his memoir *At Home* that he saw Elizabeth at tea "at the Woolves" on the afternoon of the royal funeral and that, at dinner that evening at the Camerons—the novelist had found food, at black-market prices, at a nearby restaurant—Eliot's "gravity seemed decidedly male in comparison with those exceptionally quick-witted women with their shining eyes and brilliant, rapid utterance ... outpaced by the quickness of their brains and senses."

Life went on at Clarence Terrace without George V. *The Death of the Heart*—Bowen's sixth novel, one of her popular successes ("People keep writing to her about the death of their hearts," remarked Ivy Compton-Burnett), and her greatest work of fiction—while published in 1938, grew at least in part out of a memorable weekend party at Bowen's Court in the summer of 1936, though the novel largely takes place, as noted, in a house virtually identical to the Camerons' London home. It was at this gathering in Ireland that Elizabeth's brief affair with Goronwy Rees came to an abrupt end. Rees, of working-class background, had made his way as a journalist—he was at the time assistant editor of the *Spectator*—later becoming a friend of Guy Burgess, Kim Philby, and Anthony Blunt, though it is unlikely that Rees himself was ever a spy. A Welshman and a graduate of Cambridge, Rees was an extremely handsome but unstable man; he was Elizabeth's junior by ten years. She had met him in 1931 at Oxford, when he was a Fellow of All Souls. Also present at Bowen's Court during this time were David Cecil and his wife, Isaiah Berlin, and Elizabeth's new friend Rosamond Lehmann, the mother of two children and just then in the process of leaving her second husband. Lehmann had become famous in 1927 with the publication of her superb first novel *Dusty Answer*.

Instead of devoting himself to Elizabeth, as she had expected he might, Rees found himself greatly attracted to Rosamond, as she was to him. Under the Camerons' roof at Bowen's Court Rees and Lehmann played musical bedrooms, a fact of which the hostess at first remained ignorant. When she figured it out her feelings for Rees cooled instantly. "My father went mad here," she is supposed to have said to him. "Wouldn't it be nice if you and I stayed here and went mad too?" Elizabeth Jenkins says that Bowen remarked to her of Goronwy Rees "that he was one of those trying people who won't understand that an affair has its natural termination"; apparently he wanted to have Elizabeth and Rosamond too. Oddly enough, in the next decade Rosamond Lehmann met another future lover in a home of Elizabeth Bowen's—Cecil Day Lewis, introduced to Lehmann at Clarence Terrace.

Whenever Elizabeth Bowen became involved with another man, Alan tolerated it without seeming to know anything about it. Their friends are agreed that he was willing to share her so long as she returned to him, as she always did. They tend to describe him as "impassive" on the subject of Elizabeth's affairs; at any rate he was inscrutable to them. And she was a woman who did have affairs—and for whom they were only that. It seems that Alan didn't want to know anything about them; he simply waited for them to end and rarely if ever complained. Or so we're told. If true, he was the perfect husband for Elizabeth Bowen.

The betrayal of love is a radical theme of *The Death of the Heart*, the last novel Bowen published until *The Heat of the Day* appeared eleven years later, in 1949. As a Book Society choice for 1938, *The Death of the Heart* turned out to be her best seller since *The Hotel*. The writing and publication of the novel—and Elizabeth's attempt, in it, to exorcise the aftershocks of love's betrayal—were not quite the end of the Goronwy Rees story, however. When *The Death of the Heart* appeared Rees wrote to Bowen to tell her how brilliant he thought it was. After some reflection he decided that the character called Eddie, a youthful, sexy, charming but immoral libertine, was a libellous version of himself; at one point in the novel Eddie takes a girl to a cinema but gropes her friend instead, undoubtedly a miniature snapshot of Rees's behavior with Elizabeth and Rosamond. At any rate, Rees now threatened to sue Bowen for libel. In *Glimpses of the Great*, A. L. Rowse says that Rees was talked out of any legal action by Geoffrey Faber; Victoria Glendinning declares that E. M. Forster did the persuading. Elizabeth Jenkins knows a variation on this theme: "Alan Cameron's solicitor said not to worry: if Goronwy Rees tried this on, they would produce two more young men, both of whom would say they thought *they* were Eddie: so no more was heard of that."

But Eddie is Goronwy Rees, there is no doubt about it. In the novel it is said of Eddie that he "has to get off with people because he can't get on with them." In this he embodies a central theme of the novel: the death of feeling in modern life, the substitution of a handful of dust for the human heart. And if Bowen's novel often sounds like Waugh's equally brilliant work, this is because her characters often sound like his characters. Like *A Handful of Dust* (1934), *The Death of the Heart* is a Waste Land novel, portraying hollow people addicted to and in full cry after *things*—possessions, status, influence, control—and insufficiently connected emotionally to each other. For the characters in Bowen's novel, as for Osmond and Madame Merle in *The Portrait of A Lady*—the latter, remember, admits to "a great respect for *things*"—things have replaced feelings in importance in the index of values. Here is the full passage in *The Death of the Heart* about "things," quoted earlier only in part: "Only in a house where one has learnt to be lonely does one have a solicitude for *things*. One's relation to them, the daily seeing or touching, begins to become love, and to lay one open to pain. . . . After inside upheavals, it is important to fix on imperturbable *things*. . . . These things are what we mean when we speak of civilization . . . the destruction of buildings and furniture is more palpably dreadful to the spirit than the destruction of human life." Could there be a more devastating assessment of contemporary values? *The Death of the Heart* still chills and shocks; herein lies its great power.

The novel poses the question: Is it so terrible to have a "dead" heart, or are we better off not feeling too much? How much is it good for us to know about our own hearts? Is it better to retain a few illusions on this subject—not to know too much, as well as not to feel too much? James and Conrad were fond of posing these questions in their fiction. In *The Death of the Heart* a number of characters are afflicted with emotionally "dead" or "dying" hearts: Irene, Thomas, Eddie, Matchett. Of the latter it is said: "She was only not hostile from allowing herself no feeling at all." The issue of how much we should or can know is made central here by another young girl who is also a center of consciousness. Yet again, this time in her character named Portia, Elizabeth Bowen tells a story in which corruption collides with an underdeveloped moral sense, showing innocence to be destructive and cruel, in its ignorance and idealism, when confronted with the real world and the real people in it. Anna, Thomas, Eddie, and Major Brutt (the John Beaver of *The Death of the Heart*) are all in one way or another corrupters of innocence in young Portia. At the end of the novel Brutt refuses to ruin his social chances with the Quaynes by taking in the runaway Portia; she's brought home by a servant in a taxi. How impersonal can you get?

The story of Portia suggests that you have to be innocent, untouched by the world, to feel—that the world corrupts you and kills your feelings. It is a favorite theme of Bowen's hero Dickens too. Let us recall the novel's closing colloquy:

"I suppose it's better to know?"
"No, truly it is not."

To know what? That life maims and kills? Thomas thinks: "Society was self-interest given a pretty gloss. You felt the relentless pressure behind small-talk. Friendships were dotted with null pauses, when one eye in calculation sought the clock." Everything is surface here; there is hardly any heart left to die. Innocence may be the only refuge in such a world—but as Elizabeth Bowen was fond of saying, it is both our fate and our business to lose it.

VIII

During the later 1930s and into the war years, Elizabeth Bowen was much in demand as a reviewer—primarily of fiction, but also of plays. She contributed reviews to the *Times Literary Supplement,* the *New Statesman,* the *Tattler,* the *Spectator,* the *Listener,* the *Observer, Vogue, Harper's Bazaar.* In 1937 she was elected to the Irish Academy of Letters. Visiting Ireland in that year she saw Yeats (first encountered in Oxford), "who was an angel, in his own house, less showy and more mellow: he has a superb white cat." Also in 1937 she was commissioned by T. S. Eliot to edit a volume of selected stories for Faber and produced a collection including some favorite tales by favorite authors, among them Stephen Spender, Frank O'Connor, and A. E. Coppard. As she read one story after another she came across the work of Sean O'Faoláin, who would become a friend and later on a lover.

Hugh Walpole described Elizabeth Bowen in the late 1930s as someone who might be intimidating to anyone who didn't know her well: her manner could be grand, she disliked over-familiarity, she was in some moods caustic and occasionally impatient with the slow and the inarticulate. Alan Cameron had found a likeness between her and the tigers at the zoo. Elizabeth did not mellow much as she grew older and more famous, though within her own circle she seems to have been regarded as a loving and affectionate person. By 1940 her work, as Janet Dunleavy reminds us, was routinely compared by reviewers not only to that of Virginia Woolf and E. M. Forster but to that of Henry James and Jane Austen as well. A new book by Elizabeth Bowen called forth prominent reviews in all the major periodicals of the day. *The Death of the Heart* was often said, then as now, to be her best work, though Bowen herself never agreed with that assessment. She did not say why; probably she did not want to go down to posterity remembered chiefly as the author of so pessimistic a book, the provider of such a dark passage, the bearer of such bleak insight.

Her next publication, another volume of stories titled *Look at All Those Roses,* appeared in 1941; most of its contents were composed in the period just after *The Death of the Heart*—between 1938 and 1940. *Look at All Those Roses* enters some previously untravelled Bowen territory—suburbia, for example, and the houses of lower-middle-class families. The ubiquitous autobiographical strain in her writing is represented here by "A Walk in the Woods," about a woman in love with a man ten years younger than herself. Some stories of the Blitz (1940) quickly found their way into this collection of 1941. V. S. Pritchett once characterized Jane Austen as a "war novelist," very much aware of the effects of the Napoleonic wars upon the English provincial families of her day. In this sense Elizabeth Bowen also could be described as a war novelist. She wrote about the war often from 1940 on and understood from the inside what it was like to live in the midst of it. "I could not have missed being in London throughout the war for anything," she said later. "It was the most interesting period of my life." Wartime London produced some of her most memorable tales—so much so that today, when Bowen's name is mentioned, her stories of London in the early 1940s are likely to be among the first things her readers think of.

One day in 1940 Elizabeth Bowen took her new friend Sean O'Faoláin to meet her old friend Virginia Woolf. On that very day Woolf had received from the estate of the late Lady Ottoline Morrell an antique ring-casket. O'Faoláin, writing in 1982, is quoted by Craig as describing the scene he remembered:

> The foreheads of the two women almost touched as they bent over the little casket to inhale the undying scent of its little, pale-green velvet cleft. Their two profiles, Virginia's exquisitely, delicately beautiful, Elizabeth's not beautiful but handsome and stately, were . . . like two young faces on an obsolete coin. Within months their world was under fire. Within half a dozen years it was dotted by ruins. Today we think of that pre-war world as an anachronism—until we read Woolf, or Forster, or Bowen, or Lehmann, or Waugh.

Elizabeth spent her last prewar summer at Bowen's Court, supervising the installation of a telephone system and electric lights there. She was now writing a history of the house in Ireland; *Bowen's Court* would appear in the middle of the war (1942).

But in 1940, as the war began, she wanted to find something more useful to do, to make a significant contribution to the war effort. She quickly became an air-raid warden, taking turns, as Craig puts it, "at manning her local wardens' post, answering inquiries from the public, and stomping up and down the streets in dark-blue official slacks, tin helmet and boots, on the alert for black-out defaulters." Bowen said later: "air raids were much less trying if one had something to do. . . . Walking in the darkness of the nights for six years one developed new bare alert senses, with their own savage warnings and notations." As the war commenced in earnest, Elizabeth described herself to Virginia Woolf as being in "a stupefied excited and I think rather vulgar state." She told a friend: "I am getting quite nice and thin. Raids are slightly constipating." Her description (in another letter) of London in 1940 is worth quoting at some length:

> Everyone that one sees in the streets looks dead tired, and at the same time much more grown-up than usual. And the good temper is phenomenal: one never hears people being cross, even on buses and places where feeling usually runs highest. I expect that when once this is happily over everyone will have a terrific revulsion and be as cross as cats for about a year.
>
> One minor discomfort, by day, is the extreme dirt—the air is full of queer greasy dust from the debris of the demolished houses, and this settles in one's hair, one's face, one's clothes and quite often makes one's eyes sore. It's rather touching to see people—girls—put on more and more lipstick, cheerful as ever, with the rest of their faces grey and streaked. . . . One has to walk almost everywhere, as buses, etc., owing to bomb-craters or dormant time-bombs, get 'diverted' miles out of their normal courses, so one never knows where to pick anything up. Entire districts, because of the time-bombs, become enislanded for a day or two, and cannot be got at by any means.

One result of the bombing was to push Londoners closer together. "We all have new friends—our neighbours," Elizabeth remarked. The Woolves were bombed out of their Bloomsbury house; the Camerons were bombed out of Clarence Terrace not once but twice.

In her novel of wartime London, *The Heat of the Day,* Bowen writes memorably of that time. "The very temper of pleasures lay in their chanciness," she says, "in the canvas-like impermanence of their settings, in their being off-time—to and fro between bars and grills, clubs and each other's places moved the little shoal through the noisy night." The "pleasures" she refers to here are often sexual; unusual relationships flourished. "There was a diffused gallantry in the atmosphere, an unmarriedness; it came to be rumoured about the country, among the self-banished, the uneasy, the put-upon and the safe, that everybody in London was in love." Those who stayed in the metropolis, according to *The Heat of the Day,* were precisely those "whom the climate of danger suited," including Elizabeth Bowen. Social life became deliciously unpredictable and unconventional. While the Camerons entertained the Spenders one evening at Clarence Terrace the air-raid sky was lit up by magnesium flares. The hostess made no reference to the explosions around them until the end of the party. "I feel I should apologize for the noise," she said.

We tend to think of this sort of thing as a cliché account of London during the bombing, but it was not yet a cliché when Elizabeth Bowen began writing about it; and perhaps the point is that much of what we now consider typical of wartime London, as well as of wartime writing, originated with her. If it is now a cliché, she made it so. Others, later, gave accounts of London during 1940-41, but hers came first, in *The Demon Lover* and *The Heat of the Day,* and it was indelible.

Elizabeth's wartime work was not limited to England, nor was it limited to air-raid duties. Despite her Irish origins and her tendency to describe herself as an Irish novelist, she felt identified and at one with England in its battle with Germany. Might she not, she asked the Ministry of Information, put her knowledge and understanding of Ireland, a neutral in the war, to use in some helpful way? Whether the idea originated with her or with Lord Cranborne at the Ministry of Information—David Cecil's brother—is not clear. As they had been in the Great War, the English now were greatly interested in the status of the Irish ports, used by English ships as refueling stations. Eventually the novelist suggested a series of reports on the ports in question; they would also touch on the wartime mood of the Irish, especially as it might affect Irish willingness to let English ships go on using the ports. The Ministry of Information accepted her proposal. It is not well known but nonetheless a fact that between 1940 and 1942 Elizabeth Bowen made several trips to Ireland, staying in a rented flat in Dublin or at the Shelbourne Hotel; the result was a series of memoranda sent to Lord Cranborne, memoranda having to do primarily with the conditions under which the Irish, who were fearful of German bombing, would or would not continue to permit the English to refuel their ships in Irish ports. Elizabeth's dispatches were passed, through the Ministry of Information and Lord Halifax, the reactionary Foreign Secretary who had been a member of the Cliveden Set and a leading proponent of appeasement before the war, to Churchill. Churchill wanted de Valera to guarantee British access to the most crucial ports, those in the west and south of Ireland.

Elizabeth's reports to the government must have been useful, though reading through them a half-century later one comes across many passages about the Irish character more obviously the product of a novelist's mind than a spy's. For that is what Bowen was doing: spying on the Irish for the English. She never used the word and undoubtedly, as an Irish native, never thought of herself as a spy, but that is what she was. Have other novelists spied for England? A partial listing would include her friend John Buchan, Compton Mackenzie, T. E. Lawrence, Somerset Maugham, Graham Greene, Dennis Wheatley, Ian Fleming, Lawrence Durrell, C. P. Snow, possibly Rudyard Kipling, and certainly John le Carré. But none of them spied on their native country; this was the Bowen variation.

Among other things she sent to the Ministry of Information accounts of "private" conversations she had with influential Irish politicians who did not realize they were not speaking privately. "It is the political people I see mostly: it seems a craggy, dangerous, miniature world," she wrote to Virginia Woolf. She was unmoved by and impervious to the wartime revival in Ireland of interest in the Irish language, Irish culture, Irish nationalism. Her feelings about Ireland and the Irish were always equivocal. In the mid-1940s she wrote to a friend from Bowen's Court: "To be a Roman Catholic myself would be . . . unthinkable. . . . But I do see the efficacy and all-embracingness and sublimity of Catholicism in its effects on all the people's beings and lives around here. It seems to make them hardboiled and spiritual at the same time. On Saints' Days, especially All Saints Day . . . which they call 'the day of the dead', one feels a sort of influence in the air like the flame of a candle burning." Hardboiled and spiritual at the same time is probably a good description of Elizabeth Bowen as well—Elizabeth the tiger, but the good tiger (she would use that phrase as the title of a children's book written at the end of her life) who loved the Irish even as she betrayed them in wartime.

Elizabeth spent Christmas 1940 at Bowen's Court and stayed on there into 1941 to finish her history of the house. The letter she wrote to Virginia Woolf from there in February 1941 was her last to that correspondent, for on 28 March, terrified by the threatened return of her mental illness, Mrs. Woolf drowned herself in the Thames. She was fifty-nine. Elizabeth got the news in Ireland from a friend who had heard it on the radio. "The last day I saw her," she remembered, Virginia was "kneeling on the floor—we were . . . mending a torn Spanish curtain in the house [at Rodmell, in Sussex]—and she sat back on her heels and put her head back in a patch of early spring sun. Then she laughed in this consuming, choking, delightful, hooting way. And *that* is what has remained with me." As Glendinning reminds us, Elizabeth Bowen "disliked the tragic, martyred image of Virginia Woolf which grew up after her death": "I get so *bored* and irked by the tragic fiction which has been manufactured about her since 1941," Bowen said. She told a friend that Virginia failed to understand how her words could hurt others—an odd idea, since Mrs. Woolf was so notoriously vulnerable to criticism of any kind—and that it was impossible to make sense of her to anybody who hadn't known her. Elizabeth was a loyal friend, even beyond the grave. She always remembered Virginia as fun-loving and irreverent rather than depressed and sarcastic, and no doubt that was an accurate memory of Virginia Woolf as she was in the company of Elizabeth Bowen. In later years she said that Woolf was one of the few of the dead she truly missed. But now, in March 1941, she wrote to Leonard Woolf: "A great deal of the meaning seems to have gone out of the world."

IX

And now—it is still 1941—we come to another epoch in the life of Elizabeth Bowen: in this year when some of the meaning seemed to have gone out of the world, some new meaning was about to come into her world.

A month before Virginia Woolf's death, in February 1941, Elizabeth met Charles Ritchie at a party given by the John Buchans in honor of the christening of their daughter, to whom Elizabeth stood godmother. Ritchie, thirty-five in 1941, a close friend of John Buchan's son, was seven years younger than the novelist. A Canadian diplomat stationed in London, Ritchie confessed in his diary that "The first time I saw Elizabeth Bowen I thought she looked more like a bridge-player than a poet." "Well-dressed, intelligent handsome face, watchful eyes," he added. As they became more intimate the adjectives he used to describe her grew more vivid: "mysterious, passionate and poetic . . . worldly." Their early impressions of each other are recounted in the story of the relationship of Robert and Stella in *The Heat of the Day*. The relationship of Charles and Elizabeth was not platonic, and it flourished throughout the rest of the war and way beyond: indeed, their affair would go on for seventeen years.

Ritchie inherited one role from Virginia Woolf: he became the only person other than Alan with whom Elizabeth would discuss her work. He recalled her telling him, apropos of dialogue in the novel, that each sentence "must bear directly or indirectly on the theme." Elizabeth also announced to him that every novel is a detective novel: the reader must look for clues to meaning. Bowen herself was all her life addicted to detective novels of the old-fashioned sort: she began as an Agatha Christie addict and ended as a P. D. James addict.

Ritchie was not wild about some of Bowen's Bloomsbury friends: "So far in my excursions into High Bloomsbury I have not encountered, except for Elizabeth, any striking originality of thought, phrase or personality but rather a group of cultivated, agreeable people who think and feel very much alike." Later the novelist introduced him to Augustus John, who removed a tweed cap "to reveal that noble head of a moth-eaten lion."

Some excerpts from Ritchie's diary:

- She said, "I would like to put you in a novel," looking at me through half-closed eyes in a sudden detached way like a painter looking at a model. "You probably would not recognize yourself." "I'm sure I wouldn't," I lied (January 1942).

● Elizabeth met a female admirer last night at dinner who said to her, "To meet you is like meeting Christ" (April 1942).

● I like [David Cecil] and Cyril Connolly best of Elizabeth's literary friends (April 1942).

● At first . . . I feared that I should expose [myself] . . . to her eye which misses nothing. Her uncanny intuitions, her flashes of insight . . . at once fascinated and disturbed me. . . . Now . . . I have been discovering more and more of her generous nature, her wit and funniness, the stammering flow of her enthralling talk, the idiosyncrasies, vagaries of her temperament. . . . Who could help becoming attached to her? (June 1942).

Ritchie, like Bowen, saw England with that aura of romantic strangeness brought to the view by the non-native; they loved going on excursions together. As Glendinning has said, neither felt guilty about their affair; they laughed at the same things; they loved to travel; they were both social conservatives. What Ritchie meant to her may be seen, as noted, in the story of Robert and Stella in *The Heat of the Day*: the novel shows (among other things) how thoroughly its author was in love. In his diary, later, Ritchie would refer to her as "dearest Elizabeth to whom I owe everything."

As usual, Alan Cameron seemed oblivious; he remained his wife's anchor—sensible, reliable, familiar prose to Charles Ritchie's erotic poetry. Typically, at Christmas 1943, Elizabeth and Charles went together to the service at Westminster Abbey, then returned to Clarence Terrace for lunch with Alan. If wartime bred unconventional behavior, as Bowen argues in so many places, Charles Ritchie was for her the embodiment of that unconventional spirit—conventional as both of them were in most other ways. The novelist would write in *The Heat of the Day* of Robert and Stella: "They were the creatures of history, whose coming together was of a nature possible in no other day—the day was inherent in the nature. . . . War at present worked at a thinning of the membrane between the this and the that . . . but then what else is love?"

But *The Heat of the Day* was not her next published volume. In fact she brought out three books in 1942 and another in 1945.

The books of 1942 were all works of nonfiction. *Bowen's Court* is in effect the history of an Anglo-Irish family, her own. In it Elizabeth chronicles the Bowens in Ireland from the seventeenth century on. It contains some interesting passages. Comparing Ireland's violent history with recent events, she writes here: "Fantasy is toxic: the private cruelty and the world war both have their start in the human brain." At times, describing the race, class, and society in which she grew up, Bowen sounds like Edith Wharton characterizing her New York ancestors and contemporaries in *A Backward*

Glance (1933). In *Bowen's Court* Elizabeth says this of the turn-of-the-century Anglo-Irish:

> If they formed a too-grand idea of themselves, they did at least exert themselves to live up to this: even vanity involves one kind of discipline. If their difficulties were of their own making, they combatted these with an energy I must praise. They found no facile solutions. They were not guilty of cant. Isolation, egotism and, on the whole, lack of culture made in them for an independence one has to notice because it becomes, in these days, rare.... To live as though living gave them no trouble has been the first imperative of their make-up; to do this has taken a virtuosity into which courage enters more than has been allowed. In the last issue, they have lived at their own expense.

Seven Winters, a brief (forty-eight pages) collateral volume, tells of Bowen's early life in the family home. *English Novelists,* also appearing in 1942, was her first sustained work of criticism.

The Demon Lover, her sixth collection of stories published in 1945, stands today as possibly the best of her volumes of shorter tales, inspired as she was while writing it by the war and her wartime experiences. As Patricia Craig points out, *The Demon Lover* could only be a work of the Blitz, defining as it does the "dislocation and derangement of the senses" peculiar to a bombed-out city. As noted earlier, this volume contains some premier ghost stories, another example of the "thinning of the membrane between the this and the that"; reading proofs of *The Demon Lover,* Elizabeth Bowen perceived in it "a rising tide of hallucination" she hadn't seen as she composed the tales, mostly between 1941 and 1944. "In wartime many people had strange deep intense dramas," she said later of the stories in this collection, though of course she was also talking about herself. "We all lived in a state of lucid abnormality." The volume includes a favorite of many readers, "Ivy Gripped the Steps," about a soldier returning to a house he used to visit as a boy. The title story is an indelible tale of horror about a woman's haunting by a long lost (dead) lover who leaves her threatening notes and ultimately catches up to her in a taxi. It ends with the protagonist beating "with her gloved hands on the glass all around" as the taxi and its driver (the dead lover) "made off with her into the hinterland of deserted streets." Glendinning tells the story of Iris Murdoch sharing a taxi with Elizabeth Bowen after the war and feeling once again the story's vivid atmosphere of terror, while its author, sitting placidly beside her, seemed oblivious, even as she (Elizabeth) "leant forward and knocked with her gloved hand on the glass partition to speak to the driver."

Bowen wrote all through the war, and her use of it so often as a subject in her fiction gives more weight to whatever claim she may have to being a war novelist. She wrote about a time and place in a way, as Glendinning notes, that expressed the experience of many people. Indeed, as an artist she feasted on wartime London. In *Europe without Baedeker* (1966) Edmund Wilson recalls: "It was . . . reassuring and pleasant to hear Elizabeth Bowen say that, except for some disagreeable moments when 'one of those humming things' had landed near her, she enjoyed London during the war. 'Everything is very quiet, the streets are never crowded, and the people one dislikes are out of town.'"

In the summer of 1944, however, the Camerons' house in Clarence Terrace was again nearly destroyed by bombs, and they were almost killed. "Elizabeth's nerves," Charles Ritchie wrote in his diary, "have been under a terrible strain but she is resilient and if she can get away and get some rest she will be all right. In the midst of it she is still frantically trying to write her novel"—he means *The Heat of the Day,* that quintessential work of World War II. The experience of being bombed out was transferred directly to a story she included in *The Demon Lover,* "The Happy Autumn Fields." The Camerons moved back into their house in the autumn of 1944. Early in 1945 Charles Ritchie was recalled to Canada. Elizabeth was able once again to work on her novel.

When VE Day arrived in May 1945 and the long war finally ended, Elizabeth, as usual, was watching out for material. "Small shops gradually reopening, residents creeping back. . . . The sea front is 'open' again; the miles of coils of rusty barbed wire snipped away and flung back. Soldiers about still, but not so many . . . everyone wondering what they ought to *do*," she wrote to Ritchie. She hung out flags at Clarence Terrace; unable to find any with the likeness of George VI on them, she settled instead for the image of the late George V.

Elizabeth and Alan spent the summer of 1945 at Bowen's Court, where a shortage of gasoline kept the roads free of automobiles and everything was quiet. They enjoyed themselves so much there that they decided to stay on until the end of the year. The novelist's identification with the Irish had not weakened, though she had just finished spying on them; everyone is ambivalent about the Irish, even the Irish. Bowen told an interviewer in the 1940s: "I regard myself as an Irish novelist. As long as I can remember I've been extremely conscious of being Irish"—except, apparently, in wartime. She added the familiar refrain that the novelists who had most influenced her were French, not English; Henry James was fond of saying the same thing. In the late 1940s she remarked that, as time passed, she felt more Irish rather than less: "I suppose as one grows older one reverts to type." Bowen told a friend after the war ended, "I'd much rather live my life" at Bowen's Court, adding that in England "I can't stick all these little middle-class Labour wets with their Old London School of Economics ties and their women. Scratch any of these cuties and you find the governess." A strong sense of class seems to have had a bearing on her political loyalties, both inside England and beyond it.

Alan could remain in Ireland with her because he had resigned from the BBC. The reason was deteriorating health, specifically poor eyesight brought on by diabetes. During the time she spent in London between 1946 and 1948, Elizabeth found England, with its bleak economies, its socialist government, its rationing and its ruins, depressing. "When Churchill goes I go," she had said, and she duly went to Ireland.

A highlight of the immediate postwar years for her was the appearance of Evelyn Waugh's *Brideshead Revisited* (1945), which she compared to Proust's *magnum opus* in its "overpowering sensuous emotion . . . I haven't had such a reaction to any [contemporary novel] for a long time." As noted, she and Waugh shared many of the same feelings and values, and that is sometimes reflected in themes they share in their work. Another postwar highlight for Elizabeth was the production of her play *Castle Anna* at the Lyric Hammersmith, the story of a spinster in love with her old Irish country house. The play was unenthusiastically reviewed and had a short run: like Henry James once again, she became a failed playwright. *Castle Anna* is remembered today chiefly, if at all, for the appearance in it of the twenty-three-year-old Richard Burton in a minor role, his first acting job on the stage. A less happy event of 1948 (for Elizabeth) was Charles Ritchie's marriage to a cousin. According to May Sarton, Ritchie had asked the novelist to meet him in Paris at the time Alan was having ophthalmological surgery, she elected to stay with her husband, and Ritchie married out of pique. True or not, Elizabeth Bowen and Charles Ritchie continued to write and sometimes to meet, though not always on the old terms.

Elizabeth's literary reputation, though she had not published a novel since 1938, was at its zenith in the postwar years, due at least in part to the shock of recognition so many readers had felt while perusing the pages of *The Demon Lover.* She was made a Companion of the British Empire (C.B.E.) in 1948; in the following year she was awarded an honorary Doctor of Letters (Litt.D.) by Trinity College, Dublin. She lectured at Oxford, contributed essays when asked, and submitted to interviews. One interviewer asked her how much a writer needed to live on. "I would like to have £3,500 a year net," said Elizabeth Bowen. There had been some inflation since Virginia Woolf's *A Room of One's Own* (1929) and the famous £500 a year. Elizabeth also did broadcasts for the BBC—on Jane Austen, on Fanny Burney, on Trollope, on the Kentish coast, on Bloomsbury. She, Graham Greene, and V. S. Pritchett put together a volume of essays by the three of them called *Why Do I Write?*, published in 1948. When they sat down together to discuss what should be in the book, they discovered that they could speak of no one but Henry James. In *Why Do I Write?* Bowen declares that one of the reasons one writes is "the need to work off, out of the system, the sense of being solitary and farouche." By not contributing to the general disorder of society, she concludes, writers contribute to the world at large.

Some of her earlier works were now being reprinted. Translations appeared in Italian, Spanish, Japanese, French, German, Swedish, Danish, Norwegian, even Czech, Romanian, Serbo-Croat. She had to employ a secretary to help deal with her correspondence. As always she loved parties. She has left an account of one at which the French poet Louis Aragon was guest of honor. Nancy Mitford announced: "'Aragon's marvellous—what a pity we haven't got any poets in this country!' Eliot and all the others merely lowered their heads like tortoises and blinked." Craig tells the story of Elizabeth, around this time, going to an Austrian psychologist to have her stammer cured: she wound up "telling him nothing at all about herself while he told her the story of his life." The stammer survived.

Between 1948 and 1950 the novelist lectured for the British Council in Hungary, Czechoslovakia, and Austria on such subjects as "The Short Story," "The Technique of the Novel," and "The English Novel in the Twentieth Century." Glendinning tells a story, also recounted by Graham Greene in *A Sort of Life,* of Bowen and Greene in Vienna after the war. He was working on *The Third Man* and took her to a seedy nightclub that he arranged to have raided at midnight: her papers were sternly demanded. She said later that "the British Council had not given her so dramatic an evening."

X

The Heat of the Day, dedicated to Charles Ritchie, appeared in 1949, when Bowen was fifty. This was her seventh novel. She would produce during the remaining twenty-four years of her life only three more novels, though she did publish a number of other volumes; but *The Heat of the Day* was her last major work. Unlike some authors whose books get stronger and more interesting as they go on—one thinks of Dickens, George Eliot, Hardy, Henry James—Elizabeth Bowen's later work is a substantial falling off. She was, it turned out, a writer of the 1920s, '30s, and '40s, but not of the '50s or '60s. Her subjects were embedded in the past, not the present. And in fact, interesting as *The Heat of the Day* is as a piece of wartime history and auto-biography, it is not among her greatest achievements in fiction, the best of which had reached print by 1938. The telltale sign perhaps is the lapse of eleven years between *The Death of the Heart* and *The Heat of the Day*; earlier she had produced a novel every two or three years, and they were better novels. The speed with which she composed is nothing, but the breaking of the rhythm, largely the result of World War II, appears to have been everything. "Almost anything that happens round me contributes to" the present work, she told Charles Ritchie in 1945 as she was working on *The Heat of the Day.* "It was thus the very subject of *The Heat of the Day*—the war—which held up the writing of it," as Glendinning rightly says. The novel could not be completed until the war was over.

Elizabeth Bowen is a great prewar novelist but a mediocre postwar novelist. Perhaps this is because the social world she wrote about in the 1920s and '30s did not survive the war intact: her base, the foundation of her observation, the things that interested her most, existed only in memory by the time the war ended. And so, after *The Heat of the Day,* she tended to lean in her fiction toward fantasy and away from impressionism. As a result of this her work suffered. When she was bombed out of Clarence Terrace in 1944 while working on *The Heat of the Day,* Bowen complained: "It was the last house in London which still felt like a prewar house." *The Death of the Heart* was the last of her six prewar novels, while *The Heat of the Day* was the first of her four postwar novels: therein lies the difference between them, and it is everything. Just as some writers have bloomed in their later years, so others have withered: one thinks of Thackeray, Meredith, Conrad, Lawrence.

Perhaps, then, it is appropriate that *The Heat of the Day* is about, among other things, treason. The changes that Elizabeth Bowen saw going on everywhere around her seemed treacherous; like Henry James, she too had her "treacherous" years. The war, so stimulating for her creatively, also betrayed her by taking away part of her material, taking away part of the world she knew—the world of big houses, big parties, high society, devotion to culture, protection of one's class. As these things ceased to be her subjects because they were anachronisms, her fiction changed. For all of this the metaphor is treason. Though *The Heat of the Day,* as we have seen, brilliantly sketches wartime London and its unique *carpe diem* atmosphere— "They were the creatures of history, whose coming together was of a nature possible in no other day," says the novel—it fails in many respects as a work of fiction: the plot is shapeless and at times incomprehensible, the story as a whole is vague, and the characters are shadowy and unfinished, composed more of mist than of muscle. Patricia Craig mounts as good a defense of the book's evasions as one is likely to find. "A complex novelist," she says, "can never view anything straight-forwardly"; and she cites the novel's well-known declaration that "complex people are never certain that they are not crooks." Still, there is no excuse for vagueness—James is complicated and complex, but never vague—and it is primarily vagueness, lack of focus, the novel suffers from.

That is a personal opinion. Some of Elizabeth's contemporaries were nonetheless deeply moved by the tale's depiction of the time they had just emerged from. Rosamond Lehmann pointed to its "unbearable re-creation of war and London and private lives and loves. You do, you really *do,* write about love," she told Elizabeth Bowen. "Who else does, today?" Jonathan Cape's reader commented, "She succeeds time and again in expressing what has hitherto been inexpressible." The book, Glendinning concluded in 1977, "summed up and expressed the heightened emotions of those years of war. . . . *The Heat of the Day* has become the classic novel of London in the war." The novel proved to be one of Elizabeth Bowen's greatest commercial successes immediately upon publication: she used some of the money to install bathrooms at Bowen's Court. On the strength of her renewed and revived fame, Cape now brought out a uniform edition of her works; Alfred Knopf published the American edition. The refurbished Bowen industry rumbled into gear. The first critical study of her fiction, by Jocelyn Brooke, appeared in 1952. "I was not only impressed; I learnt a good deal from it," said Elizabeth Bowen. Brooke's monograph contained this passage: "The earlier books . . . dealt with a world that has, for all practical purposes, ceased to exist: the crust of civilized life has been cracked in too many places, the abyss beneath our feet can no longer be ignored." Others who discussed her critically between 1940 and 1960, to cite Janet Dunleavy's list, include Walter Allen, Louise Bogan, David Daiches, William Frierson, Benedict Kiely, Sean O'Faoláin, A. L. Rowse, L. A. G. Strong, and William York Tindall.

Elizabeth was invited now to America to give readings, and she went often. Throughout 1950 she had been writing a "popular" history (as she called it) of Dublin's Shelbourne Hotel, and this was duly published in 1951. It is actually sort of a social history of Dublin; the idea for the book, Glendinning tells us, was Cyril Connolly's. Elizabeth often stopped at the Shelbourne on her way to and from the house in County Cork; and of course she had stopped there for the gossip during the war.

Her social life at Bowen's Court took on renewed vigor in the early 1950s. Eudora Welty and Carson McCullers came to stay, separately. Elizabeth liked the former but found the latter, because of her obsessive drinking and her habit of interrupting her hostess at work when bored, a trial. In 1986 Eudora Welty recalled her visit thirty-five years earlier to Bowen's Court:

> It was so lovely to be in that house, and I immediately fell into the way things were done. Elizabeth worked in the morning, which is what I like to do, and at about eleven o'clock you could come downstairs if you wanted to and have a sherry and then go back to work. Then you met at lunch, I mean to talk, and the whole afternoon was spent riding around, and the long twilights coming back. There was usually company at dinner time. And evenings, just a few people, or maybe more. . . . We liked to play games. Eddy Sackville-West was visiting her . . . and we all played 'Happy Families,' a children's card game—it's just like 'Going Fishing' where you try to get all of a family in your hand by asking 'May I have?' except that it's done with Victorian decorum.

In 1951 Alan Cameron, another obsessive drinker, suffered a heart attack. As part of a plan to help him regain his health, the Camerons gave up the house in London early in 1952 to reside full time at Bowen's Court. Elizabeth told a friend: "I feel not a whiff of regret for London." In this coronation year she was asked for her impressions of the new monarch, Elizabeth II. "Reigning should be enjoyable," she said. "Women, on the whole, show an aptitude for it; there are few who have not desired to try." In Ireland, Edith Somerville, of the Somerville and Ross writing partnership (Ross was dead), came to lunch, and Elizabeth liked her immensely. "Now that Virginia is dead," she wrote to Charles Ritchie, "she [Somerville] and Colette and Edith Sitwell are the only living writers whom I really admire."

Alan, though confined to bed, showed no signs of giving up liquor, except while asleep. Elizabeth tried to nurse him, but she could not put off the inevitable. He died on 16 August 1952. May Sarton said that though Elizabeth Bowen had what Sarton called "a gift of instant intimacy," that intimacy was often apparent rather than real, and many of her friends at some time or another were disappointed by her coldness. True or not, Elizabeth's intimacy with Alan was real—even if they didn't sleep together—and she was genuinely devastated by the death of this longtime companion, the rock to which she always could return when the surrounding surf grew choppy. Clearly it was not sexual passion that united them; just as clearly it was trust and familiarity that did, Elizabeth's dependence upon her husband growing out of the long habit of sharing with him the most important concerns of her life. To lose the partner of so many years—they were married in 1923—was doubly devastating for Elizabeth in the wake of Charles Ritchie's recent marriage.

Now, in August 1952, she wrote to friends of her husband's death. "I must always be glad that he went so peacefully, in a calm night's sleep, expecting to wake next day," she said in one letter. "Bless his heart. He was a happy man," she said in another. Alan was buried in the family churchyard near the house. She spent the rest of 1952 traveling in America, returning in 1953 to a Bowen's Court in which, for the first time, she was the only permanent resident. But she found she could live there happily enough. "This place sustains me and so do the people," she declared.

Throughout the rest of the 1950s Elizabeth continued to live at Bowen's Court, though she went to Rome several times and traveled a good deal elsewhere. In the early 1950s she worked on her only novel of this decade, *A World of Love* (1955), the first of the three mediocre novels of her last years. (And who's to say, in light of the evidence, that her life with Alan wasn't an important ingredient of her success as a writer?) To the house in Ireland came visitors who left their impressions. Said Veronica Wedgwood of Elizabeth Bowen after a stop there in 1953: "she's such a sane and responsible citizen . . . not a wild irresponsible like darling Rose [Macaulay] or a mania always with her nose in the *Economist* . . . but a perfectly and unobtrusively informed person. . . . She is really the only person of our way of life and thinking who isn't always putting sex first. She understands the intellectual quality of love so well." John Lehmann also visited Bowen's Court in 1953 and described Elizabeth's "stylish, rather masculine carriage, as if about to settle on a shooting stick and lift binoculars." More than anyone else he had met, Lehmann said, Elizabeth Bowen had the capacity of "making one feel completely at ease, of immediately establishing rapport by a flow of uninhibited conversation which mingles sympathy, charm, wit, and shrewd intellectual comment." This is the gift of "instant intimacy" others have commented on, with no hint of coldness. Lehmann was impressed by the novelist's energy at fifty-four: "She moved about the house like a young man setting out for a football match." She drove him around in her car "like one possessed, mainly on the wrong side of the road," and took him for "tireless, striding walks about the countryside, talking all the time."

All of Elizabeth's visitors mention her unique capacity to be what one of them called "a magic listener": she inspired others to talk about themselves because, with her, they felt that they could, that they had an interested and sympathetic audience. If one went too far with her, however—women who made passes: there were several—"she was capable of dropping people ruthlessly," as Glendinning puts it. "People's personalities are not interesting except when you are in love with them," the novelist told Charles Ritchie. She grew notorious among her acquaintances for never answering their letters: she wrote letters, a great many letters, when she chose to do so, but only to recipients of *her* choice. Meanwhile, she missed Alan. She told a friend that her late husband "never seems dead, in the sense that he never seems gone; I suppose that if one has lived the greater part of one's life with a person he continues to accompany one through every moment." If that isn't love, what is it?

XI

A World of Love, completed at Bowen's Court in 1954, was the eighth of her ten novels. It is romantic in mood and tone, and some of its themes echo those of earlier tales: an innocent girl in love with the memory of a dead soldier whose letters she reads, the impact of the past on the present, a house and a town in Ireland, the thin membrane separating the living from the dead. But the story goes nowhere: it is all, as several critics have noted, atmosphere and mood, with little substance, more like a dream than a novel. Henry James's habit of attributing psychological significance to small acts, using the grammar of conduct as a moral index, is carried on in *A World of Love* to a sort of sublime silliness, as in the late Meredith, becoming tedious in its gratuitous relentlessness. As Rose Macaulay generously said of the tale in a *Times* review, *A World of Love* "is rather fascinating, though not to everyone." The author commented on the novel in these terms: "It's on the periphery of a passion—or, the intensified reflections of several passions in a darkened mirror." Like all of Bowen's novels this one is about love—or passion, to use her word. But, like *The Heat of the Day,* it is much too vague, too dreamy, too other-worldly, and ultimately too insubstantial. The mirror is too dark: it gives no reflection.

The 1950s brought some other additions and subtractions to Elizabeth's life. She continued to travel to and in the United States, holding a fellow-ship as writer-in-residence at Bryn Mawr College in 1956; in 1955 she had been writer-in-residence at the American Academy in Rome, thus renew-ing contact with one of her favorite cities. She made several trips to West Germany between 1954 and 1958: Charles Ritchie was the Canadian ambassador there during those years. In 1956 Oxford University awarded her a Doctor of Letters (Litt.D.). Of this prestigious honorary degree she wrote to a friend: "It means the world to me—a very solemn and to me almost holy occasion . . . which I shall remember all my life. I nearly burst into tears." She was worried now about Bowen's Court. With the passage of time, the rise in taxes, and the inflation of living costs, she found it harder and harder to keep the house up; it demanded more of her income than she had to spend. In this same year, 1956, Charles Ritchie visited her in Ire-land; so did David Cecil and his wife, and Iris Murdoch. Except for her constant financial anxieties, Elizabeth Bowen was thriving in the 1950s: "Personally I am enjoying the [1950s]—it is really the first [decade], it seems to me, in which I've enjoyed being 'grown-up' as much as I expec-ted to do when I was a child." Apparently living alone had its compensa-tions.

Because of Bowen's Court's constant drain upon her resources, she went less and less often to London. And she went to America more and more often, for she could earn a great deal there for lectures and articles. Working frantically to save her Irish home, she accepted commissions to write essays for American magazines (as, for example, *Holiday, Mademoiselle, Vogue, House and Garden, McCall's*) on such topics as "For the Famine Shopper" and "The Case for Summer Romance" and "On Not Rising to the Occa-sion" and "How to Be Yourself but Not Eccentric." But she could not, as it turned out, win this financial battle. She liked to spend money, to travel and to live abroad, to entertain generously. "No one was ever, with Elizabeth, allowed to pay for anything," says Glendinning. Well, almost anything. Glendinning tells the story of L. P. Hartley, traveling third class on a train, having to fork over the excess on his ticket when he went to sit with Elizabeth in a first-class carriage. The novelist also tended to lend money when asked. Her writing did not earn enough for her to live as she liked to live and to pay the ballooning costs of running the voluminous Bowen's Court; she had what she earned and no more. (In this too she resembles Henry James.) It was not enough. She began to realize in 1957 and 1958 that she might have to sell the family home in Ireland. Yet another part of the past, for Elizabeth Bowen the most important part of her past both literally and symbolically, was slipping away.

"Much as she loved the house and the neighbourhood," Elizabeth Jenkins remarked, "I for one was not surprised when I heard she had decided to sell [Bowen's Court]. I remember once we had been walking in Regent's Park and when we came in there were letters for her on the hall table; she said: 'I sometimes wonder what I'd feel if I found a letter saying Bowen's Court had been burned to the ground.' I think that was one of the things that showed what nervous strain she lived under all the time." She had dreamt of this destroying fire for years, going back to her father's warning to her during the Troubles, when she was a girl.

Glendinning takes up the story of the end of Bowen's Court: "In 1958 and 1959 she spent months abroad, working in Rome and New York . . . closing her mind as much as possible to the situation at home, leaving bills and rates unpaid, wages unarranged-for, servants confused. Friends and relations . . . were acutely distressed about her and the situation. But she answered none of their letters about what was going on." In the summer of 1959, now sixty, Elizabeth Bowen at last faced the inevitable. Bowen's Court was put up for sale, and the first offer was accepted. In January 1960 the novelist paid a sad last visit to the place; she never saw it again. For a few months later Bowen's Court encountered a fate unexpected and unforeseen by her: it was demolished by the new owner, who wanted the property for the land and the timber, but not the house. At least, Elizabeth wrote in a late postscript to a new edition of *Bowen's Court,* "It was a clean end. Bowen's Court never lived to be a ruin." According to Molly Keane (M. J. Farrell), Elizabeth's friend Eddy Sackville-West, seeing her soon after the sale, remarked that "She looks like someone who has attended her own execution."

Once her old home was gone Elizabeth, who had lived at Bowen's Court throughout the 1950s, lived largely abroad. Her long series of appointments to American universities as writer-in-residence recommenced in earnest. After Bryn Mawr and Vassar, and on into the 1960s, invitations to lecture or reside came from Princeton, Wisconsin-Madison, Penn, Berkeley, Oregon, Washington, Reed, Amherst, Williams, Chicago, Stanford. Nearly all of these invitations were accepted. She visited some campuses more than once; the visit would be anywhere from a few days to half a year. She needed the money; she liked America, and to be admired; she had, now, no real home of her own. In *A Time in Rome* (1960) she says this: "Anywhere, at any time, with anyone, one may be seized by the suspicion of being alien—ease is therefore to be found in a place which nominally *is* foreign: this shifts the weight." As always she put her faith in place—once again a foreign place. And so the expatriate Elizabeth Bowen continued to live and work away from home, wherever that was, her feeling of anomalousness giving her comfort.

A Time in Rome testifies to the thoroughness with which she could absorb and assimilate "foreign" places. The book did not fare well with the critics—it caused Evelyn Waugh to say that she was through as a writer, in which he was largely right—but it gives a faithful account of her observations and impressions in the Italian capital. And it contains some fine writing: "Knowledge of Rome must be physical, sweated into the system, worked up into the brain through the thinning shoe-leather"; "To love makes one less clever." In this book Bowen lets her public in on the "secret" of her lifelong addiction to detective stories, which she calls "the only above-board grown-up children's stories."

Elizabeth's favorite American city was always New York, though she wrote no book about it. After her first visit there in the 1930s she had told Lady Ottoline Morrell:

> The height of the city, the air, the speed of everything are curiously exhilarating; the people I met had great charm, intelligence and variety; one seemed to live in a kind of snowstorm of impressions for all those weeks; it was a very fine autumn and long theatrical American sunshine made everything unreal, or real, perhaps in an unusual way that got near one's nerves. It was not that it was all unlike England, but oneself seemed unlike oneself, which I always rather enjoy: it was like being disembodied.

Again one notes here the relish for anomalousness, for being an outsider. In a letter written in 1958 her comment on New York is unadorned: "I must say I do love it with a passion." She became adept at borrowing flats in Manhattan, calculating nicely when their owners might be away and volunteering, in their absence, to become the occupant. From 1958 to 1962 Charles Ritchie was Canada's ambassador to the United Nations, another good reason for the novelist to be in New York. She was less happy in Madison, Wisconsin: "these are awfully nice people, though inevitably many of them are as odd as coots . . . when I did first arrive here I looked out of my window and burst into tears." Some places really *were* alien.

Elizabeth's many trips to the United States gave her the opportunity to see old friends. One of her favorite Americans was Eudora Welty, whom she visited in Mississippi. "She's very un-writerish and bien élevée," Bowen told Charles Ritchie, "quiet, self-contained, easy, outwardly old fashioned, very funny indeed when she starts talking . . . I think she's like me in preferring places to people; and any unexpected sight or view . . . makes her start up . . . with a smothered cry as though she had been stung by a wasp . . . I think she's a genius." How typical of Elizabeth Bowen to declare that she preferred "places to people." Even her unfocused last novels vividly reproduce place; her sensitivity to location is a hallmark of all of her work and lives at the heart of her literary impressionism. In this she was consistent. Her history of putting people after places may help explain why she was so notably rootless and solitary during the last two decades of her life—for her books, as she was fond of saying, constituted her connection to society.

Elizabeth's obsessive traveling, probably a reflection of her loneliness, is undoubtedly one reason why she wrote so (relatively) little during the last twenty years of her life. Another was her slowness as a writer, which became exaggerated as she grew older, a not unknown phenomenon. "I'm a slow and fussy writer," she told a publisher around this time, "but if I don't fuss I apparently can't write." Writing well remained terribly important to her. "The pleasure of creative writing was for her 'equalled elsewhere only in love,'" as Glendinning puts it. Elizabeth declared in an essay: "I am fully intelligent only when I write. I have a certain amount of small-change intelligence, which I carry round with me as ... one has to carry small money, for the needs of the day, the non-writing day." Both love and literature failed her in her final years, or at any rate failed to inspire her.

In 1962 Elizabeth rented a flat from Isaiah Berlin in Old Headington, Oxford, within view of the house she and Alan had lived in from 1925 to 1935. Here she completed the essays and other nonfiction that appeared, later that year, in *Afterthought* ("Seven Winters" was included in this volume). But living in Oxford was not, could not, be the same. Rather than an energetic, ambitious young writer on the way up, happily married but looking for new friends and endless conversation, she was now a sixty-three-year-old widow who tired easily, whose best work was behind her, and who no longer had either the patience or the desire to meet new people. Her old Oxford friends were dead, retired, or too busy and grand to hang out with her as they once did. Disappointed, she decided that Oxford would no longer do.

When an invitation came to go back to Madison, Wisconsin, for the fall term of 1962 she jumped at it, despite her previous feelings about the place. She was wanted there, and no one seemed to want her in Oxford. The surviving correspondence between Elizabeth Bowen and the University of Wisconsin clearly betrays her unhappiness in 1962, largely the result, one feels after reading what she wrote then, of the strange uprootedness of her life at the time rather than any sense or fear of failure as a writer. Publicly, her literary stock remained high. But these letters underscore, for example, her "distress and conflict of mind" (her words) as a result of giving up Bowen's Court—an event, now two years after the fact, still very much at the forefront of her thoughts. "The economic strain of supporting a big house and the psychological strain of living in it alone were becoming too much," she wrote. She added that she was now "living permanently" in Oxford—from which, in fact, she would depart abruptly three years later.

Despite her previous impressions of Madison, Elizabeth was happy there the second time around and able to get on with the novel she was writing, *The Little Girls*. "I'm thoroughly enjoying myself here: love this great big teeming university and this pretty town," she told a friend. The novel, her first in nine years when it appeared in 1964, took as its setting that part of Kent near Folkestone in which she had lived as a child with her mother during her father's illness nearly sixty years earlier, though in the story the time is said to be somewhat later: 1914, in fact. The tale's mood is hardly nostalgic, however; Elizabeth referred to *The Little Girls* as "a recall of sensory experience" book. Eleven-year-old schoolgirls on summer holiday is its central focus; this section is sandwiched between passages set four decades later, with the "girls" in their fifties.

Some critics have praised the middle section of *The Little Girls*: Elizabeth Bowen, after all, was a past mistress of any subject concerning innocent young girls, the confrontation of innocence with experience, and the past. The opening and closing sections, set contemporaneously, often have been considered weak and unrealistic, as indeed they are. Read today the novel seems largely irrelevant to and unreflective of the 1960s, or even the 1950s; the older ladies do not convince us of anything, including their own existence. Her own world gone, Bowen was an unreliable reflector of the world she had lived into. A novelist writing about the past need not be dated, of course, but the last novels of Elizabeth Bowen are very dated indeed. Glendinning recounts the anecdote of Elizabeth asking Evelyn Waugh why he never told his characters' thoughts. He replied: "I do not think I have any idea what they are thinking: I merely see them and show them." Did Bowen know what her contemporaries were feeling and thinking in the 1960s? It seems unlikely, especially when one comes across a passage such as the following in one of her letters, apropos of the antiwar agitation by then well under way in America: "these insane protests and demonstrations can only be doing more harm than good." Had these things occurred in the 1920s or 1930s she would have understood them, as she understood the Troubles in Ireland; in the 1960s she hadn't a clue. But you cannot blame a person for losing her edge as she grows older; it happens. Elizabeth Bowen, quite literally, was not the same woman who wrote *The Death of the Heart, Friends and Relations, To the North, The Last September, The Hotel.*

XII

In 1965, the year after *The Little Girls* appeared, Elizabeth moved again, and for the last time. Now sixty-six, she went back to another locale out of her past, more remote than Oxford—the town of Hythe on the Kentish coast, where she and her mother had lived between 1907 and 1912, and where her mother had died. Here, in the midst of scenes remembered from childhood, she bought her final home—thus completing, as Glendinning puts it, "her return journey." This was going back to her past in earnest. She described Hythe as "one of the few places that make me love England and Englishness." Telling no more than the truth, she characterized her urge to return there as "a back-to-the-wombishness. . . . But I can't see what's wrong with the womb if one's happy there." Though she does not say so, the novelist's feelings about Hythe must have been laced with ambivalence.

She had been deprived so suddenly and so startlingly of that womb, and she had never, as so much of her fiction shows, been quite able to forgive the "adults" for their duplicity and mendacity so many years before, when she was thirteen. Apparently nostalgia was better than nothing. The hill in front of the house the novelist bought was one she "used to play up . . . as a child," as she said. To help buy it she sold some of her papers to the University of Texas, a well-worn practice for British authors by the 1960s. She would put her friends up at a nearby hotel, "pre-paying their bills and leaving change for the meter in their rooms," according to Glendinning. Charles Ritchie, now in London as the Canadian High Commissioner, came to visit her in Hythe: he was not put up at the hotel.

Elizabeth Bowen could not help knowing that her best days, in life as in literature, were behind her. But the main thing, she told an interviewer, was "to keep the show on the road"—to keep going, she meant, with dignity. People who knew her in her last years tended to describe her as charming, funny, and energetic. *A Day in the Dark* (1965), the last volume of her stories published during her lifetime, collected much of the shorter fiction she had written since the war. The title story, vintage Bowen, concerns a young girl poised between innocence and understanding of the unsavory adults attempting to manipulate her. Much of the rest of the contents, primarily work of the 1950s, is unfortunately but predictably undistinguished.

Now, in Hythe, Elizabeth set to work on what would be her last novel, *Eva Trout,* written from 1965 to 1968 and published in 1969. Surely it is her worst novel, taking to new extremes the penchant of her later years as a writer for never explaining anything. Her last attempt to describe modern society succeeds only in aping the subtlety and ambiguity of Henry James (who is mentioned in the novel). *Eva Trout* is as close to a flat-out flop as anything Elizabeth ever produced, though of course it contains some characteristic, familiar elements. But the novel strives after effects so baldly as at times to parody itself and its author, or so it seems. The protagonist, as Patricia Craig says, is "an impossibly inflated version of the Bowen destructive innocent, and she meets an inflated end: shot dead by the other lethal innocent (her 'son') on Victoria Station." The deaf-and-dumb son has been illegally snatched away in America (shades of Forster's *Where Angels Fear to Tread*); the whole thing is preposterous. Glendinning describes Eva as "inexplicably large, and largely unexplained." The destructive-innocent theme is about all that remains of the old Elizabeth Bowen in this awful, and awfully long, tale. Eva's family, it is said, have "a genius for unreality," which also apparently embraced the author. Elizabeth was seventy when it appeared, however, and ought to be excused on the grounds of diminishing powers, including judgment. In retrospect it seems clear that she ought to have stopped writing after *The Heat of the Day* in 1949. But how could she? She was just fifty then and had no desire to cease working; being, as she said of herself, intelligent only when she wrote, she had to keep writing. After all, an achievement-and-decline view is convenient for the critic when dealing with a complicated and long career, but the artist assessed can hardly participate in the assessment; he or she can only provide the data and die.

The house in Broadstairs in *Eva Trout* is drawn from that in which Dickens wrote much of *Bleak House,* and in the later 1960s Elizabeth embarked on a return engagement with the works of her great predecessor. After rereading *David Copperfield,* she wrote to Charles Ritchie: "It has given me an almost terrifying illumination about my own writing. Here really are the roots of so many things I have felt, or perhaps of my way of feeling things and seeing them." She does not explain this, but surely a large part of *David Copperfield*'s importance for her, both now and when she first read it, lay in its examination of the lives children are forced to lead in a world regulated and controlled by adults, always one of her favorite themes as well as one of Dickens's.

From 1969 until her death in 1973 Elizabeth worked on an autobiographical volume titled *Pictures and Conversations,* published in an unfinished state in 1974. She wrote a nativity play for performance in the Protestant cathedral in Derry in Northern Ireland at Christmas 1970. The only piece of fiction she is known to have completed during her illness-plagued last years was a tale for children, *The Good Tiger,* which appeared in 1970. In the story a young tiger is brought home from the zoo by some children; fearing a loss of innocence as a tiger—becoming human is to be avoided at all costs, apparently—the tiger runs away, but later is enticed back by a cake he can eat far away from the adult world that frightens him. Even for a tiger innocence must be protected from grown-ups.

She told her publishers as she was writing it that *Pictures and Conversations*—the phrase comes from the beginning of *Alice's Adventures in Wonderland*—was not so much a conventional autobiography as a study of "the relationship between art and life." This was an appropriate topic for a writer who depended so much on "real" life, especially her own, for her fiction and who saw the novelist as a gatherer of impressions very much in the mould of a painter. She wanted, Bowen said, to examine the connections "between living and writing," a relationship she declared to be most interesting "when it is apparently not traceable." Only she knew how much of her life she had put into her books. And having read now several critical studies of her work, she wanted to get things straight: "If anybody *must* write a book about Elizabeth Bowen, why should not Elizabeth Bowen?"

She spent the autumn of 1969 at Princeton, where she described her borrowed flat as "the ideal scene for a murder" and the students, as antiwar demonstrations around the country were reaching a crescendo, as "mild" and "subdued": "Passions may be seething in their breasts, but I doubt it."

The novelist was delighted by the election of Edward Heath as Prime Minister in 1970, though she was not in the habit of expressing her political opinions publicly. "My view is that writers should keep out of pulpits and off platforms, and just write," she said. "They should not for a moment consider putting their names to petitions or letters to newspapers or matters that they do not know much about and have no reason to know anything about." The closest the novelist came in these years to ignoring her own advice occurred when she nearly wrote a letter to *The Times* to condemn the Church of England's infamous "Alternate Service," introduced in the late 1960s, to the old Communion Service.

All of her adult life, as numberless witnesses have reported, Elizabeth Bowen remorselessly chain-smoked cigarettes. In the early 1970s this life-long pattern of self-destruction caught up with her. She began to suffer from various attacks of respiratory illness. In 1971 she was victimized by both bronchitis and pneumonia. She spent the first months of 1972 at the Bear Hotel in Woodstock. After a visit to friends nearby she was observed driving away "in quite the dirtiest car I've even seen, all windows closed, the engine screaming, her smoking a cigarette and, although amongst this we couldn't hear a single word, she was still talking." As we know, when there was no one else to talk to she talked to herself. But now Elizabeth had to stop talking: in the summer of 1972 she lost her voice. Lung cancer was diagnosed, and she underwent a series of radiation treatments. She had rarely been ill and apparently was not a good patient now: "I don't take reverses and disappointments well," she admitted. A judge that year, she read over the Booker Prize entries in the autumn thinking she would recover. But the novels did not amuse her. "How strange many of them are," she told Rosamond Lehmann. "I begin to fear that women have lost their genius." She continued to smoke and to whisper. She reread Anthony Powell, Dashiell Hammett, Raymond Chandler, Somerset Maugham—and Elizabeth Bowen.

Elizabeth spent Christmas 1972 with friends in Ireland. She was ill and weak, and upon her return to Hythe she went into the hospital, taking with her the volumes she was reading as a judge for the Duff Cooper Award. Literally on her deathbed now, she devoured a book about an old friend— Quentin Bell's life of Virginia Woolf, her first choice for the award and probably the last thing she read. Charles Ritchie visited her every day in the hospital, bringing champagne. Rosamond Lehmann came, and Cyril Connolly, and Isaiah Berlin, and many others. Elizabeth Jenkins remembers her at the end, swathed in clouds of cigarette smoke in her hospital room. Bowen told her agent, Spencer Curtis Brown, to publish *Pictures and Conversations* in its unfinished state, as indeed he did. The posthumous volume would include, to lengthen it, the first chapter of a novel she had begun called "The Move-In." The fragment describes the arrival of guests at a country house. One of her last whispered conversations was with a cousin about the scent of roses at Bowen's Court in the old days.

She died on 22 February 1973; Charles Ritchie was alone in the room with her. A few days later she was buried near her father and her husband in

Farahy churchyard, just inside the gates of what had once been Bowen's Court, on the road connecting Mallow and Mitchelstown. The funeral was attended by many of her former neighbors carrying flowers, though it was the dead of winter. She had lived to the age of seventy-three, and spent much of her time and energy chronicling the life of an age long gone. And though so much of her work was autobiographical, she had managed not to inflict the secrets and the details of her own life on her readers in the tell-all, or almost-all, mode of such contemporaries and friends as John Lehmann and Stephen Spender, whose memoirs left her cold. "Most people," she said in reference to her friends' autobiographies, "do better to keep their traps shut." Her truths were in her fiction.

3

THE LAST TYCOON: ST. JOHN PHILBY

I

NEXT TO TWO framed photographs of Ché Guevara on the wall facing the desk in his spacious Moscow flat, the late Kim Philby placed a large photograph of his father, Harry St. John Bridger Philby—tycoon, philosopher, writer, linguist, eccentric, explorer, wanderer—wearing full Arab garb. Below the photograph, in another frame, reposed two pages from one of St. John Philby's holograph manuscripts, displaying neat, tiny handwriting. "Look at that," Kim Philby told a reporter from the *Sunday Times*, "what clarity of thought—only two corrections on the whole page."

Treachery, it has been said, holds a peculiar fascination for the British, perhaps because they have experienced so much of it from their public officials, perhaps because the British as a people are so prone to self-loathing. The master spy of his generation, indeed the master spy of the twentieth century—the century in which spying came into vogue both as a popular obsession and as a literary subject—betrayed his father when he betrayed his country, though St. John Philby died before he could realize what his son Kim had done. It was St. John's fame that got Kim hired by MI6 despite the reputation of Philby *fils* for subversive politics at Cambridge. As with many other youthful revolutionaries of the 1930s, Kim lacked the historical justification of a deprived upbringing, so he dedicated his life to the destruction of his own class. Nor is it any accident that Kim's colleagues Donald Maclean and Guy Burgess were the sons, respectively, of a Cabinet minister and a naval officer. You have to have something to betray if you are going to betray something. "Oxbridge," the novelist Len Deighton reminds us, "has not only provided Britain with its most notable politicians and civil servants but its most embittered traitors too." The sons of the Establishment did have something to betray; few if any British spies have come from the working classes and pushed their way up, shedding provincial accents at university. No, Britain's famous spies betrayed not only their country and their generation but also, more tellingly, their families.

Did Kim aim to betray his father and what he represented? It is highly unlikely on the face of it. St. John Philby saw himself as a victim of British politics and policy and his failure to reach the apex of political life in Britain and of the Civil Service as a betrayal of himself by the mandarin Establishment of the day. Philby *père* was also a rebel, as we shall see, and he suffered for it. Indeed, it is more likely that Kim Philby's betrayal of Britain was an act of revenge on behalf of his father rather than a conscious betrayal of his father. In this he is unique among the spies of his generation.

In his later years St. John Philby abandoned government service and lived in Jidda as an Arab, seizing every opportunity to condemn the policies of the British government. Indeed, at the outbreak of World War II he was interned for making anti-British statements. Was Kim simply following his famous father's example of dissent? By the time Kim came of age and took the path of a spy, St. John had been at odds for years with his political and Civil Service bosses and was already a bitter man. How much of this bitterness and disappointment rubbed off on his volatile and impressionable son?

For St. John Philby years earlier had, as he said himself, revolted against the political and philosophical canons by which he had been brought up, embracing instead a system of thought made up, he would declare later, of equal parts agnosticism, atheism, anti-imperialism, and socialism. His conversion at forty-five to Islam symbolized his dissociation from British ideas and ideals. So one possible view of Kim Philby is that he was following the example of his father in turning his back on Britain: like father, like son.

But St. John Philby never betrayed, and never meant to betray, his country. He would have been horrified by Kim's deliberate treachery, and it is because Kim knew this that he never told St. John what he was doing. E. M. Forster remarked that he hoped he would betray his country before he betrayed his friend. It is a typically (for Forster) muddled and fatuous sentiment, ignoring as it does the fact that a man who betrays his country betrays his friends as well. "All things betray thee who betrayeth me." Treachery is in fact a domestic act, when you think about it, because it embodies the betrayal, in the first instance, of everyone you know. Indeed, those you know are the only ones you *can* betray. Of course you betray as well those you do not know, but the person doing the betraying does not see the betrayal of those he does not know: others see it for him. He does, however, know that he is betraying friends and family, and that is what makes treachery of this sort an act so particularly and peculiarly *personal*. Seen in this light, Forster's remark seems especially idiotic.

Who was St. John Philby? Reams have been written about Philby *fils*, next to nothing about the father. And in so many ways the son was the unwitting creation of the father.

"My nature . . . could not fit into any plan or groove," St. John Philby said of himself. The question of his identity will not be easy to answer. We do know that Kim Philby's father was (for a while) an intelligence agent prone to Anglophobia: could Kim have inherited it all from St. John? Is there, as a recent book on the Philbys argues, a gene for treason? After all, there is St. John, in that photograph in his son's Moscow study, dressed as an Arab rather than an Englishman—very much the better-known contemporary, and fellow intelligence officer, of his friend T. E. Lawrence. Could Kim's betrayal have been the most stupendous of all—that of one wayward spy by another, who happened to be his son? The ultimate double cross? Who *was* St. John Philby?

II

It is typical of St. John Philby that in later years he claimed he was really the son of gypsies and that he had been inadvertently substituted for the "real" St. John Philby when he was a baby: thus his wanderlust and his exoticism. Certainly he had an affinity for Eastern wanderers. "He mixes a bit too much with the native element," one of his Civil Service superiors was later to say of him. After becoming a Muslim he took as his second wife a Saudi slave girl. For years he lived in Mecca, dressed as an Arab, ate camel meat, and kept a bodyguard of Abyssinian baboons. He spoke seven languages. But, as Phillip Knightley points out in his life of Kim Philby, St. John never really gave up being an Englishman. He stood (unsuccessfully) for Parliament. He regularly published in *The Times*. He tried never to miss a Test Match. He was a member of the Athenaeum. He was both a polymath and an explorer, charting previously unknown parts of Arabia with maps so precise they are still used today. He received medals from the Royal Geographical Society and the Royal Asiatic Society. He contributed to important geological and zoological collections from Arabia. And yet he never quite made it up the ladder of the Civil Service, falling out with his superiors at crucial points in his career. He ended up cursing the British government for what he saw as its deceit, treacherousness, and moral decline. And so in one respect perhaps he provided a model for his son Kim: the man of talent stifled and stymied by an unimaginative and unappreciative political Establishment.

St. John Philby always remembered how hard-pressed his parents were to pay their bills. He inherited his father's impecuniousness, having to cadge for money all of his life and frequently borrowing from others. He was a man, it is said by those who knew him, who went through life convinced that he was right and everyone else was wrong on the issues of the day.

When he died in Beirut in 1960, Kim Philby erected a tombstone over his grave which read: "Greatest of Arabian explorers." The grave was in a quarter of the city that saw heavy fighting in the 1980s and undoubtedly has been destroyed.

The Philbys were from Essex. St. John's father was a failed coffee planter who married into a military family in India in 1883. St. John's mother was related to the man who would become Field Marshal Lord Montgomery of Alamein. The couple had four sons. St. John was born in Ceylon in 1885 and taken to England when he was six. He was sent to a series of schools, including one run by A. A. Milne's father at Westgate-on-Sea. At thirteen, in 1898, St. John won a scholarship to Westminster and began his education in earnest at this most prestigious of London public schools. Westminster daily commemorates its founder, Elizabeth I, by singing a Latin service in the light of candles around her tomb in Westminster Abbey. The newest grave there when St. John arrived was that of Gladstone.

He never saw much of his father, the failed Ceylon coffee planter. St. John's father did not live with his family—an idiosyncrasy the son was to repeat throughout much of his own life. The old coffee planter drifted from place to place, sometimes sending money to his impecunious wife, often enough forgetting the family's existence altogether. St. John inherited his father's unsettledness and sometimes treated his large family in a similarly absent-minded way. For a while Kim Philby's grandfather was a big-game hunter. Later he took paying clients on shoots and later still served as a gunner during the Boer War. But he could not quite bring himself to live with his wife and four children, an irregularity that St. John could not help noticing and later emulating. He did not, at Westminster, answer his father's letters. "He had after all let my mother down, and that was the unforgivable sin," St. John wrote later. His father died in 1913, bequeathing to his family a few photographs, a cup and silver match box, and a Boer War medal.

As a Queen's Scholar, St. John at Westminster was expected to distinguish himself. He obliged, winning school colors for cricket and soccer, doing well in all of his academic subjects, and ultimately becoming captain of the school. In 1902 he took part in the coronation of Edward VII. For three years he studied with the Headmaster, Dr. James Gow, who had taught D.H. Lawrence at Nottingham High School. He also took up chess and debating, speaking as often as possible on the side of orthodoxy, power, and the Establishment. He favored employers over workmen in the sporadic strikes of the day and Russia over Japan in the Russo-Japanese War. Energetic and powerful, he would get up early to read plays in Greek before classes. He collected butterflies and insects, and decided early on that he was destined for the Indian Civil Service.

A glimpse of St. John Philby as captain of Westminster is less flattering than prophetic. His reign as head of the school was later characterized by a contemporary as "not a success. Autocracy was his aim and autocratic rule his avowed intention. He meant to rule with an iron hand and he had not the good sense to conceal it in a velvet glove. The result was that his year was conspicuous for internal dissensions." This account, reported by his biographer Elizabeth Monroe, goes on to describe St. John as despising the day boys, working against rather than with the masters, and failing altogether to use constructively the enormous influence available to a young man occupying his position. Philby at eighteen, according to this observer, was stiffly conventional, a reactionary, and a prig. Schoolboys are often spiteful, especially in retrospect; but it does appear that the young Philby was a fairly conventional adolescent, enamored of power and testing his strength in the schoolyard.

Westminster had long been linked through scholarships to Trinity College, Cambridge. In March 1904 Philby won an exhibition in classics; he arrived at university that October. Cambridge in 1904, as Monroe reminds us, was still the city of the Butlers, Darwins, Cornfords, Keyneses, and Travelyans. Whitehead, Bertrand Russell, and G. E. Moore were fellows of Trinity. Recent Trinity undergraduates included J. M. Keynes, Thoby Stephen, Clive Bell, Leonard Woolf, and Lytton Strachey. Fabian socialism was just becoming fashionable. Margaret Bondfield, who as Minister of Labour in Ramsey MacDonald's Labour government from 1929 to 1931 would be Britain's first female Cabinet minister, was a year ahead of Philby; Rupert Brooke was a year behind him.

Philby furnished his rooms conventionally, bought the right clothes, drank copiously, and devoted himself to athletics, hardly breaking any molds. He also played chess, did some acting, wrote some poetry, and studied a little. He spoke once at the Union. In 1906 some British officers, pigeon-shooting in Egypt, were attacked by angry villagers. One of the officers who ran for help later died of heat prostration. Harsh sentences, including hanging, were handed down by an Egyptian court, sentences endorsed by British authorities and by Whitehall. Philby spoke at the Cambridge Union in defense of the British government and against liberal criticism of its behavior in this case. Indeed, Philby was to become famous at Cambridge as a great talker and debater. He savored controversy and joined debating clubs. He proposed Jawaharlal Nehru, the future Indian prime minister, for membership in one of them, which would have been fairly daring at the time. But generally he was known by his classmates as a confirmed conservative. He joined the Sunday Essay Society, which heard papers mainly on religious topics. One Sunday evening he was scandalized by a talk called "The Ethics of the Gospels," which debunked the teachings of Christ; the speaker was Lytton Strachey. When his turn came to speak, Philby gave a paper called, characteristically, "The Convenience of Convention." Religion, he declared here, is the greatest "of all conventions," in part because it is "so strong in resistance to all opposition"—odd logic indeed. The upholders of faith, he argued, were less critical and less negative than modern philosophers. They had found, after all, a "perfectly satisfactory" system and were willing, as they should be, to force their doctrine upon waverers and prevent them from mocking tradition. Later Philby would describe his essay as "the swansong of my championship of orthodoxy." Curiously uninspired, this perfunctory platitudinizing presaged a permanent turn away from convention.

With James Strachey, Philby joined a group, founded by Leonard Woolf and Lytton Strachey, devoted to play-readings. This led to more ambitious acting opportunities. In 1906 Philby acted a small part in a production of *Doctor Faustus* in which Rupert Brooke played Mephistopheles. In the summer of 1906 Philby switched over from classics to modern languages, having got a Second in classics. He spent time in France and Germany working on his languages. In 1907 he was awarded a First in modern languages.

After passing the Indian Civil Service examination, he decided to spend another year at Cambridge reading Oriental languages and Indian history and law before departing for India. During 1907-8 Philby studied Persian and Hindustani and began to acquire that interest in Oriental nationalism that was to mark his subsequent career and thought. He sailed for Bombay and his first job in November 1908; he was twenty-three. He was assigned to the staff of the lieutenant-governor of the Punjab. The Punjab was supposed to be the preserve of those with influential families and friends, so Philby's first appointment was a lucky one. Because of its moderate climate and lush landscape, life was more pleasant there than in many other parts of India.

In 1908 the viceroy of India was Lord Minto, who had succeeded Lord Curzon in the post three years earlier. Minto was a Tory of moderate to liberal views who horrified his colleagues by appointing Indians to his Council, doing away with British majorities in provincial councils, and generally increasing Indian representation in government—all with the approval and cooperation of his minister in Campbell-Bannerman's Liberal government, John Morley. India in those days was not altogether different from the India described in Kipling's *Plain Tales from the Hills* and later in Forster's *A Passage to India.* The British deplored, or pretended to deplore, the Indian caste system while maintaining a rigid social caste system of their own.

Philby's introduction to the Indian countryside was an explosive one. The train for Lahore he boarded in Bombay proceeded to run head-on into another train, the crash awakening everyone but Philby. So he arrived at Government House in Lahore in the wrong clothes and without his kit. Philby was posted to Jhelum, a district north of Lahore on the Grand Trunk Road in some hills with a spectacular view into the mountains of Kashmir. He worked hard and quickly learned Urdu. He served as a local magistrate, went hunting and sightseeing, played polo and cricket. He got a reputation as a radical by discussing with his colleagues the issue of Indian self-government, a subject in those days horrible to Indian civil servants. In the autumn of 1909 Philby was transferred to Rawalpindi, where his primary duty was assessing damage to crops caused by British troops on parade and the amount of compensation due to local landowners. He learned the details of cattle and dairy farming in India and wrote a manual on customary law in his region. His next posting, in May 1910, took him farther south into the hot plains of the Punjab as a sub-district officer. He enjoyed the power over local life that came with the appointment.

At the club in Rawalpindi in late 1909 or early 1910 Philby met Dora Johnston, the daughter of a senior railway engineer. Dora was a good-humored red-haired beauty, an accomplished tennis player and dancer. Her grandfather had been a popular Victorian painter named Alexander Johnston; his *Flora Macdonald,* a favorite of Queen Victoria's, hung at Balmoral by her order. To his mother, Philby wrote of Dora: "She does not play bridge or smoke and I have never heard her say a nasty thing about anyone." He decided to marry her and began to borrow money in order to do so. The Civil Service frowned upon marriage so early, at any rate within the first five years of tenure: early marriage put very young men at a decided disadvantage both economically and competitively within the service and thus was seen as an extraneous complication to be avoided. But Philby decided, not for the last time, to defy tradition; he scheduled his marriage to Dora for September 1910. Of course he could not know it, but because he disobeyed his superiors so early and so decisively he would never recover their full confidence; in a real sense his career was always stymied by this premature break with tradition and the resulting conviction on the part of the Civil Service mandarins that he was a hothead who could not be trusted—that he was not, after all, one of them.

At this time Philby was very poor. Setting up house as a married man was expensive; he was also paying an allowance to his impecunious mother in England. He had nothing but his small salary, about £30 a month. But now another difficulty beset him. As the local magistrate in his Punjab district, he had to preside over a spectacular case of suspected murder. At a Muslim wedding in a small town a Hindu beggar had appeared, asked for alms, and been killed. Philby ordered a post-mortem. The local Muslim doctor, assisted by a street sweeper, declared that the late beggar died of an enlarged spleen. Philby found someone said to have given the unfortunate man a shove at the wedding and had him arrested for murder; and he had the doctor suspended from duty for giving false evidence. Local Muslims were up in arms; local Hindus were delighted. A British doctor was engaged to do another post-mortem and found that the dead man's spleen had been normal. Philby ordered the Muslim doctor and his assistant committed, without bail, for perjury—a mistake, since perjury was a bailable offense. The local police having only one pair of handcuffs, the high-born Muslim physician and the untouchable Hindu street sweeper were handcuffed together and transported to jail in an open cart in full public view. This turned out to be another mistake: the case became a sensation. Quickly the district commissioner defused it by giving bail to the accused.

In his zeal to punish, the twenty-five-year-old magistrate had forgotten or ignored the rules. The Muslim doctor and his assistant were later acquitted. And Philby's Civil Service bosses, already annoyed by his marriage, were quick to note his bumbling escalation of a small local dispute into an unfortunate cause célèbre, and they were not pleased. Civil servants have long memories; this was definitely a bad start. Philby was formally reprimanded for his handling of the case, promotion for him was ordered delayed, his salary was frozen. Desperately needing money now, Philby moonlighted as a teacher of languages and over the next few years earned a substantial sum as a tutor (about £20,000).

The next year, 1911, was a busy one for the Philbys. Dora was pregnant. Philby temporarily was put in charge of a desert town beyond the Indus—a town characterized by his biographer Elizabeth Monroe as "a howling wilderness of low scrub and worse grass in a temperature that forced him to do all outdoor work before ten and after five." Here he supervised the building of nothing less than a new town: the old one was falling into the river. In the autumn the Indus flooded. Philby was moved again, sent this time as a revenue assistant to another town, a town threatened by drought and famine. He was nonetheless pleased by his release from civil and criminal administration—"which I loathe," he admitted ruefully.

It was here, at a town called Ambala, on 1 January 1912, that the Philbys' first child was born. He was named Harold Adrian Russell Philby. Soon enough he had a nickname: Kim, after the boy-hero (and embryo spy) who gave Kipling's famous novel of Indian life its title. Years later Kim Philby remembered that, as a very young boy in India, he had spent more time with servants and other Indians than with his parents. He was able to learn some Punjabi relatively quickly. One day St. John came into the kitchen and heard his son chattering away in the local dialect. "Good heavens," he is supposed to have said, "he's a real little Kim." The nickname stuck—prophetically, for Kipling's hero was a double agent.

Philby *père* now began to work in even greater earnest on his languages. He wanted to enter the Political Department of the Civil Service and get a posting to Persia, Mesopotamia, or another country on the Persian Gulf, where life was easier than in India and the pay better. For he was, as usual, broke; he was getting nowhere in India—indeed, he got on better with the Indians than with his own colleagues. He offended the latter frequently by expressing openly and aggressively his contempt for the color bar; and he broke with Civil Service tradition (once again) by inviting Indians to his home. He went so far as to put an Indian friend up for the local club and threatened to resign if he was blackballed. The friend was admitted to membership, though this could not have made Philby any more popular among his colleagues.

His political views, clearly, were undergoing revision. Philby in his twenties seemed to have shifted significantly to the left of the boy at Westminster and the young man at Cambridge. By 1913 there was a movement afoot to allow more Indians into the Civil Service. Philby wrote to a friend: "Why we don't all plump for socialism is a mystery, but England is very dense and conservative and cannot see reason. Those who are reasonable"—a reference, of course, to himself—"are considered mad and argumentative and generally impossible," which is probably how his superiors saw him in these days. And yet Philby continued to have difficulty translating his new egalitarian views into real life. While out walking one day he met a party of schoolboys, and when their schoolmaster spoke insolently to him he boxed the man's ears. For this provocative and tactless act Philby was frozen in rank and salary for two more years: another disaster. Deeply in debt and, as always, financially desperate, Philby complained to the viceroy of his latest punishment, alleging that the circumstances in which he struck the schoolmaster "were such that a sudden loss of temper was inevitable though the practical result of it was inexcusable." The freeze was reduced from twenty-four months to nine.

In 1913 Philby was sent back to the Punjabi desert. He continued to dream of a Persian posting. The outbreak of war in Europe forced him to cancel the home leave in England he planned for 1914. But now he got a job he coveted: acting District Commissioner in Lyallpur, one of the canal colonies, which offered many of the amenities of life he missed in the Punjab. He fretted briefly at being so far away from the European war. And then along came another job: appointment to the Criminal Investigation Department at Simla. Among his new duties were censorship of the Indian press and keeping an eye on the Indian nationalists. This suited Philby. "I sit upon the slightest flicker of sedition," he told his mother. Yet he tried again to get himself into the action in Europe. His three brothers were fighting there; one was killed in France in the first days of the war. But instead of being sent home, Philby in 1915 was appointed secretary to the Board of Examiners in Bengal, which required a posting to Calcutta. Philby was jubilant: this new job should enable him to pay his debts. He began to plan Kim's education and decided that he should go to Westminster.

While in Calcutta Philby worked on his Persian and Arabic and collected material for a projected history of Urdu literature. He rode a bicycle around Delhi to see the sights, including the place where, a few months earlier, a bomb had been tossed at the viceroy. In the war, meanwhile, the Mesopotamia Expeditionary Force had requested linguists; civilian administrators would be needed when the British army, fighting the Turks, reached Baghdad. The Philbys went back to England in October 1915. In November St. John embarked for Basra. "My greatest ambition," he wrote to Dora, who stayed in England, "is to take some part in the war coupled with my work among the Arabs." Like that of many of his contemporaries, Philby's life would follow a pattern shaped by his service in the Great War. As a civilian administrator in occupied territory, he became immersed in intelligence work. Tiring quickly of practicing his Arabic on local workers pressing down packages of dates with their bare feet, he grew fond of testing his linguistic skills while wandering around Baghdad disguised as an Arab beggar.

Philby's bosses in Mesopotamia had three objectives: to cultivate local Arab chieftains; to protect the oil fields in south Persia, which supplied oil to the Royal Navy; and to foil German plans in the area. The most pressing problem the British faced was their own ignorance of local tribal affiliations, which reduced the army largely to guesswork about when to advance and whom to trust along the way. Here Philby could assist. He was set to work as the chief civilian accountant at Basra, in which capacity he oversaw the financial administration of the occupation. When he had nothing else to do he would spend the evening reading the New Testament aloud in Arabic to his Arab servants.

The British army was pinned down by Turkish forces in Mesopotamia well into 1916. A measure of the army's desperation was the attempt of T. E. Lawrence to bribe the local Turkish commander to stand down. The bribe was £1 million, and it failed. Touring one of the battlefields, Philby noted that the flies were so thick here, and so aggressive, that they "threw themselves upon the open jam tins and . . . settled on every bit of food as we conveyed it to our mouths. It was appalling . . . they settled on our clothing, turning our khaki to black." He studied ways of exploiting Arab antagonism to the Turks. Britain, he felt, must not give up Mesopotamia, but he had not as yet met any Arabs who seemed capable of leading their own nation. The war in Mesopotamia continued to be stalemated. Late in this year Philby, now thirty-one, was promoted to Revenue Commissioner and became a CIE—Commander of the Indian Empire. He was the youngest man to be awarded this honor. Kim, aged four, remained in England with his grandmother. It was at this time that his lifelong stammer surfaced, perhaps a result of early and constant separation from his parents. Kim's contemporary Elizabeth Bowen also developed a stammer as the result (probably) of early grief and separation; and so had Somerset Maugham a generation earlier. While medical science is vague on this, the connection between the condition and the symptom seems imperative.

Early in 1917 the army under Lt.-General Sir Stanley Maude began at last to advance. When the British captured Baghdad in March, Philby was sent there and took note of a growing Arab nationalism that sought to rename

Mesopotamia: the Arab name was Iraq. Philby was put more or less in charge of the Arab desk in Baghdad and wrote memoranda for the government on conditions in Arabia and among the Arabs generally. The Arabs were only now beginning the revolt against their Turkish masters. British policy was to underwrite Arab independence movements as a way of bringing down the Turks, and thus the Turks' German allies, in the Middle East. Philby was asked to go on a journey to help advance this policy. The journey was to meet Ibn Saud, the Bedouin chieftain. The two quickly became friends. Philby sought to sow the seed of revolt in Arabia wherever he could: this was his brief. Ibn Saud was quite taken with this fair-skinned lover of the desert who so desperately wished to become indistinguishable from his Arab hosts. "It was possible to distinguish Philby from the . . . Bedouin in his group only by the fact that his feet were not quite dirty enough," wrote a contemporary observer. At any rate, Philby was poised now to embark on another journey, one that would make him famous as an explorer and win the Royal Geographical Society's medal: a dash across central Arabia in pursuit of Arabian solidarity.

III

Arab tribes at this time were traditionally hostile to their neighbors; this was the single greatest barrier to Arab independence and the fighting effectiveness of the Arabs as allies of the British against the Turks and Germans. Philby's task was to go into unmapped, unexplored territory and try to convert anomalous Arab tribes to the British cause. T. E. Lawrence's labors toward the same objectives are of course better known, due in part to his passion for publicity. But St. John Philby toiled in the same vineyard.

Philby's journey to the heart of Arabia, which commenced in November 1917, was to end at Riyadh, at the court of Ibn Saud. Philby liked Arab ways. He gave up utensils and ate with his hands; learned to ride a camel; drank the Bedouin's traditional bitter coffee. As Phillip Knightley has pointed out, he also admired the austerity of the Arabs, or at any rate their strict moral code. And a political system founded on a benevolent autocratic monarch appealed to his more conventional side. Nor could Philby forgive British duplicity toward the Arabs during the current war. In exchange for help against the Germans and the Turks, the British promised the Arabs independence and self-determination when the war had ended. But the infamous Sykes-Picot agreement (1916) ignored this promise; by this secret document France and Britain agreed to carve up the Middle East to their own advantage once the war was over. The Arabs saw this duplicity multiplied by the Balfour Declaration of 1917, which promised a national home in Palestine for the Jews. From this time onward Philby seems to have adopted the (reasonable) view that the British government could not be trusted in Middle Eastern affairs. And from this time too he began to see himself as the only advisor the Saudis could trust in their relations with the British. It was, to say the least, an unusual stance for a British civil servant to take.

Philby grew a beard and dressed in Arab clothes: the long white shift called the *dishdasha*; the *thaub*, or overshirt; a colored coat, or *zabun*; the most familiar garment, the all-enveloping *aba* or *bight* of camel wool; sandals; and headcloth. He seemed to enjoy the democratic ways of the Arabs. Among them, he wrote, "there were no distinctions, traditional or natural . . . they taught me that no man could be their leader except he ate the ranks' food, wore their clothes, [and] lived level with them." For an Englishman used to rigid class demarcations, this more relaxed system seemed, as it did to Lawrence, a blessed release. He could talk to and sit with whomsoever he liked, educated or uneducated. He ate rice and dates, and learned to like them.

Philby reached Riyadh and Ibn Saud late in November 1917 and went to work. His task, as before, was to try to unite the quarreling Arab tribes against the Turks. In this Ibn Saud turned out to be a guiding force. Philby handed over to the Arab leader the £10,000 in gold he had brought with him. Meanwhile he kept careful notes and drew maps. In the midst of this uncharted expanse he recorded compass bearings, distances, times, altitudes, and landmarks. In addition to making maps he collected geological specimens and noted local customs and lore. The Arabs, he learned, believed that polygamy would sweep Europe after the war as a compensation for the expected shortage of men.

In January 1918 Philby traveled to Cairo, where he realized for the first time that his trip across Arabia to Ibn Saud had made him famous—among Englishmen, at any rate. He was introduced to General George Allenby and taken to Jerusalem, where Philby saw guns on the Mount of Olives firing at the retreating Turks. In February he returned to Riyadh and to Ibn Saud, who asked one question after another about the state of the rest of the world. One of them Philby remembered afterward: what language did Americans speak? Philby tried to spur his Arab friends to action against the Turks, but this was no easy task. When Baghdad pressed him to speed the Arabs up, Philby replied: "It should be realized that the vast majority of the people spend half their day in prayer and the other half in religious exercise, and should not be dealt with as fully reasonable beings. Their vision is hopelessly limited and their souls sour with fanaticism." By the middle of 1918 it was clear that some of his early enthusiasms for the Arabs and Arab life were beginning to be worn thin by frustration: the Arabs, despite British bribes and hopes, were not doing anything.

In the heat of midsummer Philby undertook another journey across Arabia to make maps. Many of his maps of previously uncharted Arabian terrain, produced later for the Royal Geographical Society, were sketched during this trip. The war in Arabia finally ended in the autumn of 1918 with the Turks in retreat. Philby, feeling that he had not yet completed his work there—for the Arab tribes were still at war with one another—was called back to Baghdad. After the general armistice in November 1918, a new Anglo-French declaration recommended letting the Arabs choose their own form of government without outside interference, a position Philby had been advocating for some years.

When he went home on leave in 1919 he found England in some respects less comfortable than the Middle East. Coal and food were in short supply. Servants were expensive. A general strike seemed always just around the corner. A flu epidemic came and went. Philby was acclaimed in high government circles for his exploration of the desert; he was awarded the Founder's Medal of the Royal Geographical Society. Kim, now seven, was sent off to Aldro, in Eastbourne, a good preparatory school. Here, it was hoped, he would be prepped for Westminster.

Philby was writing his first travel book, *The Heart of Arabia*, when he was asked by the Foreign Office, in mid-1919, to return to the Middle East and arbitrate yet another dispute between warring Arab factions. The first choice for this mission had been Lawrence, but Lawrence, characteristically, could not be found. In this year Philby and Lawrence met for the first time on a plane flying from Crete to Egypt. For a long time Philby talked and Lawrence listened, finally asking Philby who he was. "Oh, you're Philby, are you?" Lawrence said. He struck Philby as less interested in Arabian unity or for that matter Arabs generally than in carving out a kingdom for his ally Faisal in Syria.

The Foreign Office's arbitration job fell through and Philby was sent home again in the summer of 1919, where he learned that Dora was pregnant. Now thirty-four, he had wondered if he should have another child, and hoped that he would. While in England this time Philby played host to Arab visitors, including Ibn Saud's son Prince Faisal, arranging for them among other things an exchange of swords with George V at Buckingham Palace. He also took his guests to see *The Mikado* and the Regent's Park Zoo and Selfridge's roof garden. He continued to write and to campaign for another Middle Eastern posting.

In the summer of 1920 a rebellion against the rigid British rule of Iraq broke out in that country. Some British officers were murdered. A British mission to Iraq was formed, Philby among the number. Once there, he organized a secretariat and devised rules for the proper relation between Iraqi ministers and British advisors. Philby himself became the British advisor at the Ministry of Interior, a job which earned him £2,500 a year and brought a measure of real power. Dora came out with their new daughter Diana, and the Philbys rented a house in Baghdad. Philby worked hard and managed at the same time to turn out several volumes of Arabian reminiscences during 1920 and 1921.

Faisal was proclaimed King of Iraq by the British in July 1921, and Philby, outspoken in his support of a republic rather than a monarchy, offered to resign his post. Instead the Foreign Office sacked him. Dora, who was pregnant with their third child—another daughter, Patricia—persuaded him to take a vacation, and he took it in Persia. In the autumn he was given yet another chance to promote Arab independence, this time in Jordan. The Colonial Office, which in 1921 meant Winston Churchill, in this instance supported by Lawrence, decided that Philby was the man to bring stability to the regime backed by the British in what was then called Transjordan. He was appointed Chief British Representative there. So the Philbys—all except Kim, at school in England—moved to Amman at the end of 1921.

During his first ten days in Jordan, Philby was shown around by Lawrence himself. Philby wrote later that his famous friend was simultaneously decisive and quixotic, making snap decisions as they toured various parts of the country and then leaving office clerks to carry them out. Lawrence and Philby agreed that the latter's chief task should be to steer Jordan toward independence.

Amman at the end of 1921 has been described by Elizabeth Monroe as "still a village strung along three fissures in the high plateau of Moab; it had been the Philadelphia of the Romans, and possessed a ruined amphitheatre and some Byzantine remains but was otherwise primitive and unlovely." Amman was connected to the outside world by the pilgrim railway made famous by Lawrence's attacks on it during the late war; by some well-worn caravan routes; by a branch line to the port of Haifa; and by unpaved rough roads to Jericho and Jerusalem. Few Britons lived there. Communications from outside arrived once a week from Jerusalem. The Philbys lived in one of the nicer houses; it had no heating and no plumbing. Philby found he could write in Amman, but Dora was lonely and homesick. She went back to England in the spring of 1922. Throughout this year Philby labored mightily for Jordan's independence and for representative government there.

At the end of 1922 he returned to London for several months. He was invited to tea with Churchill, who had lost his seat in the general election of October 1922, and called on Dr. Chaim Weizmann and his wife; she was "much more nationalist" than he, Philby noted in his diary. To an audience in London he gave a speech in the course of which he unreservedly criticized British and French policy in Arabia and the Allies' failure to secure self-determination in the Arab territories after the war. "The Arab is a democrat," Philby declared. For the first time since 1911 in India (and for the last time until the 1940s) the entire Philby family was together at Christmas. Kim, who was ten, came home from school for this unique holiday.

And he was left there when the rest of the family returned to Jordan in January 1923. Petra was Philby's newest assignment; he developed it as a tourist attraction and went over the rest of the country to find other sites that might be similarly developed. Dora usually accompanied him on his travels; the two little girls were left at home with a nurse, which brought upon Philby's head a charge by the local military authorities of irresponsibility. "Either the children are safe or I challenge you to forbid tourism," was Philby's characteristically tactful reply.

In May Jordan achieved independence. Philby had no time to celebrate: he was in the midst of a nagging dispute with the Civil Service boffins. He complained about his staff, his salary, and his quarters, and got into the habit of taking his frustrations out on local Arab leaders, with whom for the first time he began to grow unpopular. Toward the end of 1923 and into 1924 the wrangle became more intense; not for the first time, Philby could not control his temper. He embezzled some Colonial Office funds to pay himself the additional salary he felt he was owed and was ordered to give the money back. A hopelessly complicated dispute followed, ending in Philby's resignation from his post early in 1924. He blamed "zionist interests" for his fall, which was actually brought about by his own impossible conduct. Before departing from Jordan in April 1924 he undertook one more expedition. "I know of nothing more pleasant," he wrote equably in his diary, "than travelling by camel over new country with a gang of Arabs." He spoke publicly of secret British plans to scuttle Jordanian independence and refused to attend a farewell dinner in his honor given by the High Commissioner. But here was Philby, now thirty-nine, without a job—and Dora was expecting their fourth child. In May they were back in England, and Philby, still a civil servant but without employment, was looking for work.

IV

One potential source of income for him now was journalism; to the astonishment and fury of the Civil Service, Philby began to publish articles arguing that Britain had betrayed the Arabs and kept them in bondage after promising independence. His theme was that everything the British had done in the Middle East was done in bad faith. Despite the lip service they paid to it, Britain and France had never recognized or accepted Arab nationalism. British policy would drive the Arabs back into the arms of the Turks; this was Philby's (highly improbable) conclusion. The British, he said, must "give up using [the Arabs] as pawns in our game with an individual Arab dynasty or with the French or with the Zionists." He portrayed himself as having been thwarted by his masters in the attempt to fulfill the promises they made; it was his duty, he declared, to state the truth no matter what this cost him.

Philby was heard. His articles appeared in the *Nineteenth Century,* the *Nation,* the *Daily Herald,* and the *Westminster Gazette.* He was courted as a speaker, and spoke his mind—to, among others, a group of Liberal M.P.s at the House of Commons. Arab nationalism, he said, would have prospered had Britain supported it as faithfully as it had supported Zionism.

British policy in Iraq and Palestine was directed by economic considerations: "The real crux is oil," an argument we have no difficulty understanding today. The more he wrote and spoke, however, the more Philby tended to contradict himself and the more shrill, inconsistent, and unstable he sounded: one is struck by this reading over his speeches and articles seven decades later. But he seemed sincere and knowledgeable, and he was taken up and lionized by opponents of the new Labour government. Throughout the rest of 1924 Philby continued to sound off, seeming to his bosses in the Civil Service increasingly fanatical, increasingly a menace.

His financial problems were eased a bit by Kim's winning a scholarship to Westminster. "I really think the proudest moments of my life have been when I heard he was elected . . . and when I took him to the school the other day," Philby told a friend. He himself now joined the Fabian Society, claiming that he had always been a socialist. This was a far cry from the Sunday Essay Society at Cambridge; and one cannot help speculating on the role played in Philby's conversion by the recent general election, which had produced a Labour government. Indeed, Philby now began to look around for a seat in Parliament, intending to stand as a Labour candidate. He also sought an academic appointment, preferably at Cambridge, and flirted with businessmen who had interests in Arabia and were seeking paid advisors. Meanwhile his third daughter, Helena, was born in September 1924.

October found him walking a more familiar path: another attempt, this one unofficial, to mediate between warring Arab tribes. The Foreign Office, which had sacked him not so long ago, quickly dissociated itself from his activities, announcing that Philby had no official standing in the British government. Undeterred, he wrote to Dora: "I can't help feeling that I have a destiny . . . to fulfill . . . I have given up the road to ordinary success and I feel that in doing so I have made my mark in the small orbit in which I have moved." Seriously concerned that Philby's gratuitous interference into Arabian affairs could be construed by others as part of official British policy, the government had managed to pull the rug out from under Philby by the time he got to Arabia. First it prevented him from traveling into central Arabia and then it threatened, unambiguously, his pension: "Mr. Philby will remember that the ordinary sequel to disobedience to direct orders is dismissal." He was still a civil servant without a job. Philby's other enemy on this ill-fated trip was dysentery, which attacked him severely enough to force his return to England in 1925. This time he had accomplished nothing.

These were hard years for Philby. His fame as an explorer and cartographer remained unimpaired: the Royal Asiatic Society, which promoted Oriental learning, gave him its Burton Medal. But he remained anathema to the British government, and this was what mattered most to him—for it was in politics, in the administration of foreign policy, that he most wished to shine. Now an increasingly bitter man, he renewed his attacks on the government. He had four young children, a small income, and few prospects. In

May 1925 he used some of his pension funds to buy a house in Acol Road, Swiss Cottage. In the autumn of this year he induced Rémy Fisher, a businessman with interests in the Middle East, to send him out to Egypt and Arabia for some first hand observation of conditions, political and economic. While in Arabia this time he tried to get Ibn Saud to hire him too. The King did allow him to open a branch, in Jidda, of a British trading company owned by Fisher's syndicate, but Philby got no further: he returned to England in March 1926. There followed once again a series of speaking and writing engagements. It was generally considered that Philby knew more about Arabia than any other private person in England. He was elected to the Athenaeum and asked to write articles for the *Encyclopedia Britannica*. He hoped to be the next Labour candidate for Cambridge; but when, in the midst of the General Strike of 1926, the party solicited his views on industrial policy, his manifesto was pronounced unsatisfactory. He wanted to talk about foreign affairs: they weren't interested.

In the autumn of 1926 Rémy Fisher's group decided to make Philby its Jidda representative at a salary of £1,500 a year for three years, plus some shares in the trading company. So back he went to Arabia, this time as little more than a salesman working on commission in a cautious marketplace. Now forty-one and rating himself a failure, Philby returned to part-time journalism with a vengeance, dashing off another series of articles on British perfidy in the Middle East. The Foreign Office was used to him by now; its Consul in Jidda told Whitehall in 1927 that in Arabia Philby "is a nuisance rather than a power of evil" and that the King, Ibn Saud, "rarely takes him seriously." With Dora and their children established in Swiss Cottage, Philby during this period of his life embarked on a series of short-lived affairs with English women: "I need a woman to bring out the best in me," he remarked, with customary tact, to his wife. He was restless and unhappy, feeling thwarted at every turn. "My chief aim," he admitted in 1928, is "to secure the immortality to be gained by the accomplishment of some great work. . . . Everything seems to indicate that the climax is not far off." His pursuit of English women abroad, as Elizabeth Monroe informs us, went on for a few more years and finally subsided when, in the early 1930s, he was named co-respondent in a divorce case. Perhaps more to the point—having become a Moslem in 1930, he was by then able to satisfy his appetite for women, at the court of Ibn Saud, with slaves and the concubines of princes. There was an endless supply. Philby enjoyed the sexual facility of Arab women, expressed without embarrassment and without comment. Later he collected erotic and pornographic handbooks of sex in Arabic, Persian, and even Sanskrit. Philby must have been one of the few Englishmen of his day who could actually use them, if he wished, to enhance his sexual pleasure.

His new interests were in part a result of boredom. He had no friends in Jidda, a city whose streets, T. E. Lawrence had written, "kept their air from year's end to year's end." Dusty, dirty, dull, quiet, and smelly, Jidda offered little to interest a cultured and sophisticated man or woman. Shunned by the few Britons there, who considered him cantankerous, dangerous, and unstable, Philby turned to the Arabs for society. They were baffled by him. He was an Englishman who spoke scornfully of the English. Was he a spy, some sort of double agent sent in to get them to talk to him, to gather and report indiscretions? Philby did nothing to dispel the mystery; indeed, he adored mysteries. Why be plain and open when he could be, or could be perceived as, inscrutable, impenetrable, enigmatic? It amused him. But was it good for business? After all, he was now a businessman who had to sell to live.

He began by selling soap at 5 percent commission, which drove him even deeper into depression. He played cards and wrote and did little else besides pursue his women friends. Not until the summer of 1927 was he given any clerical help by Rémy Fisher. During the latter half of this year he began to drink heavily. The British Consul at Jidda characterized Philby in letters home as "desperate" and "deranged." In 1928 Philby went off to look for a gold mine in Syria and failed to find it. In official correspondence during this year the unforgiving Foreign Office described Philby as an "avowed and persistent opponent of British policy." Philby himself cursed "the fate that has kept me here earning my living."

Late in 1928 things began to look up for him. He had made a few sales, mostly of transport and minted coins. The publisher Benn commissioned him to write a book on Arabia for its Modern World series. Several British constituencies wished to know if he was available to stand for Labour in the upcoming general election of 1929. (He could not afford it.) He was still capable of wildly eccentric behavior. When one of the British consuls in Jidda proposed to establish a golf club, Philby, Monroe tells us, "violently opposed it. He denounced it as racially discriminatory and a violation of Islamic law, and forbade his staff"—all two of them—"to join it. To demonstrate that he could do without human society, he paraded the baboons that he kept for company."

Throughout 1929 Philby, like Mr. Micawber, was certain something would turn up. It had better, because he was broke. It could not have been easy to be broke at forty-four, with a seventeen-year-old son at public school who wanted to go to Cambridge, with a wife and three daughters in London dependent solely on him. He negotiated on behalf of Ibn Saud for a series of radio stations to link up the country's communications, and in 1930 he was rewarded with a contract with Marconi worth £17,000. Now his old optimism began to return. He even expected to become the first British ambassador to the new country of Saudi Arabia. Of course his name was still hateful to the ears of the civil servants at the Foreign Office. A Labour government had been returned in 1929; Philby hoped, in 1930, to be adopted as a Labour candidate in the next general election, even though, as he admitted candidly, he could not pay his own electioneering expenses. He declared that he would solve "the Palestine problem" if the British government would only give him the chance to do it. But he knew only too well that he might not be given the chance to do anything. "I have to realize that the opposition is frightfully strong," he wrote to Dora, "and that I am living before my time." When she complained to him of the penury she and her daughters lived in, he serenely authorized her to sell the house in Swiss Cottage should she wish to do so: "All I ask is a study and a place in which to entertain when I am home," which was not often. He had become his father.

In keeping with Philby's revised view of his own importance he drafted in 1930, Monroe reports, a proposed constitution for a democratic republic of Palestine to be governed by a congress in which representation would be proportional under the British mandate. Chaim Weizmann and David Ben Gurion both read it and rejected it: it would, they saw, give the Arabs the greater power in Palestine. During this year Philby worked on his book about Arabia for Benn and devised an electoral scheme for self-government in a united India. Meanwhile the first British ambassador was appointed to Saudi Arabia, and it was not St. John Philby. Instead of an embassy he acquired the local Ford agency and sold fourteen automobiles to Ibn Saud. He began to think seriously about conversion to Islam. The King reminded him "how nice it would be for me when I became a Muslim and could have four wives."

There was a good reason why he should not convert: he did not consider himself a Christian and always denied the existence of God. But there were also some overriding arguments for taking the plunge: "If only I was or would become a [Muslim] I believe I could get . . . [business] concessions for the asking," Philby mused. Converting would give him more direct access to Ibn Saud and his court as well as unrestricted travel opportunities in the desert. It seemed to Philby that it would be good to renew his salad days of travel and exploration. As Monroe points out, there was more to it even than this:

> Islam is more than a religion. In the land of a devout ruler, all actions were governed by it, and no one could hope in any sense to belong to Arabia unless he took part in the prayers and readings, rejoicings and fastings, laws and personal habits that, for the Arab, constitute a way of life. The very language that Arabia speaks is bound up with it. . . . Islam's spiritual inheritance, tradition, symbolism and doctrine permeated the actions of every day. . . . Conversion wed Philby to Arabia.

Philby's thought, since Cambridge, was characterized by him as a combination of "agnosticism, atheism, anti-imperialism, socialism and general progressive revolt against the philosophical and political canons in which I was brought up." Why not become a Moslem?

V

He made up his mind to convert. It was the summer of 1930; he was forty-five, unhappy and unsuccessful. He was the first to admit, and did admit, that he needed Islam less as a faith than as a commercial convenience. A British friend later wrote of Philby in 1930:

> He made no pretence whatever that his conversion was spiritual. He had been deliberating the step for . . . years, ever since the first hot moments of his rage against HMG's Arab policy. This had now cooled . . . but his disassociation from British ideals remained and he felt increasingly cut off from things British and drawn to things Arabian.

His decision to become a Moslem may be seen at least in part as another act of defiance of British policy: you were not, after all, supposed to become one of the savages whose tribe, as a civil servant, you were governing and to whose primitive society you were bringing light. Nothing could have been more un-British, or a clearer articulation of a rebellious state of mind, than to become one of "them." The conversion, which took place in August 1930, completed Philby's translation from British bureaucrat to Arabian businessman. For this was certainly the end of his career in the Civil Service, if he had not reached it before (probably he had). Now no government post could be his. But it was commercial success he needed. To his credit he never pretended otherwise; and never did he pretend that Islam meant anything to him spiritually.

"I have too long decided on this step to feel the least excited about it," Philby wrote to Dora, "but I dare say I shall have worked up the right sort of feeling as I approach the walls of Mecca." Off he went on his pilgrimage to Mecca, changing into Arab clothes on the way. The story of his conversion was widely reported in the world press. Dora wrote to her husband in a businesslike vein: "I quite see what a difference it is going to make to you being able to get about the country." Philby replied: "I still hope to end my days in Parliament."

In 1931 he published an account of the reasons for his conversion. He wrote here:

> I regard the Islamic ethical system as a real democratic fraternity, and the general conduct of life, including marriage, divorce and the absence of the unjust stigma of bastardy, resulting in a high standard of Arabian public morality, as definitely superior to the European ethical code based on Christianity . . . I consider an open declaration of my sympathy with Arabian religion and political ideals as the best method of assisting the development of Arabian greatness.

The assertion of the superiority of "Arabian public morality" to "the European ethical code" was perhaps gratuitous and smacks of special pleading: Philby wished to flatter his Arab friends, and he always knew how to superimpose over "Arabian public morality" his own private needs and desires, which were easier for him to satisfy among Arabs than Europeans. At any rate, here was the articulation of another stage of his leisurely rebellion against Mother England. And the decision, once taken, gave Philby some genuine comfort. To a British friend he characterized his conversion as bringing to an end several years of what he called "gradual moral suicide." He blamed the British government for "having turned me adrift for my uncomfortable opinions on matters eastern and Arab." His conversion was as much (or more) a political act as it was a fiduciary act. He was getting even with the British government; a generation later his son Kim would betray his political masters more completely.

In any case, the conversion brought St. John immediate rewards. He was given the run of the palace and all court sessions. He took many of his meals with the King. He wished to make use at court of the sexual opportunities his conversion opened up to him, but he saw he must exercise some caution. "The use of contraceptives is not recognized," he wrote, "but may be discreetly indulged in, but abortion is a crime. So there are complications." The King gave him, in 1931, a house in Mecca complete with resident slave girl, with whom Philby conducted an affair over many years and whom he eventually married. Indeed, she produced for him a second family, as we shall see. The court moved to Riyadh in 1931, and Philby moved with it.

His business picked up a little. That is, he began to receive more orders for goods—radios, cars, water pumps, camp tents—but as always he had difficulty collecting payment for them. The Depression reached the Middle East in 1931 and brought commercial transactions to a standstill. The few gains Philby had made since 1929 were quickly wiped out; indeed, he had to swallow from Fisher a 20 percent reduction in salary to stay in Arabia. Dora in London was now sent nothing and could not pay her bills, including her children's school bills.

The virtual end of business activities in 1931 left Philby contemplating the possible fulfillment of a longtime ambition: more desert journeys and completion of the explorations of Arabia he had wished for so long to undertake. After all, what else was there to do? These activities would bring him no income and could not benefit his family, but so what? They would have to fend for themselves (and they did). His attitude toward the proposed exploration was highly personal and characteristically competitive: "I have sworn a great oath not to go home until I have crossed the [Rub al Khali desert] twice! and left nothing in it for future travellers," he wrote in 1931, while awaiting Ibn Saud's permission to start. The Rub al Khali was known familiarly as the Empty Quarter of Arabia. As before, Arab tribal disputes held Philby up.

His debts mounted throughout the year. He was idle and depressed, his business dead. He passed the time by "rehearsing" for his proposed journey: he went for long periods without water and tried to simulate other desert conditions. He was forty-six now, not exactly the same young man who welcomed the challenge of the desert with such energy two decades earlier.

Finally, in December 1931, things calmed down in the Empty Quarter, and Philby was allowed by Ibn Saud to set out. He left Riyadh in a fog in January. He expected to disappear off the known map for three months, and he did. He failed to achieve some of his cartographical objectives but by no means all of them. He was at one stage almost murdered by his bodyguards: this was when he insisted on exploring an area known as the Waterless Desert. They demurred and carried the day. Later Philby wrote bitterly that the Arab, unlike the white man—that is, himself—"clings frantically, desperately to life however miserable, and when that is at risk, loses heart and head. . . . I felt like Moses in the wilderness when the multitude clamoured against him." But Philby managed to collect much valuable information and material during his journey across part of the Rub al Khali in 1932. Monroe remarks: "Philby was never too tired to take notes and use his own instruments to determine where they were; his thumbed notebooks . . . record every change of terrain and shift of direction, each plant observed, each snake or insect seen, each trace of bird or animal." The Royal Geographical Society would make much of his findings, and the British Museum would welcome many of them into its collections.

But Philby had, for once, a close call. The last of the water was used out of sight of a resupply, and Philby's Arab companions had begun to butcher and eat their camels when civilization was regained. Philby had gone without water for fifty-five days just to see if he could do it. He now (March 1932) persuaded a remnant of his escort to explore with him the Waterless Desert, and the party set off, knowing it could not find water for the next 350 miles, through country without living vegetation of any kind. It almost destroyed Philby, who grew so parched and weary he feared he would have to give it up. He characterized this ordeal later as a continuous marching into the sun. Finally the party reached the other side of the desert, a place that was unused to foreign visitors and had seen no rain for twelve years. Philby pushed on. His objective was to get to Mecca, through hundreds of miles of country unmapped and virtually unknown to outsiders. At all points he was drawing maps, many of them still used today, and challenging his guides to interpret every feature of the landscape they encountered. He collected butterflies and insects and geological and ornithological specimens, all sent eventually to the British Museum: the Arabian collection of bird skins there became the best in the world due to Philby's contributions. He spent his forty-seventh birthday in a sandstorm on the road to Mecca, which he reached in April 1932.

The story of Philby's latest exploit was published in the newspapers shortly after his return. Dora wrote: "Kim is wild with excitement." Philby replied wearily: "I think that I have done with desert exploration for good." "Bursting with my epic in embryo," he asked Dora to negotiate his next book with a London publisher; he began immediately to write an account of his most recent travels. He returned to London in May, a hero. The story of his crossing the Rub al Khali was by then known to everyone. He was honored by the Royal Geographical Society and the Royal Central Asian Society. He was asked for lectures, newspaper articles, radio talks. His three-part account in *The Times* of his travels was widely read. He became reacquainted with his family—his three daughters and Kim, now twenty and stammering painfully, and routinely receiving thirds on examinations at Trinity College, Cambridge, the first of his many rebellions.

Philby and Dora returned to Jidda at the end of 1932. Here he found that his fame as an explorer was earning an unexpected financial dividend. American developers bent on extracting oil from Saudi Arabia, where petroleum in commercial quantities had just been discovered, wished to use Philby as an intermediary with Ibn Saud. Offering his services, Philby ultimately agreed to consult for Standard Oil of California on the following terms: a salary of $1,000 a month; a payment of $10,000 if Esso got the rights it sought in Saudi Arabia; another payment of $25,000 should Esso be able to exploit its oil lease commercially over a long term; and 50 cents per ton exported, up to an additional $25,000. Other oil companies now entered the bidding to retain Philby's services; he wished to oblige them all, though he had to be (uncharacteristically) discreet about his activities. As it turned out, Esso retained an advantage over the others because it was the only company prepared to pay everyone involved, including the Arabs, in gold. And so the perennial problem of Philby's finances, of household debts and school bills, was solved, at least for the time being.

By the spring of 1933 Esso and Ibn Saud had agreed to terms, largely through Philby's mediation: £50,000 down, £5,000 a year in gold, and a royalty of four shillings per ton on production. Yet again Philby was excoriated by the British Civil Service, which saw him as an enemy of Britain for promoting American oil interests in Arabia. Why shouldn't the British, for so many years the protectors of the Arabs, obtain the oil leases themselves? Because they hadn't been quick enough or generous enough, and because they didn't agree to pay in gold: that's why. Philby betrayed nobody; he just looked after himself. The coming of American capital to Saudi Arabia was not an unmitigated success for him, however. The Esso presence brought in other corporations. It appeared that Philby's Ford agency would be swamped in 1933 by the large franchise granted to General Motors. He buried his automotive disappointment (short-lived anyway, as it turned out) in another success. Standard Oil of California now put him on an annual retainer of £1,000 in addition to his other income from them. And now that the Arabian desert was opened to oil prospectors Philby became even more widely sought: he was the only European on the scene who knew enough about the interior and had the languages and the contacts to make use of his unique expertise. At the end of 1933, with Saudi Arabia on the brink of war with neighboring Yemen, he found that he could sell Fords again after all, since everyone wanted mechanized vehicles. It was a very good year.

Preparing for a career in the Foreign Service, meanwhile, Kim Philby was living in Vienna in order to improve his German, or so he said. Information recently come to light suggests he went to Vienna on orders from the French Comintern, having already been recruited by the Soviet Communists while at Cambridge. At any rate, in Vienna he proceeded to fall in love with his communist landlady, a Jewish divorcée a year older than he. She would be the first of a long line of ladies loved by Kim Philby; he married her in February 1934. St. John took an immediate dislike to the new bride; his abuse of the marriage was at times astonishingly public. Kim had graduated from Cambridge in June 1933 with a second-class degree in economics; he used his modest Trinity College prize of £14 to purchase the works of Karl Marx. Now, nearly a year later, at twenty-two, he had no job and no money and apparently had handicapped himself by making this quixotic marriage. At Cambridge he had openly advocated Communism; now he found himself unable to get a place in the Civil Service. In these days he was straightforward about his divided loyalties, admitting that should a conflict between them arise—for example, a choice between the British government and the Communist party—he could not be certain what course he might follow. Kim's father found yet another reason to denounce the Civil Service. No one, he declared, should be victimized for "views honestly held"; Kim, he said, was entitled to his "leanings toward communism." St. John had apparently taught his only son the value of free-thinking. At Westminster Kim had allowed himself to be confirmed, though he was an agnostic; he never forgave himself for this attack, as he later saw it, of moral cowardice, for giving in to the views of others. Nor did he do so often in subsequent years.

St. John wrote, prophetically, to a friend in England: "The only serious question is whether Kim definitely intended to be disloyal to the government while in its service"—that is, had he been accepted into the Civil Service. Had he so intended, said Philby *père*, he should not have tried to get into the service at all. And he went on in this same letter to distinguish carefully between disagreement with a government and actual disloyalty to it: "Some people may think . . . that *I* was disloyal to the government, but that was never the case. I was in opposition to its policy and always made this clear, and I resigned in order to have freedom to express my views more publicly." Even though this is not strictly accurate—Philby was sacked for embezzlement of government funds—an important difference between father and son is articulated here. While St. John Philby believed in expressing disagreement "publicly" but not by being actually disloyal, Kim Philby would become adept at hiding his real views while he betrayed the government he worked for. Nor would he ever resign.

At this crossroads of his son's career, St. John, characteristically, urged Kim to speak out and take the consequences, whatever they might be. Kim replied that, after all, the Civil Service commissioners "certainly would not choose anyone who at a critical moment . . . could not be trusted." Equally characteristically, Kim went on: "The ideal would be for people of extreme views to keep them dark from everyone, their own families included. But it is very difficult to hide views . . . and indeed unless they [stay] extreme there is no incentive to do so." Dora was keeping an eye on Kim and sent periodic reports to Jidda. "I do hope he gets a job to get him off this bloody communism," she wrote to St. John. "He's not quite extreme yet but may become so if he's not got something to occupy his mind." His new wife, Dora thought, egged Kim on and urged on him her more radical political views.

Kim eventually landed a subediting job with the *Review of Reviews* in London. For the next several years he developed his "cover" as a communist agent by cultivating and espousing extreme right-wing views, even joining the pro-Nazi Anglo-German Fellowship and advocating appeasement. When he found that his communist wife had become a professional liability, he unloaded her. And when he lost his job at the *Review of Reviews,* St. John helped him along at *The Times,* suggesting to his friends there that Kim should be sent to Spain to report on Franco and his forces. Kim was duly sent to Spain. Indeed, he became at twenty-five *The Times'* youngest foreign correspondent. In Spain he spied on the fascist enemies of his Soviet masters while pretending to sympathize with Franco—who was, as St. John had suggested, his beat in this war. Kim's career as an undercover agent was unwittingly helped by Franco himself, who personally decorated the young *Times* correspondent with the Red Cross of Military Merit—this for nearly being killed by a shell fired, ironically, by a Soviet gun. "As the war ground on," Phillip Knightley has written, "Philby continued to write his undistinguished dispatches, neatly tailored to suit the [pro-Franco] prejudices of his newspaper and cleverly circulated to enhance his reputation as a serious young Englishman of impeccable right-wing political views." St. John was baffled by his son's new politics. "He's not only reporting for the Franco side," Philby *père* was to complain in 1939, "but he seems to think that they're right." British intelligence, also taken in, was to recruit Philby *fils* largely because of his work in Spain. The right-wing masquerade was necessary to get Kim back into the good graces of the British government, which was to give him a job when the civil war in Spain ended.

There was another war in the mid-1930s, this one in the Middle East and scarcely remembered. Saudi Arabia and Yemen, by 1934, were battling over borders; St. John was busy organizing purchases of arms for Ibn Saud and writing articles on the fighting for *The Times.* The war ended in April. St. John spent the summer consolidating his business position, which the war had improved—making especially giant strides with his Ford agency, which had thrived on many of the usual requirements of war. Indeed, he was doing well enough now to acquire a car (and chauffeur) of his own. Thanks to his automobile and oil concessions, he prospered during the rest of 1934 and on into 1935. Typically, however, making money, once he had mastered it, began to bore him. "Money-making is a very dull business and I hate the sight and sound of motor cars," he remarked. He still yearned for the big stage, to participate in events of international and historical importance. He began to grow impatient with Ibn Saud's maladroit administration and for the first time criticized his old friend openly.

VI

Philby's books had not done well. He resolved early in 1935 to gather material for another one. Now nearly fifty, he had never lost his wanderlust. He spent most of 1935 and 1936 traveling and much of 1937 on home leave in England. The journeys across Arabia were taken by car now instead of camel: the roads were primitive but they existed where before only wilderness and camel trails could be found. His explorations in 1935 took him across Arabia from sea to sea in six months. The trip in 1936 was commissioned by Ibn Saud; Philby was to map Arabia's southern boundary with its defeated neighbor Yemen. This would be his longest journey in terms both of time and distance. In the course of it he collected another bonanza of geological, zoological, and ornithological specimens, at times treating his guides with such bad temper, and even violence, that some of them left him before the end. Philby noted how the physical strain of travel by camel during earlier explorations gave way on motorized trips to mental strain born largely of uncertainty about the group's reception in uncharted land. He wrote:

> The physical exertion of desert travel is as nothing compared with the nervous—especially in the desert borderlands where tribal loyalties can never be taken for granted. In fact, we met with nothing but friendliness—a striking tribute to the desert's fear of the desert King [Ibn Saud]—but each day's success had to be paid for by the anxieties of the night before.

The people he visited in this way generally took him for a spy. "Who was this Christian who prayed like a Muslim?" one of them asked. The local British authorities did not consider him one of themselves and gave him no help when he traveled through British protectorates, which infuriated him.

The British viewed Philby as a supporter of Ibn Saud and an enemy of the British Empire. For his part, Philby delighted in thumbing his nose at his compatriots by demonstrating that he could travel wherever he liked in Arabia without their protection or even their permission.

During the last months of 1936 and the first months of 1937 Philby completed both his inspection of Saudi Arabia's southern boundaries and his frontier maps, which were to be extremely valuable to later travelers. He suffered from boils and malaria, but persevered. From a coastal plain he was one of the first Europeans to see, he wrote to Dora: "The garden of Eden must be very much like this valley and the human beings one meets from time to time might have stepped straight out of Genesis, naked except for a loin-cloth and sometimes a rifle, and with very fuzzy greased hair." He had to complete the last stretch of the trip by donkey, a backbreaking experience. It was emblematic of his life, perhaps, that at the end of this journey he got off his donkey and stepped into Ibn Saud's Rolls-Royce, which took him the last few miles to Mecca. Philby spent the latter half of 1937 in England, lecturing and writing articles; among his new clients was the *New York Times*. A familiar theme of this round of lectures and essays was the propensity of perfidious Albion to cheat, or try to cheat, the Arabs of their land and its income.

He went back to work in Mecca early in 1938. His Ford agency was once more mired in hard times, but his royalties from Esso continued to be paid. By midyear he was again restless and bored. "The years are passing," said Philby, now fifty-three, "and I am rather wasting my time in Arabia." Again he craved some measure of political power; again he offered to stand as a Labour candidate at the next general election. He did not ingratiate himself any further with the Foreign Office by continuing to complain that the British government was trying to steal territory away from the independent Arabs. By what right were the British attempting to annex territory in Arabia, Philby asked. He wished to know, he said, what benefits of civilization the British were bringing to people whose villages it bombed from the air as punishment for disobedience. He developed these themes in all company and on every occasion; and for the first time questions about his loyalty began to be raised inside the Foreign Office. During a lecture in England Philby claimed that British representatives in Arabia "wanted to shoot me." If they didn't before, they did now. Requests for articles continued to pour in. Philby was asked by the British papers to write not only about Arab affairs but about the proposed partition of Palestine into Arab and Jewish sectors, a plan that he favored (though Ibn Saud did not). Philby worked in Jidda throughout the rest of 1938, returning to London early in the next year for a secret conference on Palestine in the course of which he hosted a luncheon for Chaim Weizmann and David Ben Gurion.

He was back in Jidda in March 1939 when Hitler invaded Czechoslovakia. Like Nancy Astor an ardent appeaser, he advocated even now a British non-aggression pact with the Germans, arguing that "no cause whatever is worth the spilling of human blood." It was largely his pacifism that caused the Epping Labour party to turn him down as a prospective candidate. "It really would be most amusing to be up against Winston," he wrote at this time—"no chance of getting in, of course." Indeed, the new conflict in Europe justified Churchill's persistent warnings and made him even more formidable in his Epping constituency and throughout the ranks of the Conservative party. (Churchill would come to power at last in May 1940.) Philby wrote letters and articles advocating pacifism and placating Germany, Italy, and Japan to avoid world war. He now joined Lord Tavistock's British People's party, a fascist and anti-Semitic group that argued for non-involvement in wars "which in no way affect the security and national independence of our peoples" and pressed for the protection of the average taxpayer against big business. In June 1939 Philby agreed to stand for Parliament as a member of the British People's party, and in July he returned to England to fight a by-election at Elizabeth Bowen's once and future home town, Hythe, a safe Conservative seat. He was supported by, among others, Oswald Mosley. Philby polled only 576 votes out of 22,169 cast and lost his deposit. Nevertheless he continued to speak and write in favor of appeasement, declaring in September that Poland's fate "should warn us to cease from the folly of refusing to recognize Germany as a principal factor in the shape of things to come." Generally his political conduct throughout 1939 can be described as craven, discreditable, despicable, and irresponsible; his opposition to all foreign policies of the British government had trapped him on the edge of a truly lunatic fringe. No one could suggest, as has been done for Nancy Astor, that St. John Philby was politically naive. He knew what he was doing; but his fatal recklessness and especially his hatred of the government in Whitehall were greater than any impulse he may have had toward moderation and common sense. Nonetheless, he never went over to the other side—to England's enemies.

When war finally broke out in earnest Philby offered his services to the government as an Arabist. He was told he was being considered for a job in military intelligence overseeing intelligence and counterintelligence in the Arab theater. But he was not approved. His pre-war associations were much too unsavory and his public statements too bizarre; his record was bad, and of course he was well known as an independent spirit. Philby declared later that "I had already sacrificed my career by my fight for Arab independence." But it was his identification as an appeaser—in 1939-40 hardly anything could have been worse for a politically ambitious person, as Lady Astor found out—that did him in. He now launched himself briefly into a scheme to raise money for Ibn Saud from the Zionists. The idea was that in return for £20 million, the Jews would be permitted to take over part of Palestine. The King angrily dissociated himself from this plan as an unseemly attempt to let himself be bribed. (Chaim Weizmann, however, pursued the idea with President Roosevelt.) Philby's final exploit before leaving England this time was to associate himself with publication of "Stop the War" pamphlets distributed by the British Council for a Christian Settlement in Europe, another lunatic organization whose activities were observed by the police.

In December 1939 he finally tired of waiting for the British government to find a position for him and returned to Arabia. He was again depressed and oppressed by his failures, admitting to Dora that "I would rather run an empire than a house." Kim was closer to the war, having been sent to France as a correspondent for *The Times.* During the summer of 1940 Kim was recruited by the Secret Service on the recommendation of his Cambridge friend Guy Burgess.

In Arabia, St. John was in one of his most contrary moods. Ford had fired him as their agent there; the British did not want him for the war effort; he had virtually nothing to do but gossip. He spoke wildly of the impending German victory and British surrender, declared that the Allies were responsible for the war and that they could not win it. Dementedly, he characterized Hitler as "un homme tres fin" and compared him to Christ and Muhammad. When the war heated up in the summer of 1940, Philby remarked that the sooner Hitler took Paris the better for everyone. He seemed to have gone mad. In July Ibn Saud reported to London that Philby had become "mentally deranged. He never ceased heaping curses and insults and scorn on the British government." When he announced that he planned to travel to America and India in order to conduct anti-British propaganda, the British authorities decided to transport him back to England, where he would be less of a menace than anywhere else, and to keep him there. In August, in Karachi, the fifty-five-year-old Philby was arrested under the Defence of the Realm Act, Section 18b, as a risk to the security of Britain. He was taken to a police station and from there shipped directly back to Liverpool. "Those who tell the truth are traitors," he wrote in his diary.

Arriving in Liverpool in October, he was hustled off the ship, a bitter man; he was not even allowed to see Dora. Indeed, he was permitted no visitors at all due to the seriousness of the charge: "activities prejudicial to the safety of the realm." He was taken by police van directly to Walton Prison. His notes and manuscripts were confiscated; he was locked in a cell six feet by eleven. Philby noted in his diary that his conscience was not guilty; his criticism of England had—mistakenly, he thought—been interpreted as treachery and disloyalty. What he had said was treacherous and disloyal, not to mention idiotic and indefensible; but it's true that he did nothing actually to betray Britain: that would be left to the next generation. In November St. John was moved to the Mills Circus ground at Ascot, where his fellow inmates, he noted, included "priests, professors, peacemongers *et hoc genus omne.*" Friends and former colleagues petitioned the government for his release, arguing that he had always enjoyed being cranky and disobedient but had never been disloyal or unpatriotic.

Philby, in prison, read a great deal: G. H. Hardy and Hitler were among his selections. He also took this opportunity to outline a sort of personal philosophy of life, in the course of which he advocated among other things free medicine and competitive examinations for places at the universities. Brief reflection on metaphysics led him to note tersely that no doubt "the materialist or realist explanation of the fundamental nature of the universe [is] the correct one." He also produced a mass of punning poems called "Quatrains from Quod." In December he was finally allowed to see Dora—for fifteen minutes in the presence of a prison officer.

In February 1941 Philby was summoned before a tribunal, which he proceeded to lecture on the failings of British foreign policy in the Middle East. The tribunal decided he was a harmless fanatic. According to Kim Philby, who was by then working in War Office intelligence, "He bored them into submission."

After six months of detention St. John was released. He spent much of the next few years in Wales, writing a history of pre-Islamic Arabia. It was clear he could get no war work, and he saw no point in undergoing the inconvenience of a bombed-out London. By June he was celebrating Hitler's invasion of the Soviet Union as "certainly the best thing (apart from America coming in) that we could wish for"; "we" were the British, and his subsequent comments on the war tended to be more sane and moderate than those of 1939.

What effect did all of this have on Kim? Declaring that "One view of Kim Philby is that he followed St. John's example, like father like son, and turned his back on Britain in a similar manner," Phillip Knightley argues with conviction that, "outspoken as St. John was, there was never any evidence that he worked actively against his country. If he had been given a worthwhile job where his talents could have been put to good use, then there is every reason to believe he would have swung wholeheartedly behind the war effort." This is undoubtedly true. It is also probably true that the government's detention and humiliation of his father helped justify in Kim's mind the betrayal of his country, which at least in part must have been an act of revenge. England had imprisoned his father for the expression of political opinions, thus demonstrating once again, if further demonstration were needed, the hypocrisy of its so-called commitment to democracy and civil liberties. So Kim must have thought. Revenge has always been a weighty motive, and there can be little doubt—though in fact this theory has not been offered before—that Kim Philby's persistent disloyalty to his country over a quarter-century was in some measure an act of revenge against the tormentors of his father in 1939-40.

Throughout 1941 and 1942 St. John in Wales worked on his history of Arabia, the world falling to pieces around him. For once he played no part in the events of the day. Several times he was consulted about maps and the geography of the Middle East, but that was all. He offered himself as, now, a Conservative candidate for a parliamentary by-election in Putney, declaring that he could "give the country an inspiring lead on the way to a new spirit of empire," but the application of this latest Tory recruit was ignored. He was still identified in the public mind as an appeaser. Soon afterward he joined yet another political party, a new one called Commonwealth, which advocated, according to Elizabeth Monroe, common ownership of resources, "socialism for the middle classes," abolition of the House of Lords, the defeat of Conservatism (whose candidate he had so recently wished to be), and the substitution of merit for privilege as a criterion for advancement. Does one sense that St. John's political convictions during these years were, shall we say, fluid? Commonwealth soon enough had its fill of Philby. He was criticized for intemperance in promoting party doctrines: "he is not a suitable person to be entrusted with the public exposition of Commonwealth policy," party leaders declared. Philby indignantly articulated for his new colleagues his current beliefs: "I have always disapproved of war as a method of settling international disputes," he wrote. "The fact that we are at war does not justify any change in that attitude, though I am not and never have been a pacifist." He concluded: "I am as convinced as anyone else that being actually at war we should do our best to win it in order to make future wars impossible."

It is a hard thing to be rated by your peers untrustworthy and unreliable, especially in time of national upheaval, and Philby was having a bad time of it. For the most part during the war years he stayed in Wales and wrote—not only his history of Arabia, called *The Background of Islam* and printed privately, but also a gigantic and ultimately unpublishable autobiographical tome (largely on Athenaeum notepaper) called "Out of Step," which he put away for good in 1943. Writing books never published, giving advice not heeded, composing self-justifications ignored by others, Philby got through the war years, but only just. Again he was short of money: Esso's royalty payments to him were cut off when he left, or rather was propelled out of, the Middle East, and he could get nothing published; there was no longer any demand for speeches and articles by H. St. John Philby, who had been arrested in wartime for anti-British activities.

Throughout 1944 Philby bombarded the government with requests to reinstate his passport; it was clear to him now that Arabia was the only place in which he was still held in high enough regard to earn a living. His passport was restored as soon as the war in Europe ended, and in July 1945, now sixty, Philby embarked for Arabia on a troop ship headed for the war in the Far East. He reached Jidda on the day of the general election in England in which Labour buried the Tories and sent Churchill into a surprising temporary retirement.

VII

Kim Philby, meanwhile, had spent the final years of the war working in Section D (for "destruction") of the Secret Intelligence Service (SIS). His job was to help stir up resistance to the Germans in Europe, largely through acts of sabotage. Philby *fils* also served as an instructor of other agents in courses in underground propaganda. As a propagandist Kim was briefed on Britain's projected post-war policies, information that duly found its way to the Russians. In the last years of the war Kim got the promotion he had all along been coveting—to Section Five, the counterespionage department. The deputy chief of MI5, before making his decision, invited Kim to lunch along with St. John, an old friend of his.

"He was a bit of a communist at Cambridge, wasn't he?" the deputy chief inquired of St. John.

"Oh, that was all schoolboy nonsense," St. John replied. "He's a reformed character now."

No doubt he believed it.

And so Kim was hired. He had moved quickly into a position to penetrate SIS for his Soviet masters. The very nature of his new work, counterespionage, opened the door to virtually all of the service's most important secrets. By the end of the war the SIS, Phillip Knightley reminds us, was "a decrepit and incompetent service, riddled with nepotism and run by a chain of command remarkable for its feebleness." SIS was ripe for Kim Philby: "It deserved him, and he devastated it." When the war ended, Kim was immediately put in charge of a section (Nine) whose responsibility was to carry out offensive espionage operations—that is, to penetrate communist countries and mount espionage operations against them. Needless to say, this was a perfect job for someone who wished to turn all such ventures into crushing failures, and that is what Kim Philby proceeded to do: he could now protect Soviet operations against Britain while undermining all British operations against the Soviet Union. In the immediate post-war years his position was one of incredible importance, giving him sway as it did over the new Soviet satellite countries of Eastern Europe. His MI5 brief was soon expanded to include responsibility for the gathering of intelligence in the Soviet Union. Largely because of Kim Philby, that nation's post-war espionage triumphs were assured; indeed, its intelligence victory was more or less complete.

St. John, meanwhile, found post-war Saudi Arabia largely unchanged except for the introduction of air travel. As usual, he was nearly broke. More and more he devoted his days to Ibn Saud's court and neglected his sagging business affairs. He was to have a stroke of luck, however, in 1946. In this year a British consortium bought out his automobile and oil interests, a transaction that provided him with a significant amount of capital and, for some years more, a generous retainer as manager of the Saudi Arabian concerns of the consortium. Always at court and in a position to hear the latest gossip about business propositions and rival firms, St. John was undoubtedly a valuable asset to any commercial interest.

Ibn Saud's opposition to a Jewish state in Palestine, however, did not command Philby's support. The King foresaw that a Jewish state in the Middle East would "become one of the most powerful governments, equipped with arms and wealth and everything else. They will be against the Arabs and at the same time difficult for them." He preferred the outdated British mandate to continue. Philby told him that the Arab tribes would go communist if Britain tried to go on ruling them. As the battle in Palestine raged throughout 1946 and 1947, Philby in spite of himself began to admire "the courage and fanaticism of the Jews as much as I deplore the futility of the Arabs." Some members of the Saudi Arabian court concluded that he was a Zionist spy—he was, after all, an Englishman—and others that he was a Communist, supporting the party line favoring partition. Philby in the post-war years was fond of referring to himself as a Communist fighting western imperialism in the Middle East. Each Philby, *père et fils,* in his own way, supported Soviet objectives after the war, undoubtedly with little understanding of the other's views and certainly with no understanding of the Soviet Union's views.

In 1947 Ibn Saud gave Philby an order for £1 million in tents, an order that St. John could fulfill only by traveling to India. It was his first visit there since 1915. Now he observed at first hand the plans going forward for the handover of power from the British to the Indians, as well as the incipient birth of Pakistan. Invited to lunch with the viceroy, Lord Mountbatten, Philby saw British splendor in India in its last moments. He was asked to speak to the country on All-India Radio and did so in a dinner jacket.

Throughout the late 1940s Philby regularly visited England and his children and grandchildren. Kim by this time was stationed in Istanbul; father and son saw each other more regularly than ever before. St. John remained ignorant of Kim's real activities.

The post-war oil boom in Saudi Arabia had its drawbacks for St. John. The country was so full of foreigners, he told Dora, that "I regard myself as a stranger at Jidda." Riyadh was transformed: "Whereas in the old days a man would walk fifteen miles to spare his camel, nowadays he uses his car for every small errand to the bazaar." And so Riyadh passed into the twentieth century and became subject to traffic jams. St. John complained to Dora in 1949 that it took him hours to travel a mile: "The cars and trucks must have been at least six abreast and hundreds deep . . . moving inches at a time," a far cry from the country town he remembered in the 1920s. "That he had been the Sorcerer's Apprentice never seems to have crossed his mind when he grumbled about such changes," as Monroe observes. "He had always pressed cars and radios and modernity on the country, but was content with innovation only so long as he was dispensing it." During these years he continued to keep a young (sixteen when he first saw her) Arab slave girl as a mistress; between 1947 and 1949 she bore him two sons, both of whom died. The King presented Philby with a new house in Riyadh said to be worth £15,000, a gigantic sum in post-war Arabia. "Evidently [Ibn Saud] expects me to spend the rest of my life here, which is more or less my idea too," Philby wrote to Dora in England. "If there is to be another war," he added in a speculative vein, "I shall stay safe in Arabia as I have no desire to be in gaol as a Communist in one war having been there as a Fascist in another." There is acknowledgment here that he would probably always be at odds—"out of step," to use his phrase—with British policy of the day, whatever it was, as well as some rueful awareness that his views had never been doctrinaire or rigid. Clearly he was aware too that Arabia, not England, had become his home. He embarked on a book about the seventy-year-old Ibn Saud, telling the story of the King's life since his capture of Riyadh in 1902. St. John took to following the old sovereign around his palace like a Boswell; on one occasion he was rewarded by hearing Ibn Saud remark to him, "Although you talk through the top of your head at least you keep me awake."

By 1950 Philby was restless again. Looking through his maps made him nostalgic; he wished, through another round of explorations, to bring them up to date. He was sixty-five now, but age did not deflect him; on the contrary, he was determined not to be superseded by the next generation of explorers. He bought a Land Rover and thought about going out to look for pre-Islamic Arabia, the primary subject of his writings for many years now. This would require a journey through northern Arabia, which was still poorly mapped: Philby settled on this course. The 4,000-mile trek, once undertaken, did uncover information of genuine historical importance, though on this occasion Philby's guides sold all his stores along the way, making the going particularly hard. Rather than take the time to acquire additional stores, he wore every garment until it fell to pieces and traveled light. Philby noted of his trip through the North: "It was virgin territory, as nobody had ever been here before but me on such a quest; and I did my best to leave nothing for my successors to discover."

In 1951 he was off again. Monroe tells us that the Saudis on the whole are not interested in the history of their country before the founding of Islam. But Ibn Saud decided to support Philby's next venture, which resulted in the first official Saudi expedition in search of pre-Islamic antiquities. (One of the King's conditions for support was that the venture should include no Jews, a condition Philby unhesitatingly accepted.) This would be a journey into southern Arabia; it departed Jidda in November 1951. Philby was able to revisit a part of the country he had not seen since 1936. Among other things he found this time some rock drawings of animals long extinct. He returned to Riyadh in February 1952 having collected 13,000 new inscriptions and traveled 3,000 miles along a route two-fifths of which, Monroe tells us, had never been mapped before, not even by Philby.

Late in 1951 the Saudi government sent him on a shopping expedition. He was to look along the coastline for sulfur, gold, and iron deposits whose existence had been surmised in the nineteenth century by the explorer Richard Burton. No one since then had investigated to see if anything was actually there. It was thought that Sir Richard may have been over-optimistic about sulfur and gold but that some iron ore might be found. Philby spent the last months of 1952 and the first of 1953 on his travels, accompanied this time by mining engineers. As it turned out, a good deal of iron ore was discovered; and Philby was able to complete his map of Arabia as far north as the Saudi border with Jordan. When he returned in March 1953 he was, unusually for him, exhausted. Now sixty-eight, Philby described himself, uncharacteristically, as "weary enough of our long and strenuous journey." This was to be his last major exploration.

Life went on. His Arab mistress bore him healthy sons in 1950 and 1952, and Philby now took as much (and as little) interest in his new Arabian family as in his more elderly British one. His Esso royalties, repaid from the time of his return to Arabia after the late war, had become more lucrative each year. Philby branched out, acting as agent in Arabia for British companies to build roads, oil tanks, and water pipelines. He helped to bring to the Middle East radio telephones and jet planes.

In November 1952 Kim Philby was tried—not in public but instead privately, by his SIS colleagues—for high treason. This was the culmination of a year and a half of comprehensive but inept investigation of his past and present activities by the security services.

On 25 May 1951 Donald Maclean and Guy Burgess had defected to the Soviet Union, though this was not generally known for some time afterward. They had been friends of Kim's at Cambridge; he was especially close to Burgess. Suspicion centered on Kim as "the third man," the friend who had advised them to leave England before they could be interrogated; in all likelihood it was Anthony Blunt who played that role. Kim managed to get the better of his accusers by the end of 1952—Harold Macmillan even went so far as to "clear" him publicly—but he was nonetheless asked to resign from the service because of those suspicious friendships. Still, he managed to hang on. His ultimate unmasking, it should be said, did not take place for another decade, by which time his father was dead. Indeed, St. John never took the charges against his son seriously. "One of the really surprising things about Kim," he wrote to Dora, "is that he has such dim friends on the whole." And he added: "Kim has always been very loyal to his friends. Although he seems to have got a bit tired of Guy [Burgess] lately, his long association with him could scarcely go unnoticed." The truth never dawned on St. John. To him it seemed only that Kim was a bad judge of character and a loyal friend. He described the business as if it were an unfortunate falling out between pub-crawling buddies. But then he never had any idea what Kim was actually up to: he hadn't a clue.

In Arabia, meanwhile, Ibn Saud was dying. Ordered to have a blood transfusion, the King said: "Give me some of Philby's. He is never ill." The last time Philby saw him, Ibn Saud muttered: "A man's possessions and his children are his enemies." He died in November 1953. Philby's verdict on the King's last years was not favorable. He wrote to Dora: "It is sad to see such widespread decadence in a country that had a greatness of its own when it was poor." But he missed Ibn Saud, his best friend at court; and he quickly began to find that he was not quite so welcome there as he had once been. "I begin to wonder how long I can stick it," Philby wrote, "but life in retirement doesn't appeal to me and I am more or less stuck." He traveled leisurely through Italy, Switzerland, Germany, France, and Belgium with Dora during the summer of 1954, returning to his Arabian wife (he had finally married her) and their two boys when Dora went back to England.

He now took up his writing again, polishing the account of the 1936-37 mapping journey he undertook for Ibn Saud and revising his history of Saudi Arabia for the Benn series. He published articles on the late King and contemplated another volume of autobiography. He wrote more about the history, as he saw it, of British encroachments on Arab lands. And he supplied to British periodicals articles on the new ruler of Saudi Arabia, King Saud. Nonetheless, he wrote to Dora, "since the King's death I have felt quite rebellious against the whole country. . . . Beirut might be a good place for us when we get old." Philby spent the autumn of 1954 in Cornwall with Dora, who told a friend: "You don't know what a terrible temper he used to have. We were all terrified of him."

At the end of this year his *Saudi Arabia* was published and caused a storm in his adopted country. For in the book Philby took the new generation of rulers to task. He complained of corruption, poor administration, waste, and debt. He noted that the religious ban on alcohol was evaded by the highest families. King Saud was displeased by Philby's criticisms and chose to believe they were the result of foreign influences. He ordered Philby out of the country—unless he wished to write to the new King a letter of contrition. Philby did not. In April 1955 he left for Beirut, having been allowed by the Saudi government to take with him only a few of his by now vast accumulation of possessions. Among these were his Arabian wife and their children. Now seventy, he was embarking on what he called "my last journey." At the Saudi border he noted: "I think I must be quite the only person who has ever left the country with no share of the spoil." And one can certainly say of St. John Philby, at least, that despite what must have been astonishing temptations and opportunities, he was not at heart a corrupt man.

VIII

It was a blow to Dora to learn that she would not after all share with her husband his Lebanese exile. To her he had always denied that he had an

Arab family; and to her credit, she had always assumed he was lying. Now she learned that she was to be left behind in England during what must be her husband's last years. Kim had known about St. John's Arab family all along and, as Monroe reports, considered it just another of his father's many eccentricities. St. John couldn't understand why Dora minded so much. When she declared that "this last straw had been the deadliest of them all," he pretended to be astonished by her putative ignorance: everyone had known of his other family, hadn't they, and besides, hadn't she always told him that she did not care what he did in Arabia so long as she didn't have to know about it? But now she did know about it, and she cared deeply. Why had she spent all those years living uncomfortably without him if it wasn't so that she could live comfortably with him in retirement at the end of their lives? Was she supposed to spend her final days by herself when she had a husband living?

Kim was no help to her. During these years he began to drink heavily, no doubt one result of the increasingly precarious double life he was leading. Kim, Dora now told St. John, was "slowly deteriorating and losing confidence in himself." In the autumn of 1955 Kim, now forty-three, was investigated again, and again "cleared." This gave Dora another topic to complain about: "It's a pity [Kim] can't sue them for defaming him the way they did." And she told St. John: "I don't think I can live alone much longer."

In Beirut Philby became a minor celebrity. The story of his banishment was by now well known, and he was asked for interviews. He continued to work on his Arabian maps and notes, and wrote for the *Sunday Times* a series of muckraking articles on contemporary Saudi Arabia, titled by the newspaper "The Scandal of Arabia." Philby's pieces underlined the prodigality and corruption of the new regime. The Saudis responded by doing what they could to blacken his reputation. Philby remained serene. "Now I see Arabia in retrospect . . . I have no desire to go back there," he told a friend. (But go back there he did for brief visits in 1956 and 1958.) Taking pity on Dora, he invited her to join his *ménage* in Beirut—thus forming what he called "a Philby colony in one of the nicest countries of the world." But nothing came of this proposal, including Dora. Philby calmly worked on, finishing his autobiographical memoir, *Forty Years in the Wilderness*, in 1956.

This was the year in which the world's attention was focused on Nasser, Egypt, and the Suez Canal. From Lebanon Philby deluged newspapers and magazines with articles and essays extolling the virtues of Nasser and his policy of pursuing the economic independence of Egypt by cutting it off from the West. Philby was consistent; at seventy-one he was still fulminating against European imperialism and advocating Arab independence. "The East does not trust the West," Philby wrote, "and there is no means of inducing it to do so until every vestige of the old Western imperialism is removed from its lands." In September 1956 Kim arrived in Beirut to report

3.1 St. John Philby with his daughter-in-law Eleanor Philby (Kim's third wife) and his grandson Harry (Kim's youngest son) on the terrace of Kim Philby's flat in Beirut, 1950s; by permission of Phillip Knightley.

3.2 St. John Philby with Kim Philby and two of Kim's half-brothers, St. John's sons Khalid and Faris, in Saudi Arabia, 1958; by permission of Phillip Knightley.

Υ Υ Υ

on the Middle East for the *Observer* and *The Economist*. He had been exonerated in all of his various secret trials, but the SIS felt that his usefulness as an intelligence agent was at an end; so he had gone back to his first profession, journalism. St. John introduced his son to his large circle.

In the spring of 1957 St. John was invited to become a visiting professor of Arab Studies at the American University in Beirut. He was considering whether to accept this invitation when he got word, on the last day of June, that Dora had died in her sleep back in England. He had not seen her for three years, though they corresponded regularly. In her last letter to him she had written: "It always makes me feel mad when I've seen for years people picking your brains for nothing." St. John spent the latter half of this year in England clearing up his affairs and Dora's. Among her papers he found a note: "No mourning. No garden of remembrance, no in memoriams." She had kept all of his letters to her, dating back to 1910.

He returned to Beirut. Unlike most men who lose their wives, St. John Philby had another one living. During the winter of 1957-58 he served as visiting professor at the American University. He taught one class and gave two public lectures on contemporary Arabia. His students, according to Monroe, found him lively, talkative, and approachable. "I don't prepare anything but just let myself think aloud," he said; he had no notes and was always oblivious of time. His auditors found him interesting but inclined to long-windedness.

In March 1958 St. John and Kim spent some time together in Riyadh. Kim's second wife had just died, he felt cut off from England and his five children there, and he had grown gloomy and depressed. St. John thought a sojourn in Arabia might cheer up both widowers, father and son; he himself missed his Arabian life and determined to stay this time for as long as the government would tolerate him. At the border St. John changed into his Arab costume. Kim was soon reporting to the woman who would be his third wife (Eleanor) that his father's domestic life in Riyadh was "an annoying shambles": St. John and his Arab wife regularly engaged in "the most frightful shouting matches."

The British and American landings in Lebanon in 1958, undertaken to stabilize unrest there and in Jordan, incensed Philby. In articles and letters of this period he attacked, as so often before, the notion that "the best interests of . . . Arab countries can only be served in some form of subordination to British imperial policy sweetened by lavish British financial aid"; and, as before, he articulated his conviction that "only in unity *inter se* can the Arabs ever realize . . . their destiny." He declared that the British "cause [was] lost beyond recall." He continued to attack the West and to praise the East, urging the Arabs to ally themselves with the Soviet Union. But he criticized Nasser too, when the latter allied Egypt with Syria, for "picking quarrels and forming unions that prevent the attainment of unity." And he reiterated another familiar refrain: "It is up to the Arabs themselves to achieve the unity which alone can give them strength." At the end of his life he was still pointing out to the Arabs the disadvantages of their disunity. Nor could he resist the urge to denounce once again Saudi extravagance and corruption. "The present regime has given us nothing but palaces," he declared.

In his last months Philby abandoned political commentary for authorship. He worked on a long account of his experiences in Transjordan, challenging Benn to publish every word or none. Benn chose none: the book was not published. He wrote new articles for the *Encyclopedia Britannica*, translated the Koran, and revised yet again his book on the history of Islam. He walked his young boys to school every day. In 1959, after King Saud had abdicated, Philby went off with the new King, Faisal, on a desert journey, this time in a luxurious caravan equipped with a bathroom. He spent his seventy-fifth birthday, in April 1960, "watching the bulldozers knock down half of my property for a new road through the town," as he wrote complacently.

Philby passed the summer of this year in England and then traveled to Moscow to attend an Orientalists' congress, where he was treated as a sort of grand old man; his stories of desert exploration were treated with attention and respect. Afterward he visited Kim and Eleanor in Beirut. It was here that he died of heart failure, on 30 September 1960. His last words, uttered from the hospital bed to which he was confined, were "God, I'm bored." At Kim's direction, the funeral was held in a local Muslim cemetery. And Kim now ordered the tombstone, mentioned earlier, with the inscription, "Greatest of Arabian explorers." The death of St. John Philby was widely noted in 1960: he was a famous man.

"Sure of his worth, but unable to make Englishmen see it," as Elizabeth Monroe has written, Philby "sought abroad the name that he reckoned he deserved." The Arabian desert suited his talents. "There he was his own master, unhampered by rules, in control of his companions, seldom gainsaid." True enough. Like his more famous son he was not very good at being an Englishman and ultimately gave up trying.

IX

His father's death sent Kim on an extended alcohol binge. He had never told St. John the truth about himself, about his true loyalties, the work he was actually doing. How would St. John have taken it? Kim would never know, though surely he had a good idea. Recently he had had ample opportunity to open up the subject with his father. But despite the fact that he had been more or less forcibly retired from spying, as we have seen, he never spoke candidly to St. John. "If he had lived a little longer to learn the truth," Kim wrote of St. John, "he would have been thunderstruck, but by no means disapproving." Perhaps; perhaps not. It sounds like special pleading. Because for all his Anglophobia, Philby *père* remained in many ways essentially British. As noted earlier, he read *The Times* every day, followed cricket avidly, scanned the Honours Lists, haunted Lords and the Athenaeum, wished to sit in Parliament. Like Kim he had, in Kipling's phrase, two separate sides to his head; but would he have condoned outright treachery, which even at his lowest ebb in 1940-41 he stoutly denied having drifted into? Didn't he tell the SIS recruiter that Kim's precocious Communism was schoolboy nonsense, something he had grown out of, like acne? Didn't he tell Kim himself, "Don't do anything you are not allowed to, but, if you do, don't mind owning up"? Didn't he advocate expressing one's political convictions publicly rather than hiding them, and didn't he do this himself? Wasn't it Kim, not his father, who said he believed that people with extreme views should keep them "dark," even from their families? Didn't St. John declare that if Kim intended to be disloyal to the British government he shouldn't have entered the Civil Service? At any rate St. John never knew the full story, which certainly left Kim free to imagine his approval. Perhaps this is why he never told his father in the first place. Kim, after all, had mastered the techniques of deception, and he continued to exercise them even among members of his family. Spies have to do this. Instructed, possibly, by the lesson of his father's life—great promise and opportunity, punctuated by disappointment and frustration—Kim Philby learned never to reveal his true feelings. Even his putative autobiography, *My Secret War* (1968), is largely fiction.

A recent book on Kim and the Philbys—*Treason in the Blood,* by Anthony Cave Brown (1994)—argues that, for Philby *fils,* treason was a habit inherited from his father: that St. John was always a closet socialist who set out to deceive and undermine the Civil Service and his country and failed only as a result of his own ineptitude. But there are a number of insurmountable problems with this reading of St. John. Philby *père* did not lead two lives: he led one that kept turning him in different directions. That is to say, in politics he was both indecisive and opportunistic, as we have seen, approaching the political parties one after another in hope of adoption and sponsorship. He was no idealogue. If he was motivated by anything throughout his life it was self-interest—shortsighted desire to distinguish himself, to rise to the top of the greasy pole; he never wished to pull the pole down. For St. John ideology and self-interest were indistinguishable. Unluckily for him, he was no good at the game he wanted to play. Cave Brown's idea that St. John led "a life of conspiracy against, and disloyalty to, England" is preposterous. Perhaps nothing makes clear how different St. John and Kim were than the fact that Kim's first assignment for the K.G.B. was to spy on his own father! The Soviets wished at the time to gain a strategic foothold in the Middle East, and one way of doing that, they thought, was to penetrate the court of Ibn Saud and learn what they could of the leading figures there, including St. John Philby and his associates and contacts. If there really was "treason in the blood," why didn't Kim share this great joke with his father? Because St. John would have been outraged, that's why. Because he would have been, as Kim himself admitted, "thunderstruck." Kim was the ideologue of the family. He hated England and the English and longed to betray them, to hurt and destroy them in any way he could. St. John only wanted to represent them in Parliament.

When Kim Philby died in May 1988 his obituary in *The Times* of London took up the entire space devoted to deaths that day—three full columns, with a photograph. The obituary writer devoted one brief paragraph to Kim Philby's father, who was described (erroneously) as "a tea-planter's son":

> St. John Philby, an eccentric, flamboyant character, had served as an intelligence agent in the Middle East during the First World War. He later became a Muslim, took a Saudi slave-girl as a second wife, "went Arab," became an advisor to the Arab leader Ibn Saud, and was detained briefly in the Second World War under Regulation 18b for anti-British statements.

And that's all. In the end he was just Kim Philby's father.

Like many sons of men once famous, Kim Philby wanted to be more famous than his father, and obviously he got what he wanted.

4

LADY OF THE HOUSE: NANCY ASTOR

I

IT IS TYPICAL of everything else in her life that Lady Astor was neither English nor an Astor. Nor was the first woman to sit in the British parliament either a Liberal or a Labour politician. She was an American divorcée who married a British peer, stood for Parliament as a Conservative, was elected seven times, lived in a house next door to the Libyan embassy that now sports a blue plaque with her name on it, and was buried under a Confederate flag.

One might have expected a socialist—a member of the Fabians, say—to become the first woman seated in the House of Commons, and surely one might have expected that woman, whatever her politics, to be British. But Nancy Witcher Langhorne of Danville, Virginia—a small town near the North Carolina line—was none of these things, and indeed throughout her life she had a habit of doing the unexpected. She did not see it that way. "I was born a Virginian," she would say later, "so naturally I am a politician."

Miss Langhorne, the fifth of eight surviving siblings—four sisters and three brothers; two of the latter drank themselves to death—was born on 19 May 1879, the same day on which her future second husband Waldorf Astor came into the world. Her mother, Nancy Witcher Keene, was from a Virginia family of Irish extraction. Her mother's father was also born in Virginia, in Lynchburg. Chiswell Dabney Langhorne, Nancy Astor's father, had been a tobacco planter who owned a slave plantation in Virginia and was ruined by the Civil War. He fought, of course, on the Confederate side. After the war ended he worked as a night porter in a hotel, as a security guard in a clothing store, and as an auctioneer; for a brief spell he kept himself alive by playing poker. He "was so good at it that he thought people would get suspicious," his famous daughter remarked years later. When, a decade after the war ended, contracts to rebuild the old railroads and construct new ones became available to open bids, Langhorne saw that an understanding of how railroads operated had nothing to do with the matter: you only had to make the winning bid and the contract was yours, to succeed or fail with. It was sort of like poker. He collected some contracts, hired others who knew something about the work to do it for him, and gradually, like many others, grew very rich during Reconstruction, a time made to order for would-be millionaires with daring, intelligence, and an instinct for gambling.

Lady Astor claimed in later years that she knew what it was to grow up without money, but this can hardly have been true: her father made his pile during the first decade of her life. Certainly she worried all of her life about having enough money, but this is by no means the same thing. In her behalf it can be said that she devoted herself to charities, both public and private, in aid of the poor, the injured, the helpless. But as a public figure both rich and famous and seeking political office, she could hardly do otherwise.

After living some years at Richmond, the state capital and inevitably the center of the booming railroad industry in the region, Langhorne bought an estate called Mirador, near Charlottesville. In Richmond and at Mirador his five daughters and three sons grew up. Except for riding none of the girls was taught much of anything, which was the practice in the 1890s. Those of Lady Astor's contemporaries who thought her stupid, and there were many, may have mistaken stupidity for ignorance. She was not a stupid woman, but she was an ignorant one. In a word, she was uneducated; and most commentators agree that she had no taste. She knew she was ignorant and often lamented her lack of education. She could have educated herself, of course, like Edith Wharton—but what for? If anyone during her youth had told her that at forty she would be elected a British M.P. she would have found this an amusing hallucination. Why should she, unlike most American women of the day, need a formal education, or any education at all?

Her elder sister Irene married the graphic artist Charles Dana Gibson, who used his wife as the model for the original Gibson Girl, the standard of feminine beauty in the United States in the 1890s. Nancy Langhorne was also considered beautiful, and her father was rich. What would she do with an education? Her sister had received sixty-two proposals of marriage (excluding Gibson's) and knew no more than she did. So why worry? She set to work developing an illegible hand in order to disguise her (lifelong) imperviousness to the rules of spelling.

Her "education" away from home took place during three brief interludes. When she was seven and living in Richmond, Nancy was sent to a day school run by Julia Lee, a cousin of the Confederate commander. At nine she attended another Richmond day school at which the teacher, Lady Astor wrote long afterward, "gave me a thirst for knowledge and a real liking for learning." Nancy now began to read—though she never read much, either now or later. Her one other experience of formal education was not so pleasant. When she was seventeen and the family was at Mirador, she attended briefly, and unsuccessfully, Miss Brown's Academy for Young Ladies, a finishing school in New York—the New York of *The House of Mirth,* of the Gilded Age. Here, where the girls talked only of money, clothes, and men, one's appearance and background were one's fate; learning in women was no more valued than it was in Jane Austen's day, and Nancy Langhorne (had she known of it) would have been equally at home in the world of *Northanger Abbey.* Nancy asked to go home from Miss Brown's and was allowed to depart. She had by this time received sixteen proposals of marriage—not nearly so many as her sister Irene, but enough to enable her to believe she would not long remain without a husband.

Back at Mirador, bored with her life, Nancy Langhorne started visiting homes for the elderly and the disabled and found she enjoyed doing this and that the people she saw liked her. She wondered if perhaps she ought to be a missionary. Her mother was intensely religious; the daughter inherited the practice of churchgoing and, gradually, a fervent faith that, in various trajectories, was to last the course of her life. One might not be prone to see missionary zeal as forming a significant part of the life of Lady Astor, yet it was there all along, and from her earliest years.

She also at this time began to notice the nature of her parents' relationship. Her mother, she saw, was the stronger character of the two, but her father had the money and therefore the true power in their relationship, his wife being dependent upon him for virtually everything. "I felt if Mother had had independent means she would not have had to stand that," Lady Astor would write. "I felt that men put women in this position for this very reason, that it rendered them helpless. They had no kind of independence. It seemed to me wrong."

In 1897, when she was eighteen, Nancy Langhorne paid another visit to New York, this time to stay with her married sister Mrs. Gibson. One day they went to watch a polo match. When it was over one of the players, a "rather spectacular young man" as Nancy described him, came up and introduced himself to the sisters. This was Robert Gould Shaw, a Bostonian of good family and ample means. He proposed to Nancy shortly afterward. She was dazzled and flattered but realized she was not in love with him. They shared a passion for riding but not much else. Shaw's great-uncle was the famous Boston abolitionist who died in South Carolina in 1863 at the head of a regiment of black troops; the film *Glory* sketches the last months of his life. Shaw's mother's father, the Harvard zoologist Alexander Agassiz, was also famous.

The Langhornes thought the match a good one and urged it on Nancy. She and Shaw became engaged; she had second thoughts and broke it off;

the engagement was renewed. At almost the last moment Nancy's father, hearing stories about his future son-in-law, rushed up to Boston to ask the Shaws if there was any reason why their son should not marry his daughter. The Shaws said their son was wild and often foolish but no more so than other sons of rich families before their marriages. They thought he was ready to settle down and that Nancy would help him to do so. Langhorne came back to Mirador and advised Nancy not to marry Shaw. Shaw *père* begged her to honor her promise. Now that it was a matter of having her own way or being dictated to by her father, Nancy decided to marry Shaw. It turned out to be a terrible decision.

Probably even his parents did not know that Robert Shaw was already a hopeless alcoholic and emotionally unbalanced. But, with all ambivalence temporarily pushed aside, Nancy Langhorne and Robert Shaw were married at Mirador in October 1897. The honeymoon, at Hot Springs, Arkansas, lasted about twenty-four hours. The first night was a shock to Nancy: like most young ladies of her day and class, she knew nothing whatever about sex. Unacquainted with the facts of life and a Puritan *enragée,* as A. L. Rowse has put it, she fought Shaw like a wildcat and then went home to Virginia. Her father sent her back to Shaw. She never said much about this passage in her biography, though years later one catches a glimpse of her feelings in something she wrote: "To wish to attract attention to your figure is just a desire to attract the male sex through its most vulnerable point. Is that really worth doing? Don't we women have to pay for these methods in the long run?" Shaw also had made a mistake. He thought he was marrying a quiet Southern belle and was unprepared to have a tiger by the tail. On both sides the parents advised perseverance and compromise, and the newlyweds decided to retry the experiment.

So they went to live in a fashionable Boston suburb called Prides Crossing. It was now that Nancy Langhorne Shaw discovered to her horror the extent of her young husband's addiction to alcohol. In his drunken rages he would sometimes strike her. She was already pregnant, and in 1898 the Shaws had a son. It was after the baby arrived that Nancy left her husband for six months, what today would be called a trial separation. Shaw was supposed to stop drinking, and Nancy would come back to him: that was the bargain. He could not stop drinking and in her absence found solace elsewhere; and in 1902, by which time Nancy had left and come back half a dozen times, the couple decided to live apart permanently. Nancy was twenty-three.

In those days grounds were needed for a divorce, and by 1903 Nancy had them: she divorced her husband on the ground of adultery. On the very day the divorce became final, Shaw married his mistress—legally, having married her illegally (that is, bigamously) earlier. He had wedded a "nice" lady and been unhappy with her. Now Shaw married a not-so-nice lady and was happy with her for the rest of his life. Therein, somewhere, lies a moral. Nancy, meanwhile, was given custody of Robert Shaw, Jr. ("Bobby") and left the marriage with a lifelong hatred of liquor and those who consume too much of it. Not only did she herself not drink; she became an ardent temperance reformer, and visitors to Cliveden were to find this a great nuisance: the only way one could get a drink there in Nancy Astor's day was to bribe the butler. At any rate, she came back to Mirador now with her small son, a casualty in her early twenties of what Jane Austen called "the marriage-trade." "Your beautiful daughter is back again, unwanted, unsought, and partly widowed for life," she told her father. Nancy's mother decided a trip to Europe might cheer her up; in February 1903 they went off to Paris and London, where the Gibsons were now staying.

Nancy declared she hated men and loved England; the second notion turned out to be accurate. "I had this strange feeling of having come home, rather than of having gone abroad," she said later, and some American visitors to England will understand this. Nancy's sister introduced her to an American expatriate, Mrs. John Jacob Astor. The two women liked each other, and when Mrs. Astor invited Nancy to stay with her for a month the invitation was gratefully accepted. Mrs. Langhorne went home to watch over young Bobby. And so Nancy was given a taste of a winter season in London during the reign of Edward VII. The Astors, of course, knew everybody. Oddly enough, Nancy left England in the spring without having met her future second husband—but just in time to see her mother before she died, without warning, in the summer of 1903, aged fifty-five. "There was sorrow such as I had never known or imagined," Nancy would write later. "The light went out of my life. I was ill for months, in a wretched, nameless fashion." As late as 1951, at age seventy-two, she was grieving for her mother: "The memory of those days is like a shadow on the heart still." She tried without much success to run Mirador for her father and even took to gardening, which she had always disliked. The only hope for the future she had at this time, she recalled later, was "that my little son . . . would grow up sober." She was deeply depressed by the death of her mother and her own failures, in her eyes, as a wife and a daughter.

One day in 1904 Mr. Langhorne asked her if she would like to go back to England for the hunting season. She jumped at the chance and by November was settled at Market Harborough. On her first day in the field she was thrown by her mount into the mud of a ploughed field. When a man stopped to help her remount, she rewarded him by shouting, "Do you think I would be such an ass as to come out hunting if I couldn't mount from the ground?" She began to grow celebrated among the horsey set for her boldness and unpredictability, her friendliness and fierceness, and the bite of her *repartée*. The English hadn't seen many Americans chasing after foxes, and soon enough Nancy Langhorne Shaw became a personality, someone others wanted to meet. Who was this beautiful young divorcée who drank nothing stronger than tea, went regularly to church, and treated would-be admirers as if they were ridiculous?

But not all of them. There was one man who fell in love with her and she, briefly, with him, though this story is not well known outside the pages of Christopher Sykes's biography of Lady Astor. The man was Lord Revelstoke, head of the family banking firm of Baring Brothers. He was forty-one when he met Nancy Shaw in the hunting field in 1904. They were engaged for a short time—until Nancy broke it off. She called him her bald Apollo; her father, who came over for Christmas that year, thought he was a terrible snob. This was confirmed in Nancy's eyes when he asked her if she thought she could "fill the position" required of his wife and entertain kings and queens and ambassadors. Also, she discovered, there was a mistress in the background: it was Lady Desborough, and Nancy accused her ever afterward of intriguing against her. Revelstoke pursued Nancy with letters and on several occasions personally during a motoring trip she took through France in the spring of 1905. But she had been spooked by him, and by marriage. By the time she went back to Virginia in July it was over. Again she left England without having encountered the man she would marry.

Before departing she had asked Herbert Asquith, whom she had met in London, for his advice as to whom, if anybody, she should marry. (She had just received a proposal from a Russian grand duke who was honest enough to inform her that his wife would have to take second place in his affections to his mistress.) When Asquith failed to answer she berated him for tardiness. Back in Virginia she received an answer from the future prime minister:

> You must not reproach me, my dear Mrs. Shaw;
> It's not like a Redskin selecting a squaw;
> For there's no tougher problem, in logic or law
> Than to find a fit mate for the lady called Shaw.

II

Mrs. Shaw found a fit mate after she sailed for England again in December 1905. Waldorf Astor, the same age as she down to the very day, was the son of William Waldorf Astor, chief heir of the huge family fortune and possibly the richest man in the world. (After she became his daughter-in-law Nancy called him "Old Moneybags.") Astor *père* had settled in England in 1889 after an unsuccessful political career in America. A strain of romanticism had induced him to write several historical novels and to purchase the vast, elderly house at Cliveden; an autocratic temper and the desire to air his views on everything led him in later years to buy the *Pall Mall Gazette,* the *Observer* newspaper, and *The Times* of London. Editors of these organs were regularly sacked for refusing to publish the proprietor's unsolicited contributions.

Waldorf Astor had been to Eton and Oxford, was English by circumstance, and had become a naturalized British subject in 1899, when he was twenty. He had once told his father to go to hell, but they remained close. When Nancy first met him Waldorf was having an affair with Princess Marie of Rumania, five years his senior. Unlike his father, Waldorf Astor was a serious, responsible, conscientious man who believed that the wealthy owed the state enlightened public service. His own major interests, however, were less political than sporting; his primary obsession was the raising and racing of horses. In this he and Mrs. Shaw shared a passion. In his midtwenties Waldorf had developed heart disease and was already a semiinvalid when he met Nancy Langhorne Shaw. A modest and a quiet man, he had great strength of purpose. He was handsome, courteous and charming, and Nancy found herself attracted to him. They became engaged in March 1906 and were married in May at All Souls Church, Langham Place, after the Bishop of London, hearing the circumstances of Nancy's divorce, gave the couple permission to use the Anglican marriage ceremony. Their honeymoon was spent in the Swiss Tyrol.

Who were the Astors? As Nancy's biographer Maurice Collis has discovered, the family was originally Spanish and called Astorga. In the eighteenth century they emigrated to Germany, where the final "ga" in their name was lopped off. During the latter third of that century the head of the family was an unprosperous butcher living with his family in the village of Waldorf, in Baden. The butcher had three sons. The eldest went to London, where he became a successful manufacturer of musical instruments. The second son went to America. The third son, John Jacob Astor, went to London in 1779 when he was sixteen and spent four years there learning English and working for his brother. In 1783, the year in which England acknowledged the independence of its fractious former colony, he joined his other brother in America, sold some flutes he had brought from England, and set himself up in the fur trade. He bought his stocks cheaply from the Indians, who had been unable to do any business with the colonists during the long years of their war for independence. John Jacob Astor founded the American Fur Company and eventually opened offices all over the new country. Later he acquired his own fleet of merchant ships so that he could export his furs to Europe and the Far East. He grew rich and looked around for suitable investments. New York, he guessed, would grow in size far beyond the 100,000 inhabitants of the early nineteenth century, and he decided to buy all the available land he could find in and around the city. By the time he died in 1845 the Astor fortune was said to be second only to that of the Rothschilds. It had been done in one generation.

The next several generations of Astors nurtured and increased the great pile. Waldorf Astor's uncle, John Jacob II, having bought all the land in

New York his father failed to buy, began to build on it and eventually became the owner and landlord of thousands of dwellings. His *income* alone in the 1870s was said to be over $100 million annually, of which—it was also said—he spent only a "miserly" $750,000 a year. Indeed, before Waldorf's father came along the Astors had never been big spenders—only big earners, careful and cautious, rarely taking a holiday from work and going regularly to church: pillars of the community, in short. A few years before his death John Jacob II handed over his vast fortune to Waldorf's father because he wished to avoid public probate of his will, which might have led to disclosure of his net worth. But of course there was no income tax in those days.

Up to this time, then, the Astors had been hard-working, sober, realistic, and unpretentious. William Waldorf, Nancy's father-in-law, was different. He retraced the route from America to England because he wished to lead a larger and more cultured life. He was less interested in the family business than in literature, history, art, and architecture. Having tried and failed to get himself elected to Congress—he did serve briefly as President Arthur's ambassador to Italy—he decided to leave America, to remain in Europe, to settle in England. Leaving his younger brother to run the family businesses, William Waldorf, as we have seen, became an English citizen and had his children naturalized. "The landlord of New York," as he had been called, could not get into the U.S. Congress, but he could get into the choosiest society on the face of the earth, and this he proceeded to do. The future first Viscount Astor bought three houses in London; and for his country seat he purchased Cliveden, a palace in a park on the Thames at Maidenhead. (His pursuit of English society was not always sure-footed. At a ball at one of his London houses he appeared at eleven o'clock, just when the guests were warming up, to tell them that he was going to bed and their carriages were waiting.) He did use some of his money for the public good; among other things he founded the Great Ormond Street Hospital for Children.

This was Nancy's new father-in-law and this the family she was now joining. Her husband was clearly of the old-school Astors: earnest, thoughtful, the opposite of frivolous. It turned out to be nearly a perfect match, and of course it made possible Nancy's social and political careers. William Waldorf was delighted with his daughter-in-law and gave her the famous Sanci diamond as a wedding present. It had been owned by, among others, Charles I, James I, and Mazarin; Louis XIV wore it at his coronation; it was said to be the size of the last joint of the thumb. Waldorf's wedding presents from his father were Cliveden and several million dollars. And so the great diamond worn by at least three kings traveled in the jewelry case of Nancy Langhorne Shaw Astor to the Tyrol and came back with her to her new home.

The Cliveden of 1906, third house on the site since the seventeenth century, had been built in the middle of the nineteenth century by Sir Charles Barry, architect of the House of Parliament and the Reform Club, for the Duke of Sutherland. As Maurice Collis reminds us, it was modeled on the Villa Albano in Rome and stands on a wooded ridge about two-hundred feet above the Thames on the eastern (Buckinghamshire) side of the river just above Windsor and Maidenhead Bridge. The only other house in the vicinity is Taplow, the seat of the Desboroughs. Nancy of course had a grudge against Lady Desborough, and her guests were expected not to go to Taplow while staying at Cliveden: it was just about her only rule for guests. In later years there was a thaw and she did get to know the dashing Grenfell boys before they were both tragically killed in the Great War; there is some extant correspondence between the two families.

After he bought Cliveden from the Duke of Westminster in 1893, William Waldorf Astor redecorated it, largely following his taste for things Italian and French. A mosaic floor was laid in the great hall and an eighteenth-century French fresco depicting classical scenes appeared on the ceiling of the dining room. The dining room table had been made for Madame de Pompadour's hunting lodge. Parisian tapestries, Roman statuary, early Christian sarcophagi, and antique vases were imported and distributed around the house and gardens.

"The Astors have no taste," Nancy remarked after seeing Cliveden for the first time. The fact is, however, that her father-in-law's taste was far more cultivated and informed than her own. She had the mosaic floor in the hall replaced by parquet and removed the dining-room fresco. She tossed out the statuary and sarcophagi and vases. Her main contributions to Cliveden were new curtains and electric lights. She substituted chintz for the tapestries and antique furniture. Imagine Laura Ashley redecorating Versailles.

Running Cliveden, once she got it going, turned out to be nearly a full-time job for Nancy, but it was a job that she came to love. The guest wing could accommodate forty visitors and had an inside staff of thirty-four. In the family wing there were twenty indoor servants. Cliveden also employed forty outdoor servants. Altogether there were forty-six bedrooms, many of them occupied at weekends as the social éclat of the Astors began to soar. It was considered de rigeur to go there: you met interesting people and had a good time, since the hostess left her guests alone and let them do what they liked; nothing was ever "planned."

And so Edward VII asked to come one weekend, and was duly invited. He spent most of the time playing cards and bored Nancy to distraction. At one point he asked his hostess to play with him. "I wouldn't know a king from a knave" was the rather undiplomatic reply. Henry James and Edith Wharton visited Cliveden together on his sixty-ninth birthday. Some 180 politicians were asked, but the heyday of Cliveden as a political force was still many years off. In inviting guests to Cliveden the only policy Nancy Astor seems to have followed in these days was that of exposing as many Englishmen to as many Americans as she possibly could, believing as she did that the peace and happiness of the world depended in part on Anglo-American friendship. According to Nancy, Winston Churchill in his thirties thought he disliked Americans, and she was always careful to put one on each side of him at dinner. Some of her guests were not asked back. Hilaire Belloc at first offended her with his anti-Semitism (later, when she grew equally anti-Semitic, they became great friends), Lord Birkenhead with his arrogance. She also tired of Kipling: "I found him dour. He was very poor company. He didn't seem able to take things lightly . . . He would sit on the sofa with his wife, an American, and before answering a question ask her opinion." James Barrie, she said, was spoiled by his success, turned snobbish, and "became ridiculous." John Buchan, who in later years would be a close friend of Elizabeth Bowen, was another snob, according to Nancy. Lord Kitchener, who collected antique porcelain primarily by expressing admiration for this or that piece wherever he went to stay and then graciously accepting it as a gift from grateful hostesses, was told bluntly by the mistress of Cliveden: "I am not going to give you anything." But she approved of Lytton Strachey: "He was nervous, but excellent company, so droll and lively." Liveliness was what attracted her most, and the liveliness of Cliveden in those days was what attracted her guests there. Only rarely was someone asked with ulterior motives: she invited Sargent, who painted her portrait. Others who came to Cliveden then and later included the Queen of Rumania, Bernard Shaw, Charlie Chaplin, Sean O'Casey, George V and Queen Mary, the Archduke Franz Ferdinand of Austria and his wife, Lord Curzon, Henry Ford, the King of Sweden and Lady Louise Mountbatten (the future aunt of Prince Philip), and the Prince of Wales, later Edward VIII, with whom Nancy played golf and to whom, she said, it took considerable skill to lose.

At meals in the Pompadour dining room Nancy would sometimes startle her guests by popping a huge set of false teeth into her mouth and, while chewing gum, do impersonations. Her favorites were a horsey, profane, toothless, shrewish, upper-class Englishwoman who hated Americans, and a Southern belle telling stories about "her" Negroes. She would fan herself with a dinner plate and push back her diamond tiara as if it were an old hat. And Waldorf? Nancy encouraged him in his passion for horses; given his resources, he soon became one of the most successful breeders of racehorses in the country. Between 1907 and 1950 the Cliveden stables won 460 races (though never the Derby) and earned nearly £500 million pounds in purses and stud fees. Neither Waldorf nor Nancy ever placed a bet: she preferred hunting.

William Waldorf Astor offered his son the editorship of the *Pall Mall Gazette,* but Waldorf preferred something more galvanizing than office work. Eventually he decided that at the first opportunity he would stand for

Parliament as a Conservative. Offered at once a safe seat, he turned it down. He had studied genetics as part of his preparation for breeding horses. Now he said he wanted to study politics before he stood for election and that when he did stand he preferred that it be for a contested seat—otherwise election would mean nothing to him. In the event he did not stand until 1910; but he had time to prepare himself.

In August 1907 their first child, William Waldorf Astor, was born, and this gave them both a great deal more to do. A year later, in July 1908, the Conservative Association of Plymouth adopted Waldorf Astor as the party candidate, and in 1909 the Astors bought a house in Plymouth, a place in which they were destined to spend a great deal of time for the next thirty-five years and a city that still remains in some English minds at least associated with the Astors. Waldorf had got his wish: the prospects of a Conservative victory at Plymouth in the next general election seemed remote.

What Waldorf actually got was not one general election but two, for 1910 was a tumultuous year in British politics. Edward VII died and was succeeded by George V. The Liberals had triumphed in 1906, and Labour was growing in strength. Asquith's government wished to restrict the powers of the House of Lords, which had stupidly thrown out the People's Budget in 1909. There was fear of civil war in Ireland and of aggression in Europe by the Germans, and much disagreement on both topics as to what, if anything, should be done. In the first election, in January 1910, Waldorf proved an able candidate and Nancy a zealous canvasser; she visited hundreds of working-class homes and talked informally to thousands of people, most of whom liked and remembered her. She even made a few speeches, astonishing herself. She said later of this first campaign: "All through my life I have found that if you go out to people in a friendly spirit, that is how they will receive and listen to you. The trouble with so many English people is that they cannot, however hard they try, be quite natural with other people. It is difficult for them not to be just a little patronizing. I don't know why that is. Maybe it has something to do with the climate over here." In mid-campaign Waldorf's heart condition flared up and he had to abandon the hustings until the last few days of the campaign, which he lost to the Liberal candidate.

But another election had to be called in December 1910, and this time Waldorf was successful in his Plymouth constituency. In the next few years he would be re-elected to Parliament, he would serve briefly as Lloyd George's parliamentary secretary (a reward for voting against his party and for Lloyd George's Health and Unemployment Insurance Bill, a direct result of Waldorf's observation of social conditions in Plymouth), and—no doubt urged on by his wife—he would energetically support all temperance measures. A few years into his first parliamentary term he accepted Lloyd

George's invitation to become chairman of the State Medical Research Committee. He also took some interest in family affairs, persuading his father to buy the *Observer* from Lord Northcliffe in April 1911.

Nancy, meanwhile, was making headway as a political hostess, specializing in liberal Conservatives of her husband's stamp. Lloyd George, for example, was a frequent guest at Cliveden. Nancy had some influence, but in these days Cliveden stood for progressive conservatism if it stood for anything, and its visitors, though often well known, were rarely controversial. Certainly the Astors at this time were seen as belonging to the left wing of the Conservative party. In 1912 they were asked to dine alone with the Asquiths at 10 Downing Street. And to this period belongs one of the better-known anecdotes of a collision between Nancy Astor and Winston Churchill, the first of many. Churchill, then a Liberal, was holding forth one morning during breakfast at Cliveden when Nancy interrupted him to say, "If I was your wife I'd put poison in your coffee." Churchill, who all his life hated to be interrupted, replied: "If I was your husband, I'd drink it." Also to Cliveden in these years came Nancy's father, an unreconstructed American who chewed tobacco in the drawing-room, drank when he felt like it, and took great pleasure in getting his disapproving daughter's drinkless guests drunk.

Between 1911 and 1914 Nancy Astor went through a disconcerting period of ill health and invalidism, forcing her in some cases to make her bedroom the venue of small dinner parties. A daughter, Phyllis, was born to the Astors in 1909, and another son, David, in 1912. Bobby Shaw was now sixteen and at Shrewsbury, headed for Sandhurst. He was a difficult adolescent, as the sad history of his parents presaged. The oldest Astor child, William, was seven. Nancy, just thirty-three in 1912, found herself unaccountably exhausted. Various physicians tried various cures. Twice she had surgery for what was termed an internal abscess. But in 1913-14 she discovered another of what was to be one of the strongest passions of her life: Christian Science, the belief in cure through prayer. Having digested Mary Baker Eddy, she told her doctors to go away, recovered her health, and continued, as she put it, to "hunt between babies." From now on she would do her Christian Science reading, prayer, and meditation every morning for an hour or two. Christian Science is not an especially tolerant religion, and eventually this new mania was to affect her brain in an unwholesome way. It helped turn her into a virulent anti-Catholic, like Belloc, and like another bigoted friend of hers, G. K. Chesterton, himself a Catholic. All three—Belloc, Chesterton, and Nancy Astor—were unrepentant and unreconstructed anti-Semites. As a Virginian she found it natural to believe in the superiority of some races and religions and the inferiority of others; indeed, bigotry remains a remarkably enduring fact of life in the American South. These attitudes would affect the politics of Nancy Astor, driving her so far to the right that eventually she was forced to give up her seat in the Commons before she was ready to do so—and also before she had concluded her long investigation into the question of whether there was a Jewish plot against "civilization." But all of that was not yet. The seeds were planted; only time was wanting.

This period just before the outbreak of the Great War also saw the Astors' purchase of a house at 4 St. James's Square, where they entertained their many guests (dinners for sixty, balls for 1,000) when Parliament was sitting, and another at Sandwich, a modest holiday retreat with a mere fifteen bedrooms. As the fashionable English did in those days, they went to their place in Scotland for the months of August and September. It was as if they were living in a Palliser novel. This period also saw the death of Waldorf's cousin John Jacob Astor III, who went down with the *Titanic*. After the great ship struck the ice and its doom was pronounced to the passengers, Astor and his valet changed hurriedly into full evening dress so that they might, in the parlance of the age, "die as gentlemen."

The age was about to end.

III

During the Great War, which began in August 1914, Nancy divided her time between Cliveden and Plymouth, where Waldorf built a series of canteens for troops stationed there; later he constructed some public playing fields. Nancy immersed herself in hospital work. The grounds of Cliveden were turned into a large hospital for Canadian soldiers. The Astors paid most of the medical bills. By the end of the war five years later 24,000 men had been treated there; the house itself had been converted into a convalescent home. Nancy's bedside manner was unusual, to say the least. Hearing that two badly burned men had lost the will to live, she bent over them and murmured, "You're going to die, and I would too, rather than go back to Canada." This roused them wonderfully, and Nancy went on to preach a lesson to the nurses on keeping their patients interested in life. By immersing herself in matters of morale rather than medicine, Nancy was able to keep her faith in Christian Science intact while helping to administer a medical hospital. Waldorf, disgusted with himself for being unfit to fight when his fellow thirty-five-year-olds were universally under arms, asked the army to give him the most disagreeable job it could find. He was requested to oversee army waste. This only inflamed Waldorf's guilt at living in comfort while so many of his contemporaries were in dire discomfort in France. Indeed, his own stepson, Bobby Shaw, was serving there in the Royal Horse Guards. In 1916 Waldorf's father turned over to him the editorship of the *Observer*, which gave him more to do.

"After two years . . . we did not look at the casualty lists any more," Nancy would say later. "There was nothing to look for. All of our friends had gone." Now and then during these years she may be glimpsed in a harsher light—such as when she complained to Mrs. John Buchan that the war had robbed Cliveden of all interesting company. "I would welcome the butcher's boy from Maidenhead to tea," she declared with great sorrow. There was some diversion in the birth of her son Michael in April 1916. It was this son who would serve, years later, as M.P. for a Surrey constituency and whose maiden speech in Parliament would be greeted by his mother in the Gallery loudly enough to embarrass him: "Where did you learn to do this? I feel like Balaam when the ass spoke."

In the new year's honours list for 1916, William Waldorf Astor was made a baron by Lloyd George; in the next year he was elevated to a viscount. This would have far-reaching consequences. The Astor peerage was an hereditary one. When William Waldorf died, whenever that might be (he was sixty-nine in 1917), his son would automatically succeed him in the peerage, whether Waldorf liked it or not. Since peers could neither sit in the House of Commons nor (in those days) renounce their titles, this meant that Waldorf's political career was effectively over. When his father died he would have to sit in the Lords—no place for a progressive and a reformer—give up his Plymouth seat, and forget about political advancement. Waldorf was furious with his father for seeking and accepting the peerage and accused him of ruining his life; but of course the old *emigré*—who must have made at least two enormous contributions to Liberal party funds in face of the upcoming general election, though this is nowhere recorded—found the lure of a British peerage irresistible. Could any native-born American resist British honors? And so William Waldorf became the first Viscount Astor. One of the viscount's first actions was to leave all of his money to Waldorf's sons instead of to him outright. It was meant as revenge upon his son, but in fact the new tax laws enacted after the war turned this act of spite into a shrewd maneuver, and in any case Nancy and Waldorf were not materially affected. The ennobling of William Waldorf, though apparently a trivial event, would turn out to be one of the things directly responsible for the seating in Parliament of its first female member.

It was now that Lloyd George, having succeeded Asquith as Prime Minister, made Waldorf his parliamentary private secretary. This was a genuinely interesting and important job; finally Waldorf could forget about army waste. He worked in a hut in the garden of 10 Downing Street and felt for the first time that he was doing something useful. In this same year, 1917, with the encouragement of Lloyd George, he turned one of his passions into a pamphlet, *The Health of the People,* which started discussion in the country of forming a new Ministry of Health. With all of his new duties, as well as the *Observer* to run, Waldorf found he could rarely get down to his Plymouth constituency, and Nancy began to represent him at meetings there. Opening one on the alleviation of ignorance, Nancy remarked: "I am very keen about education because I suffer from the lack of it, and if you want an ignorant woman to take the chair at an educational meeting, you could not have found a better one if you had searched Europe." Quickly her platform manner, irreverent and amusing, became popular, and she began to attract crowds to the halls in which she appeared. Back at Cliveden she had the less agreeable task of opening a cemetery for soldiers who had died in the hospital there. A smaller contribution of the Astors to the war effort was the loan of their house at Sandwich to Lloyd George whenever he needed a day or two's rest (there was no Chequers then).

In 1918 the Astors' last child, called John Jacob, was born. In the autumn of this year the big house in St. James's Square became a rest hotel for American officers and remained so until the end of the war in 1919. The place was (perhaps inevitably) dubbed by its occupants the Waldorf Astoria.

During the war women had taken on many tasks, and after it was over, when everything seemed changed, some attitudes of mind also had changed. Opposition to female suffrage was no longer widespread; to some it now seemed ridiculous to oppose it. The same thing happened at the same time in America and a few years earlier in Canada. Bills to give the vote to women over thirty who were householders or married to householders and to permit them to sit in Parliament were introduced in that body in 1917 and 1918 and quickly became law. Women were given the entrée in time to stand during the general election of December 1918. Seventeen of them stood, including the redoubtable Christabel Pankhurst, and sixteen of them, including Mrs. Pankhurst, were defeated. The lone victor, an Irish nationalist with the unlikely name of the Countess Markievicz (née Gore-Booth), was in prison at the time. In any case all of the Sinn Fein members—she was one of them—refused to take the oath of loyalty to George V, and their elections were invalidated. So the first woman *elected* to the British parliament never sat there. In the same general election Waldorf Astor was returned with a huge majority from the Sutton division of Plymouth, as his constituency was now called; he polled 11,756 more votes than his Labour opponent. At that moment he was parliamentary secretary at the Ministry of Food; later he moved to the Local Government Board. In July 1919 he had the pleasure of seeing his cherished scheme turn to reality when a Ministry of Health was established. Transferred, he served in it for the next two years. Indeed, it must be clear that had it not been for his father's vanity and selfishness, a genuine career in government would have been open to Waldorf, who was a capable man. But as the embryo second Viscount Astor, he and all around him knew that his days in the House of Commons were numbered. How closely they were numbered no one realized until they ran out altogether.

The fateful date turned out to be 18 October 1919. William Waldorf had been a baron for one year and a viscount for two, and that was that. Protocol said that Waldorf, now Lord Astor, must resign his seat in the Commons and go next door and sit in the Lords. Waldorf had hoped to become the next Minister of Health; he would not go without a struggle. Here was a man who wished to evade honors and titles in order to do some useful work. The system said he could not avoid his fate; he decided to challenge the system. He wished either to renounce his peerage or get legislation passed allowing peers to sit in the House of Commons. "Some people find it hard to get titles," the new viscountess remarked, "but Lord Astor is finding it even harder to get rid of his." Waldorf discovered quickly enough that he had to go to the Lords: there was no alternative except death, and even death as a disqualification was questionable. It all happened too quickly for the Conservative central office to settle on a suitable candidate for the Plymouth constituency Lord Astor had to leave behind.

An early decision needed to be made. There was speculation in the press that Lady Astor might stand. The title was her husband's; she held no title in her own right and thus was eligible to sit in the Commons. Waldorf's huge reelection majority, the death of his father, the new legislation enabling women to sit in Parliament and giving them the vote—all of these things occurred within the space of a year, an astonishing series of events that made it possible now for Nancy to be the candidate of the hour. The press was in a frenzy: Will She or Won't She? It seemed at first certain that she would stand. Then it was certain that she would not. Another rumor began to circulate that the former prime minister Mr. Asquith, who had been defeated in the 1918 general election and was looking for a new seat, might choose the Sutton division of Plymouth. The press now began to anticipate a "dream" by-election co-starring Nancy Astor and Margot Asquith in an epic battle of tongues and lungs. Finally the *Pall Mall Gazette* carried a story saying that Nancy Astor would run for her husband's seat if adopted by the Conservative association of Plymouth; since the *Pall Mall Gazette* was owned by the Astors this seemed definitive. And Asquith? Word came that he had never considered standing at Plymouth. On 24 October 1919 the Conservatives of Plymouth formally and publicly asked Lady Astor to run for the seat. There was no immediate answer from her ladyship; Lord Astor told all callers that the decision must be his wife's alone. Two days later she accepted the invitation to stand at Plymouth.

Under the circumstances her adoption by the Conservatives at Plymouth was not surprising. An Astor had represented the place for nine years and was widely liked. Nancy Astor was now forty. She had worked hard in Plymouth, helping to establish maternity centers in the poorer neighborhoods. She had given generously to private charities there. She had acquired the habit of calling the citizens of Plymouth "descendants of Drake" and had loudly praised the valor of its sailors in the late war. Though she was an unknown entity as a candidate in Plymouth, everyone knew who she was, which is always a good start in politics.

The press had an interesting story but treated it as most stories are treated in the British press, then and now: irresponsibly. One daily carried a banner headline announcing that a peer's wife had entered the lists in order to fight against the workers at Plymouth. "Dux Femina Fecit," screamed another, and went on to remind everyone of the Tories' anti-feminist position. Typically, G. K. Chesterton's *New Witness* commented that since there were so many Jews in Parliament, one more foreign member, an American, would not matter.

The Liberals at Plymouth nominated a respected local lawyer who had stood before. In this constituency with a historically growing Labour vote, a Labour candidate also was found; his pacifism would turn out to be unwanted extra baggage in the wake of the war. And then there was the Conservative candidate, an American woman untried and untested in this arena. The election, everyone agreed, would be close. Lady Astor might be seen to have an edge, but then no woman had ever taken a seat in Parliament....

One of the first things Nancy had to do was disguise from her constituency her strict views on temperance. Prohibition had just been enacted in America, and Britons, quite sensibly, looked on the temperance movement with fear and loathing. Advised by Waldorf, Nancy averted disaster by saying, when asked her position, that she was against drunkenness but no friend of Prohibition, which of course was untrue. Her political education had begun.

She adopted the manner most congenial to her—that of the breezy, amusing woman who likes to tell stories against herself and does not take things too solemnly. This manner was natural and seemed to please the electorate. She turned out to be a sure-footed campaigner who could speak extemporaneously. Asked to comment on the "new" feminism, Nancy declared that women were not looking for superiority over men, since they already had that: what they wanted was equality with men. A large audience of women wanted to know why they had been wedged into such a tiny room. "Because the meeting was arranged by men," said the candidate. It seemed to her hearers that probably she could hold her own with the other sex when called upon to do so at Westminster. Lady Astor believed in women's rights but had never fought for them. It turned out to be fortunate for the cause of women in England that, though the first woman to sit in Parliament had not actively campaigned on behalf of women, women's rights should at first be represented by a woman who was neither identifiable as a feminist nor as, in Christopher Sykes's words, "the dreaded unsexed ogress of popular and not always misled imagination": it put the whole question on a general basis.

No one could accuse Lady Astor at Plymouth of being subtle. Her manner was often confrontational, and she enjoyed trading barbs with the occasional heckler. A woman asked her to state her position on reform of the divorce laws and referred to the relatively relaxed statutes of America, obviously intending to dredge up the ending of Nancy's first marriage. Sounding concerned, the candidate replied: "Madam, I am sorry to hear you are in trouble." "I do not believe in sexes or classes," she told another meeting.

Referring to the pacifist Labour candidate, Nancy remarked that he "repre-
sents the shirking classes, I represent the working classes. If you can't get a
fighting man, get a fighting woman." She drew big crowds, composed largely
of women, which in these days was unusual; stump crowds were generally
small and male. Soon she became known in the constituency as "Our
Nancy," the highest accolade she could have hoped for, or so Waldorf told
her, for in the beginning the candidate refused to let anyone call her by her
first name.

All the national papers, and many urban American dailies, were covering
this interesting by-election. Almost overnight Nancy Astor became a
famous woman, with the papers in the United States trumpeting her American origins. During the (blissfully short) two-week campaign, she went on
making speeches, visiting local institutions, and staging impromptu street
theater. There was also the occasional not-so-funny joke, as when she
advised working-class mothers to try soothing their infants by putting
ropes of pearls around their necks. Since Waldorf was a stolid supporter of
Lloyd George the Liberals did not send their big guns against her, while the
Conservatives did dispatch several speakers on her behalf, among them the
newly elected M.P. Oswald Mosley.

On election day Nancy went off to vote. Outside the polling booth a
woman holding a baby approached her and asked what she should do with
the child when she went inside: "I can't vote and hold him." What good was
the suffrage if she couldn't vote? "Give him to me," said the candidate, "I've
had five of my own." When the result of the poll was announced, Nancy
had received 14,495 votes; the Labour candidate, 9,292; the Liberal, 4,319.
Waldorf's majority had been halved, and Nancy portrayed herself as disappointed; she had expected, she said, a majority of at least 8,000. But she had
a comfortable margin of victory and polled more votes than her two opponents combined.

So this was the beginning. She would be returned six times after this and
serve until 1945. Never having marched with the suffragettes, she had
nonetheless benefitted from their years of hard and often dangerous campaigning. She was by no stretch of the imagination a socialist, or even a liberal. She was not even English. She was an American divorcée married to an
English lord, and she believed in Christian Science and teetotalism and the
Conservative party. Nevertheless here she was, on the verge of being the
first woman to sit in Parliament.

Nancy's only real regret was that her father did not live to see her elected:
he had died in February 1919. She must have reflected on the fact that if her
parents had not suggested a little foreign travel for her after her divorce
from Shaw, none of what was now happening could have taken place. But
she had not yet actually been seated in the House of Commons, and one
heard muttered wishes that she never would be—from, among others,
Winston Churchill and Austen Chamberlain, and generally from the Con-

servatives, though she was one of them. More diverting and problematical for Nancy was the question of what to wear when she went into Parliament. There was no precedent; what she decided to do now could be precedent-setting. She might, of course, make a terrible blunder, disgrace the cause of women, and justify the mutterings of the reactionaries.

The question of clothing was settled first. She chose a black dress with a white blouse open at the collar, white cuffs and white gloves, and—after great soul-searching—a small, black tricorne hat. Having made her choice, she had enough copies of this costume ordered up so as to be able to wear the same thing every time she went into the House, a practice she followed for the next quarter-century. (A boudoir and a lavatory for women members had been installed, and Nancy was to have the sole use of these places for the next two years.) She was thus attired, and carrying her election writ but no handbag, when, on the afternoon of 1 December 1919, she was introduced into Parliament by Lloyd George and Arthur Balfour, the only two sitting M.P.s who had served as prime minister. (Both had also supported women's rights; Nancy checked). She had chosen a seat on the Opposition side where the overflow from the Government supporters sat. The chamber was packed for the historic event about to occur. Three of Nancy's children, her two sisters, and her husband watched from the Gallery, which was also full.

At the end of Question Time, the Speaker proclaimed, "Members desirous of taking their seats will come to the table." As a new Conservative member for Croydon was introduced, Balfour and Lloyd George took up their position next to Nancy, under the Gallery and below the bar of the House. Lloyd George proceeded to march off without his two companions, who had to recall him. He went back and they started again. The two men went too fast for the new member, who stretched out her hands and drew both back level with her. At the point where all three were supposed to bow to the Speaker, Lady Astor was clearly heard to prompt her companions, "Bow now," which they did, but not together. Then the two men retired to the Front Bench while the new M.P. surrendered her writ to the clerk. She took the oath, holding a Bible in her right hand and a printed text of the oath in her left. And she signed the roll. At that point the ceremony was over and she should have gone to her seat, but instead she chatted briefly with the Speaker, who was too astonished to send her away. She moved to the Front Bench and talked to the leading members of the Government as if she was admitting them to her house and they were going through a receiving line. Chamberlain, who was then Chancellor of the Exchequer, not knowing what else to do, took off his enormous top hat and bowed to her. Nancy saw no point in not talking to them; after all, she knew them. But this was a breach of etiquette, and the serjeant-at-arms was dispatched to take her to her seat. She found herself sitting next to William Young, a Liberal from Perth, who told her that in his opinion women had no business being in

Parliament. The new M.P. listened to the speeches for awhile, at one point clapping her hands at something Chamberlain said; her neighbor explained that one could only express approval vocally. She stayed a while longer and then left the House. On the evening of that historic December 1 the Astors gave a big party in St. James's Square to celebrate the great event. Later that night there was a division, and the member for Plymouth obediently went back to the House of Commons to cast her vote for the Government. On her way out she stopped to chat with a friend. Hearing the Speaker call "Order! Order!," she looked around for the excitement, saw none, and continued her conversation. Her interlocutor finally told her that she was again in breach of etiquette; and so she left.

Thus ended her first day (and night) in Parliament. And thus did Nancy Witcher Langhorne Shaw Astor, of Virginia, at forty, become the first woman ever to sit in the House of Commons. It was 1919.

IV

"Parliament was like a men's club," Nancy said later. "No one wanted me there." Churchill pretended he couldn't see her. Annoyed, she finally asked him why. "When you took your seat I felt as if a woman had come into my bedroom and I had only a sponge with which to defend myself," he declared. "You are not handsome enough to have worries of that kind," came the reply. This did not patch things up between them. But she would not allow herself to be put on the defensive if she could help it. "I have been in [Parliament] a week, and I never saw a house where more women were needed," she told a female audience. She could sometimes be tactful. For years she stayed out of the members' smoking room and only occasionally used the members' dining room, both of which the men considered exclusively their own. During tea breaks in the Commons she would go out on the terrace and practice her golf swing. She was given a room of her own in which she could sit and, with her secretaries, grapple with her correspondence. Women from all over the world wrote to her about their grievances and desires; her mailbag was enormous for many years.

But Nancy Astor was no reformer once she got away from cranky obsessions such as temperance. She never mastered parliamentary etiquette: during her parliamentary career she continuously infuriated colleagues by her audible running commentary during speeches (for example, when Aneurin Bevan rose to speak: "it really is intolerable when this old gas bag gets up and gabbles away") and by talking directly to them instead of addressing the Speaker when she was on her feet. The only things that interested her as M.P. were temperance and women's rights, and the latter only from time to time. She strongly supported and helped to get passed a bill prohibiting the sale of liquor to anyone under eighteen years of age; when another member rose to argue against passage she walked over to him, pulled on his coattails,

4.1 Nancy Astor in 1920, the year after her first election to Parliament; by permission of the National Portrait Gallery.

and tried to make him sit down before he had finished speaking. She said she wanted to do something to improve the position of women; but here, as Astor family biographer Lucy Kavaler has written, her poor education was against her: she was never able to master parliamentary law or even the background of many issues.

Lady Astor made her maiden speech on 24 February 1920. A member had proposed that all wartime restraints with reference to the strength, supply, and consumption of alcoholic beverages be abolished, that the (wartime) Liquor Control Board be disbanded, and that restrictions on licensing hours be done away with. This was a controversial issue, especially in view of passage of Prohibition in America. The Government opposed the motion to remove restrictions, and Nancy asked to speak against it. She could hardly have chosen a more unpopular course—but this was *her* issue. The debate began. The House and Gallery were packed. The mover of the motion emphasized the fanatical nature of teetotalers; referring to Lenin's brief experiment with prohibition he conjoined teetotalism with Bolshevism, characterizing temperance as the product of crazy theorists. Lady Astor rose. At first her voice was hoarse with nervousness, but it gained strength and clarity as she gained courage. First she tactfully thanked the House for making her feel welcome, though it wasn't true: "I know it was very difficult for some honourable members to receive a woman into the House . . . it was almost as difficult as it was for the lady to come in. To address you now on the vexed question of drink is harder still. It takes a bit of courage to dare to do it. But I do dare." Her chief argument was that the restraints placed during the war on licensing, sales, and the strength of liquor had greatly reduced drunkenness, of which the chief victims were always women and children. Working-class women in particular had suffered great abuse when there was no restriction on the sale of liquor. "I could talk for five hours on the benefit to women the [Liquor Control] Board has been [roar of protest from Hon. Members]." She would not urge Prohibition now, she said, but she hoped it would come some day. Here she had gone too far, and this remark was greeted with genuine anger and resentment. She said that the House was really debating the welfare of the community versus the prosperity of trade. She showed with statistics that the wartime restrictions really had reduced the incidence of drunkenness, which had tripled since the end of the war. But she went on too long, and there were shouts for her to sit down, an unusual occurrence during a maiden speech. "I do not want you to look upon your lady member as a fanatic or lunatic," she ended. "I am simply trying to speak for hundreds of women and children throughout the country who cannot speak for themselves."

The motion to abolish the Liquor Control Board was defeated and the wartime restrictions were retained; indeed, some of them remain in place today. The Government promised it would not pursue Prohibition. But the big story was of course the first speech in Parliament by a woman, to an audience of five-hundred men. Despite some lapses, Nancy had conducted herself well, and the measure she spoke against had been defeated. Lloyd George congratulated her, telling her that her voice was her fortune. She expressed reservations about the cogency of her argument. "It's not what you say that matters," the Prime Minister remarked, "but whether you hold your audience. That you did from start to finish"—a slight exaggeration, as we know.

Four days later she was able to show that her first success was not a fluke. Parliament was deciding whether to lower the voting age for women, which was thirty, to that of men, which was twenty-one, or to make the voting age twenty-five for everybody. Women, said an honorable member in the course of the debate, introduced an element of undignified frivolity into political life—as witness, he said, the recent by-election at Plymouth, more like a circus than a poll according to press accounts. This was too much for Lady Astor, who waited her chance and then jumped up to speak. She had not intended to speak and so could not have had Waldorf's help in preparing her remarks. She began by saying that, after hearing the debate, she felt someone ought to say something on behalf of men since there had been so many gallant defenders of women. This piece of calculated irony got a big laugh, and she went on. Women, she said, matured earlier than men, were more idealistic than men, and more reform-minded. She thought they ought to be able to vote at the same age as men. She concluded by asserting that whether or not the election at Plymouth had been a circus, she could say at least that the clown had not been elected. This was good stuff; but again she made the mistake of going on too long, got off the subject, and came to a lame ending. However, she showed she could speak in public without elaborate—or any—preparation, and this was an important thing to establish. On this occasion her cause was not successful in the Commons, and for a while longer the voting ages stayed as they were. Later in this session Lady Astor also supported a bill that sought to remedy the absurdity that British women who married foreigners automatically lost their citizenship.

After drink and women's rights, it may not be surprising to find that the next subject to engage Nancy's attention was divorce. This time she was genuinely afraid of the issue; and though other commentators on her career seem oddly perplexed by her terror, the facts that she herself was a divorced woman and that this was not, after all, universally known are sufficient to explain the real distaste and nervousness with which she approached the debate—one in which, as the only woman in the House, it was quite naturally expected that she would participate.

The debate took place in April 1920. The measure being debated recommended that in addition to adultery, grounds for divorce should be conceded for desertion (after three years), cruelty, drunkenness (if habitual), insanity (if incurable), and imprisonment (if for life). Incompatibility, or irreconcilable differences, was still considered a frivolous reason for divorce.

Lady Astor astonished the House and the press by joining the reactionaries and opposing the bill. She spun out a long religious argument, and ended: "I am not convinced that making divorce very easy really makes marriages more happy or makes happy marriages more possible." The bill was later thrown out on its second reading, perhaps due in part to Nancy's opposition to it, and another fifteen years would go by before Parliament effectively reformed the divorce laws.

This was not one of Nancy Astor's more shining moments as a human being. Suppose she had had to wait fifteen years to divorce Robert Gould Shaw? Had she been poor she might have had to, and it is here that her chief offense surely lies: for the bill was designed, of course, to put divorce within the reach of those who were not as rich as the Langhornes and the Astors. For the first time she got a decidedly bad press, which she richly deserved. The educated public began to see how deeply conservative this daughter of the Confederacy really was. Conan Doyle declared in public that her behavior in the House was shocking. Here, for once, she had studiously ignored women's rights—or women's wrongs.

And she was to pay the price. The 8 May number of *John Bull* carried a spectacular banner, "Lady Astor's Divorce," with the subtitle "A Hypocrite of the First Water—The Poor and the Rich." The whole story of her divorce from Shaw was told, to most of the public for the first time. The most damaging part of the article in *John Bull* was that which showed how Nancy Shaw had made use of a number of provisions of the American divorce laws that she had condemned and voted against as a British M.P. Could anything be more hypocritical? The piece ended by quoting from *Who's Who*, Burke's *Peerage*, and other reference works Waldorf Astor's statement that in 1906 he had married the *widow* of Robert Gould Shaw, which of course was untrue.

Deeply hurt, at first Nancy said nothing. She decided to defend herself in her constituency but got tangled up in the law during her speech, and *John Bull* retaliated by repeating all the original charges. She let the matter drop. But she and her reputation had been injured.

On the plus side—while she was not the most effective M.P. in the House, Lady Astor was one of the most conscientious. She rarely turned down an invitation, either social or political. She attended the House assiduously, spoke in the House regularly and out of the House peripatetically. During the summer of 1920 she gave speeches at Sheffield, Bradford, Leeds, York, and Hull. She also, now and later, spent a lot of time in her constituency; there and in the House she looked after the needs of the Royal Navy, one of whose principal bases was at Plymouth and about which she had to keep herself well informed. She was successful in her adroit campaigns of 1920-21 to get women admitted into the Civil Service and to prevent the Government from carrying through its plan to disband the Women Police; though passed, the former measure was not implemented until many years later. Whenever the opportunity offered itself, she would recommend that the British try the American prescription for perfection, Prohibition, and eventually on this subject she exasperated everybody. As for women's rights, apparently the ex-Mrs. Shaw was willing to let women do anything they wanted except leave their husbands legally, even if those husbands were drunkards. Since that is what she herself had done, her ill-conceived position on this issue cannot be defended.

In September 1921 Nancy's splendid isolation as the only woman in Parliament came to an end. Mrs. Margaret Wintringham was elected as the Liberal member for Louth, inheriting a seat held by her late husband Thomas. Though her new colleague had of course defeated a Conservative to get into the House, Nancy Astor sent her congratulations. Mrs. Wintringham thus became the first native-born female member. At the end of this decade Britain would see its first female Cabinet minister—Margaret Bondfield, Minister of Labour in Ramsey MacDonald's Labour government from 1929-1931. (She lost her seat in the general election of 1931.) And there would be other women in the Commons. Nancy now had to share all those nice little rooms near the House chamber originally set aside for her.

Lady Astor often spoke at Plymouth. She was usually given written-out speeches (many by Waldorf) to deliver, but frequently ignored them and spoke extemporaneously. Thus we find her, at the end of 1921, musing in front of an audience: "I cannot stand humbug, yet know that I myself am self-righteous, for which I am sorry. It is really a terrible temptation for people who are trying to do right. Every now and then I find myself saying—Thank God, I am not like other politicians." She went on: "I am not highly educated, I am not brilliantly clever. I have just got a little knowledge. Sometimes I wish I could understand things better; I wish I could understand the Budget [laughter]." This was Nancy at her best. "I saw today an old lady of over a hundred," she told a Plymouth audience. "Another lady, introducing her to me, remarked: "'This is Lady Astor, my dear. Some people likes her and some don't.'"

Nancy was delighted to be invited to address the Women's Pan American Conference in Baltimore in April 1922. The meeting was sponsored by the International League of Women Voters. For the first time in ten years she would revisit her native land.

In her speech at Baltimore, Lady Astor urged women to take an interest in world affairs and attacked America's self-imposed isolationism in the wake of the war. Be responsible, come back to Europe, and join the League of Nations: this was her message, largely ignored in the United States but politely received—with one exception. Her religious fanaticism reared itself in the spontaneous and inaccurate remark that America "had been founded by Protestants in the Protestant faith." In Washington a few days later she lost the thread of her argument after another extemporaneous excursion and turned to her husband: "Waldorf, what was I talking about?" She visited the White House and met President Harding, whom she pronounced nearly as enlightened as herself. On the floor of the Senate she adjusted one senator's tie and asked, "Why don't you fix yourself up?" She was given lunch by General Pershing. And then she was off to Richmond and Danville; the former Miss Langhorne received tumultuous welcomes in both of her home towns. Unfortunately, she remembered nothing about Danville and no one there, and was saved from severe embarrassment by a local newspaper reporter who was first sworn to secrecy and then briefed her thoroughly about people and places she would be expected to know. From Danville they went to Charlottesville, where Nancy spoke at the University, and then on to Chicago, Toronto, Ottawa, and Montreal before returning to New York at the end of May. Here, in the last formal speech of her tour, Nancy repeated her criticism of the United States for staying out of the League of Nations. Just before embarking for England she managed to enrage her cousin (by marriage) Vincent Astor, speaking out against his chief financial asset. "It is bad business to tolerate slums," she declared, adding that bad housing wrecks the health of its tenants.

During this trip Nancy Astor made approximately forty speeches, formal and impromptu. Most of them were brought together to compose a book she published in 1923 called *My Two Countries*. She and Waldorf returned to England early in June 1922. Lloyd George's coalition government appeared to be losing its grip; an early general election was widely predicted.

V

Nancy Astor enjoyed campaigning in her Plymouth constituency. She would go down a street, Lucy Kavaler reports, and shout until enough heads came popping out of windows, and then she would start orating. Eventually hecklers would appear, a tamer brand than in our day. "Come on," she'd cry, "I'm ready for you." "You have enough brass to make a kettle," one would yell at her. "You have enough water in your head to fill it," came the reply. A farmer accused her of knowing nothing about the needs of rural folk because she was too rich. "How many toes are there on a pig's feet?" he asked the member for the Sutton division of Plymouth. "Take off your shoes . . . and count for yourself," was the answer. Nancy's knowledge of "rural" matters was confined to the Cliveden cow the Astors took with them on trips within the country so that their love of milk would not expose them to the danger of drinking the product of a strange and possibly tubercular animal; that neither Waldorf nor Nancy nor anyone else in their entourage was versed in pastoral matters may be reflected in the fact that along with the Cliveden cow they brought with them a Cliveden farmer whose only job was to milk it for them.

Nancy had been adopted again by the Plymouth Conservative association despite the great repugnance in her constituency to any attempt to infringe further upon the licensing laws. The M.P. for Plymouth, utterly immune to popular feeling on this issue, had introduced a private member's bill in the last parliament to restrict access to drink. The bill died a quick death, but it was resented by many of Nancy's constituents. Still, many of them also seemed to feel that they could tolerate this small strain of lunacy in an otherwise generous character. Nancy's foes in the election of November 1922 were another Conservative, financed by the liquor industry, and a Labour candidate. Prudently she said nothing about temperance during the campaign, which turned out to be one of her most difficult. Two Tories, a capable Labour man who had fought valiantly in the recent war, no Liberal candidate, Nancy's unpopular position on drink, and the fact that the coalition her party belonged to had traded in the popular Lloyd George for the inert Bonar Law as its leader threatened, in combination, to put the Labour candidate in her place. Fortunately for her the left wing of the Labour party frightened voters with radical schemes, a not-unfamiliar phenomenon; in 1922 it was a capital levy that put voters off. Nancy said her opponents were the candidates of the brewers; they said no "alien" should be representing the city of Drake and meddling with the English way of life.

Nancy got 13,924 votes, the Labour candidate received 10,831, and the maverick Conservative, 4,643. Nancy's majority was reduced to 3,100. Nationally the Conservatives also won. Bonar Law became Prime Minister, but his poor health forced him to give way to Stanley Baldwin. Besides Nancy and her parliamentary colleague Mrs. Wintringham, no other women candidates were sent to Westminster in the general election of November 1922; thirty-one were defeated. From now on the chief opposition to the Conservatives, who had a majority of eighty-seven in the House of Commons, would be Labour. Churchill, labeled a warmonger and blamed for wartime military disasters in Greece and Turkey, lost his seat.

So Lady Astor's career on the public platform continued; taking political moderation as her new theme, she denounced both the far left and the far right. She shocked the annual conference of a Conservative organization by declaring: "People who live in two houses do not realize what it is to live in two rooms. That's what is wrong with the Conservatives." When some of her hearers complained audibly, the speaker retorted: "Why, you're worse than a Labour audience." They continued to howl. The member for Plymouth observed that reactionaries were as great an enemy to Great Britain as Bolshevists; it's a pity she forgot this in the 1930s. An uproar ensued; Nancy lost control of the meeting altogether.

She saw that one way to bring conservatives and liberals closer together might be to introduce the two extremes to each other. In March 1923 she invited to St. James's Square for dinner George V and Queen Mary and the leaders of the Labour party, who were thought by some to be radical revolutionaries and who had raised a few tentative questions about the usefulness of the royal family—a question last raised seriously in the 1870s, with Queen Victoria in seclusion and refusing to perform her constitutional duties. The King and Queen were willing to come to the Astors, though the Labour leaders, as Collis points out, up to then had never been invited to meet any members of the royal family anywhere. Labour strength in the country grew rapidly as the Liberals completed their self-destruction; there was a chance that Labour might form the next government, though few people, in March 1923, thought this would actually come to pass. At any rate everyone accepted the Astors' invitation, including the Labour leader, Ramsey MacDonald. Court dress was required, which caused some befuddlement among the Labourites, but they complied. Lady Astor entered the dining room on the arm of George V, whispering to one of the Labour M.P.s as she went by to pull his socks up. After dinner the King invited the Labour leaders to visit him at Buckingham Palace, which Labour's far left, not being invited, denounced as part of some unspecified conspiracy. When MacDonald became prime minister nine months later, he and the King had the Astors to thank for smoothing the path to friendship and cooperation. Labour did not regard the royal family as hopeless reactionaries; and the royal family did not regard Labour as lunatic revolutionaries. This was Nancy's anti-extremist position fruitfully at work.

Stanley Baldwin, the new Prime Minister, decided in 1923 that a protectionist economic policy was the only hope for England's unemployment woes. In this he was opposed by the free-traders in his own party; and of course he turned out to be wrong, as he so monotonously was throughout his life. There was only one way to resolve the issue, however, and for the third time in four years Nancy Astor had to face the electors of Plymouth. In this general election of December 1923 Nancy had only one opponent: the same Labour candidate she had out-polled a year earlier. Nancy continued in Plymouth her campaign to push, or rather drag, the Conservative party slightly to the left. She talked of town planning, public housing and public health care, pensions for widows and orphans, retention of women police, raising the school-leaving age from fourteen to sixteen, reform of the penal system and of the lunacy laws. The extreme right continued to object to her, even in her own constituency, and spoke darkly of nominating a "real" Conservative at the next general election. Her election meetings were packed. One of them was so crowded that the candidate was unable to enter it through the door and had to climb through a window instead.

The country had swung to the left, and it is likely that Waldorf and Nancy planned her third campaign with this fact in mind. A Conservative with less progressive views certainly would have lost the seat at Plymouth in 1923. As it was, she staggered home with a further reduced majority of under 2,700 in a field of two. Around Great Britain the Conservatives were less successful. The result in the Commons was a standoff, and when the Liberals threw their support to Labour in January 1924, Ramsey MacDonald formed the first Labour government. Now a member of the loyal opposition, Lady Astor and the positions she had taken seemed vindicated. Had the Conservatives adopted a more tolerant attitude toward social reform—had they been more liberal—they might have retained power, as the re-elected member for Plymouth declared in a letter to *The Times.* But "tolerant," "reform-minded," and "liberal" were terms that could hardly be applied to Stanley Baldwin; indeed, in the next decade there was good reason to question not only his intelligence and his integrity but also his loyalty. Critical as she was of her Conservative colleagues, however, Nancy Astor could never bear to hear them attacked by others who were not Tories. "My own party may be reactionary, but at least they are honest," she blurted out on one occasion.

As time passed the paper-thin majority of the Labour/Liberal government caused administrative problems. It finally disintegrated altogether under the combined weight of MacDonald's inept handling of Anglo-Russian relations and his disinclination to listen to the Liberal chief, Asquith. And so in October 1924 Lady Astor found herself having to fight her fourth election campaign in five years, her third in three years. Her standing in the constituency was not hurt by a gift she and Waldorf had made earlier in the year: £10,000 to build workmen's dwellings in Plymouth. She was always admired for her charitableness—so much so that people she did not know and had never met would come to the Commons and send their names in to her; she would invariably come out to meet them, and if she thought them needy she would help them on the spot. (Beggars who lined up at 4 St. James's Square rarely if ever were turned away.) Nancy's constituents were beginning to see her as a lady with a lamp, a sort of fairy godmother ministering to their needs, and this was no disadvantage on polling day.

It was this campaign, the "Red Letter Election" of October 1924, that witnessed the startling effect of the so-called Zinoviev letter. In it Zinoviev, president of the Communist International, allegedly called on English Communists and working men to take on the army and raise a revolution in Britain. The letter ultimately turned out to be a forgery. But the Labour party, perceived as closer in sympathy to the Bolsheviks than the other parties, suffered mightily from the electorate's fear of the red menace, and the result was a huge Conservative victory. Running against the same Labour candidate for the third time, Nancy raised her majority to 5,100. Baldwin came back as prime minister. Asquith lost his seat; the number of Liberals in Parliament was reduced to thirty-nine. Three women were elected this time; Margaret Bondfield and Mrs. Wintringham were among those turned out by the voters. Nancy had survived; but she was bitterly disappointed that the new government offered her nothing, not even an under-secretaryship. She had probably offended too many Tories with all her talk of reactionaries and reform; and of course there remained prejudice against her gender, especially among her fellow Conservatives.

During this Parliament, which went on for five years with a large Conservative majority, Lady Astor brought in private member's bills to control prostitution, to raise the legal drinking age, and to raise the school-leaving age. All were defeated; the Commons was growing tired of her puritanism. On one notable evening in the House she threatened to disclose everything she knew about the discreditable company allegedly kept by a Labour member with a dozen children: he had contradicted her during a debate. She was called to order by the Speaker and reminded yet again not to address her colleagues directly.

Through the middle and late 1920s, the prospect of annual general elections gone for the time being, Nancy and Waldorf spent a good deal of time at Cliveden. The house was one of the favorite haunts of the egregious Prince of Wales, the future Edward VIII, and he and Nancy became firm friends. One of the things she liked about him, she said, was his modern democratic outlook; since he was one of the most reactionary men alive this was an anomalous response. Surely she was wrong to rate the father, George V, more old-fashioned than the son. She thought it wonderful and generous of the Prince to make personal sacrifices in order to perform public duties— which he rarely did—perhaps because he complained so much about having to do so little. He was after all doing his job, though inconsistently and resentfully; he did only what he was required to do—no more, and often a good deal less—and he did it reluctantly and with an ill grace while enthusiastically taking advantage in every way he could of his unique position. He hated being deprived even for an hour of his private pleasures. No matter what this may have augured for the future, Nancy Astor thought he would make a wonderful king. Of course she knew nothing about him. She saw his gallantry to herself, but not his selfishness and his frivolity and his loathsome politics.

It was in 1927 that Lady Astor shouted "Rats!" while listening to what she rated a poor speech in the House of Commons. George Bernard Shaw, who despised the House of Commons as a matter of principle, read an account of her interruption and was amused. He arranged to meet Nancy Astor. It looked like an impossible friendship: the brilliant seventy-one-year-old socialist playwright, born an Irishman, seemed to have nothing in common with the quarter-educated forty-eight-year-old Tory socialite viscountess, born an American. They hit it off immediately, largely because they shared an hilarious irreverence. At their first meeting Shaw was asked if he really believed what he was saying about something, and Nancy interrupted: "Of course you don't believe a single thing." Shaw was charmed. They both enjoyed these bantering conversations. She got him to visit some working-class nursery schools with her; he took the occasion to ask a group of five-year-olds if they had read any of his plays. "No," they said. "I am glad to hear it," replied George Bernard Shaw. He was fond of pretending that he knew the Astors were Communists.

Nancy Astor and Bernard Shaw remained friends for twenty years, largely through a shared sense of fun, a taste for witty conversation, and the streak of puritanism they shared. He gave her presentation copies of his plays, which she did not read; indeed, she really had no idea what he thought about anything: she simply enjoyed his company. She knew he was a Russophile. An ardent Russophobe, she offered publicly to pay the expenses of any family stupid enough to wish to spend two years living in the Soviet Union. To Shaw's delight, a man took her up on this offer and returned two years later to say how much he loved it. Shaw wrote *The Apple Cart* at Cliveden in 1928-29 and read out passages of it in the evening, changing his tone and expression to suit the various characters. Invited for three days, like the man who came to dinner he stayed for three weeks, along with his wife, insisting at every meal that he be seated on the right hand of his hostess. On Boxing Day 1928 he dressed up as Santa Claus at a party for the Cliveden staff and their children. Twenty-two years later, when Shaw lay dying, Nancy Astor was the only one he would allow to cheer him up. Through Shaw the Astors met T. E. Lawrence, who often visited them in Plymouth on his motorcycle. Nancy was taken for several excursions on this famous and ultimately fatal machine—an invitation extended to very few and probably to no other woman. They managed to cycle without touching each other; their last ride together occurred just two weeks before his death, which happened to occur on Nancy's fifty-sixth birthday. Lawrence was buried obscurely without military honors; among the tiny group of mourners at his funeral were Lady Astor, Augustus John, and Winston Churchill, who wept. But that was later. Now the Viscountess explained to Lawrence that anyone thought "bad" was not asked to meet the Astors: the "guilty" party in a divorce, for example, or anyone leading a "sinful" life, if known to the mistress of Cliveden. (H. G. Wells was a spectacular example.)

More guests came. Kavaler describes Gandhi turning his spinning wheel on the floor of the Cliveden drawing-room. At their first meeting Lady Astor harangued Gandhi about the so-called destructiveness of his policy in India. He gave her his attention for a while and then asked her whether she would prefer to listen to him or go on talking. He quickly won her sympathy for the national movement in India—a widespread sympathy thought by many politicians, including Churchill, to be treasonous. Gandhi left telling his secretary that Lady Astor loved humanity and was therefore a friend. She thought he was a great figure and called him "the wild man of God."

Nancy would on occasion attend her younger children's lessons, sometimes interrupting in her assumed negro dialect to say things like, "Me and Mistah Jesus, we gonna help yew." She would visit her elder sons at Eton, delighting to stop any boy of any age and asking him in a tone of intense seriousness if he had brushed his teeth that day. In the autumn of 1926 she took her three eldest children to America for a brief sojourn. She also visited Palestine and managed to come and go without committing any indiscretions.

Their children, in the late 1920s, gave the Astors' faith in Christian Science a severe testing. When William Astor fell seriously ill at Oxford during the winter of 1927-28, the Astors and the university authorities got into a nasty fight over the question of whether the future viscount ought to have medical attention. The question was finally left to William to resolve, and he immediately summoned a physician. The incident impelled H.A.L. Fisher, then Warden of New College, to write his famous refutation of Mary Baker Eddy. Entitled *Our New Religion,* and an astonishingly effective piece of sustained destructive criticism, Fisher argued eloquently that Eddy was a colossal fraud and that her embrace of Christian Science, as Christopher Sykes puts it, contained a mixture of megalomania, self-delusion, and conscious hoax. The following year saw the Astors' daughter Phyllis badly injured in a riding accident. Again the parents wished to do nothing but pray, but this time the pressure put on them by friends, and the threat of permanent disablement or even death, induced the Astors to allow proper medical attention to be given, and a complete recovery was the result. Nancy claimed ever afterward, inaccurately, that her daughter had not been attended by a doctor.

Meanwhile the Prime Minister, Stanley Baldwin, lethargic, lazy, and reactionary, had managed to make the electorate impatient with his large Conservative majority, which faithfully reflected its leader by doing nothing. Confident he was popular, thinking he had the support of women after the Franchise Act of 1928 finally gave them the vote at twenty-one instead of thirty, and as usual deluded about everything, Baldwin called a general election for May 1929. Typically, his slogan for this election was "Safety First." And so for the fifth time Nancy Astor went before the electors of Plymouth. She was now fifty, and had sat in Parliament for ten years.

This time around she had both Labour and Liberal opponents. The contest was a fierce and divisive one, as indeed it was around the country. As always, Baldwin had misjudged the electorate. The strikes of the 1920s had alienated many working-class voters from the Conservative government, aptly characterized by Lloyd George as "torpid, sleepy, barren." The campaign in Plymouth started with a bang when the Labour candidate was serenaded with "The Red Flag," Lady Astor with "God Save the King," and the member for Plymouth knocked off the hat of the Labour candidate's manager, who had kept it on during the national anthem.

One little-known fact about Nancy's fifth race is that she took a few days off from it in order to stump for her friend the member for Stockton, Harold Macmillan. She followed the Duchess of Devonshire to the platform. "I admire a man who is courageous enough to let his mother-in-law speak for him," Lady Astor declared.

Unlike many Conservatives in the 1929 election, Nancy had a fighting chance to keep her seat because she was seen, rightly or wrongly, as sitting on the left wing of the Conservative party, and she had supported a number of progressive measures. Indeed, at times she seemed to be running against the smug and inert leadership of her own party, which was good strategy. "Every single thing I told the Conservative die-hards that they were wrong in not doing, the party has done since," she declared. She enjoyed playing the role of a maverick, and it may have saved her seat. The Labour candidate, seeing some American warships come into Plymouth harbor, speculated wistfully that perhaps they had come to take the member home.

The Viscountess sniffed the air and knew she would have to perform audaciously if she were to come through again, and this she proceeded to do. Three days before the poll, taking some reporters with her, she invaded the poorest neighborhood of Plymouth, where communist sympathies were said to be strongest. She managed to draw a crowd; and then, squarely planting her feet, a large umbrella clasped by the ferrule in one hand, like a club, and her smart hat at a rakish angle, she addressed it.

"So you are a pack of Bolshies, eh?" She waved the umbrella at them menacingly. Voices in the crowd warned her to go away. "Don't you think mothers ought to stay home with their children?" someone shouted. "I think children ought to stay at home with their mothers," came the reply. She asked them if they thought her too proud to represent them. At this point, providentially for her political career, a small dog started running through the crowd; bricks were tossed at it for amusement. Like an avenging angel with her umbrella, Lady Astor jumped down to the sidewalk, picked up the dog, and then addressed her audience.

"Twenty years you have known me," she said, referring to the earlier days when her husband was the member for Plymouth. "And this man [the Labour candidate] is brought against me. Who and what is he? He has only just come, and we do not even know what he looks like. I tell you . . . this is the beginning of the revolution. They are out to smash the British government. Believe me, don't believe . . . idiots who come round touting false promises." There was a pause. Then came the familiar shout: "Good old Nancy!"

Her majority in this election was sliced to a razor-thin 211 votes over the Labour candidate. Had there been no Liberal in the race, Lady Astor would have been defeated. It was the nearest she ever came to losing her seat. In the country Labour out-polled the Conservatives, and again with the support of the Liberals Ramsey MacDonald formed the next government. The Tories lost 154 seats; so much for Baldwin's reading of the country's mood. In addition to Nancy, thirteen women were elected to Parliament. It was now, in 1929, that Margaret Bondfield became the first woman to sit in a

Cabinet: MacDonald made her Minister of Labour. And so George V became the first British monarch to have his hand kissed by a female Cabinet minister—an event that, he said, pleased him greatly.

Encouraged and stiffened by Bernard Shaw, whose ideological effect on her has never been properly measured, though it lasted from the mid-1920s to the mid-1930s (no longer), Nancy Astor in the new Parliament, though again in opposition, continued to campaign on behalf of some favorite causes: the women police and widows' pensions, penal reform, the plight of women prisoners. She also made herself an expert on nursery schools and the status of babies born in prison. Also at this time she and Waldorf gave a large resident dormitory for students to University College Exeter, now the University of Exeter.

In April 1930 the socialist Harold Laski published a long essay in the *Daily Herald.* Called "Lady Astor," it argued contemptuously that millionaire reformers could not be taken seriously. According to Laski, Nancy knew nothing and did nothing. He went on to argue that any compromise with capitalism in light of the economic depression exported from America to Europe would be suicidal. Lady Astor's response was to add some new causes to her list. She worked for more humane slaughtering of animals, for preventing boys under sixteen from working in mines, and against the death penalty. But for the next few years the member for Plymouth would not be so prominently featured in the news of the day. Capitalism was now in disrepute, and the Astors were notable capitalists. Favorite issues of hers such as women's rights, temperance, and public health ceased to interest those in the grip of the Depression, which temporarily put an end to at least some political partisanship. After the repeal of Prohibition in America the House of Commons heard Nancy on the iniquities of liquor with less and less patience. As usual, she never knew when to stop talking.

Nancy's son Bobby Shaw, now thirty, a handsome, witty man, a skilled horseman who had fought bravely in the Great War, had always been a rebel. The more Nancy talked to him about teetotalism, the more he drank; it was rumored that he ran his own private "speakeasy" in his rooms on the top floor of Cliveden. His father having died in 1930, he spent more and more time with his mother. Now he was a senior subaltern in the Royal Horse Guards. Found drunk on duty one night, he was asked to leave the Guards, and he did so. This scandal was quickly followed by another: arrest for "homosexual activity," and imprisonment for four months. Nothing had changed in Britain since the days of Oscar Wilde. What actually happened was never clear. The Astors with their wide connections, especially in the British press (they still owned the *Observer* and *The Times,* which was now edited by Waldorf's brother John Jacob), managed to keep the incident unpublicized; only their circle knew about it. Certainly Waldorf and Nancy were better at containing publicity than helping Bobby Shaw; they kept his name out of the papers but were advised by "friends" to do nothing to keep

Bobby out of jail, as it would undoubtedly "do him good." And so they did nothing. It was embarrassing that the great champion of temperance could not keep her eldest son sober; such bad publicity should be avoided at all costs. The Astors' great influence was thus used to obtain press silence rather than the release from jail, on a ludicrous charge, of Nancy's son. She continued to speak serenely about the virtues of Prohibition. In the course of one speech in the Commons around this time she reminded her colleagues of the many great fortunes made out of the sale of stimulants—so many indeed that the peerage, declared the Viscountess, might well be renamed the beerage. She was called to order by the Speaker: "The noble lady must not say anything disrespectful of the other House [laughter]." But nothing could stop her talking in public about drink, not even the spectacle of her eldest son being cashiered out of the Royal Horse Guards for being drunk on duty.

VI

In March 1931 Waldorf and Nancy Astor celebrated their silver wedding anniversary at Cliveden. It was shortly after this that Bernard Shaw was invited to visit the Soviet Union for nine days, and asked his hosts if he could bring the Astors along. David Astor and three others were also to come. It never occurred to the Soviets that Shaw would be bringing with him the kind of capitalist aristocrats the Stalin regime had been murdering. Because Shaw was a socialist they thought him sympathetic to the Soviet government; they knew nothing of Lady Astor's politics. But Shaw's plays were widely read, attended, and admired in the Soviet Union, and this was enough to secure him the invitation.

So in July 1931 the unlikely party traveled by train to Berlin and from there to Warsaw and Moscow. On the same train was Maxim Litvinov, the Foreign Minister. "Now tell me honestly," said Lady Astor to Litvinov, "wouldn't you rather not have had a revolution at all?" The reply, if any, is lost to history. On they went. Lady Astor's first view of the Soviet Union included the sight of barefoot women with shovels working on the rail line: forced labor in fact.

At Moscow Shaw was the great hero. For once, no one paid any attention to the Astors—until the elevator got stuck in the Metropole Hotel and the member for Plymouth had to be dragged out of it through an aperture. Meanwhile Shaw was telling the press that he had been a socialist before Lenin was born.

They were taken sightseeing in Moscow. What remained of the crown jewels (the rest had been sold) did not impress Nancy, who was heard to say that she had more jewelry than the late Tsarina. They saw prisons and factories and collective farms. Then on to Leningrad; here they stayed at the Astoria Hotel, where the elevators did not break down. They saw the Winter

Palace and the Hermitage. Shaw's account of what may be the world's greatest collection of paintings is astonishing: "We marched past acres of pictures but they all looked alike to me." They were taken to see workers' holiday homes; a school for sick children; the Peterhof, Peter the Great's rococo palace; the divorce courts and the marriage registry; and a convent.

The party returned to Moscow on 26 July, Shaw's seventy-fifth birthday, where in his honor the Soviets, knowing that all Englishmen were passionate sportsmen and loved horses, laid on a day at the races. Declaring he was the only Irishman who had never been to a horse race, Shaw got bored and fell asleep during the Bernard Shaw Handicap, while the member for Plymouth fanned the flies away from him. Shaw and Nancy were taken to see Lenin's widow, but no account of this meeting survives. Shaw, being photographed on top of a giant Tsarist cannonball, told reporters: "I think the Russian government had better have a five-year aesthetic plan."

It was now, at the end of their visit, that Stalin decided he wanted to meet Shaw and invited him to the Kremlin. The playwright asked if he could bring along his traveling companions, and permission was given so long as whatever was said at this meeting remained private. Fat chance. And so Nancy Witcher Langhorne Shaw Astor was invited to meet Stalin. Navigating the maze-like corridors of power in the Kremlin, she said later, felt like going into a prison. The group was ushered into the presence and found before them a man neatly dressed in uniform and long boots. He shook hands with each of them. The interview took place at a round table in Stalin's study and went on for two and half hours. Litvinov and an interpreter were also present. "He has a clear rather kindly eye," Waldorf wrote of Stalin afterward, and "is a man of very few words . . . He seemed shrewd rather than big mentally. He had quite a sense of humor and knew how to parry questions he did not wish to deal with." Waldorf also described Stalin as quick and lucid. Nancy, meanwhile, startled everybody by summoning up her endless capacity for tactlessness and asking Stalin why he had slaughtered so many people. The interpreter refused to translate the question; Stalin demanded to know what she'd asked him. The others no doubt had pleasant dreams of Siberia while this was going on. When it came, Stalin's answer was polite and evasive. The conversation turned to British politics, with Stalin asking the questions. He was especially interested in Churchill; he wished to know if Churchill would be given any job when the Conservatives got back into power. They all assured him, correctly, that Churchill would not. Stalin asked why Churchill was so anti-Soviet. Shaw said Churchill just had a bee in his bonnet and was hopelessly old-fashioned. This did not satisfy the dictator, who had a high opinion of Churchill's abilities, having seen him perform during the war as First Sea Lord and Minister for War, but who also distrusted him, largely because while in office Churchill had done everything he could to support the White Russians against the Bolsheviks. (Interestingly enough, a few years later Hitler would make similar inquiries of British visitors about Churchill; both dictators instinctively sensed in him an implacable foe.) At any rate, Lady Astor now displayed her talents as a political pundit by informing Stalin that Churchill, then fifty-seven, was a spent force, that he might never win back a seat in Parliament, and that he would certainly never be prime minister. (Churchill was to regain a parliamentary seat in the next general election and begin his political comeback.) Nancy was fond of saying that "Shaw knew nothing whatever about politics"; the same with equal justice might be said of her. She did get one thing right. "Chamberlain," she said, referring to Neville, not Austen, "is the coming man." And Churchill, persisted Stalin—was this really the end of him? "*Churchill?*" said the Viscountess, and now she gave a scornful little laugh. "Oh, he's *finished.*" She went on to touch upon some of her favorite subjects, including child care and welfare, telling Stalin that Soviet children were too drilled, too supervised, too regimented. Stalin's reply was that if a Soviet parent beat a Soviet child, as children in Britain were routinely beaten, the Soviet child could sue the parent in court.

When they returned to the Metropole of course they had to honor their promise not to speak to the press, at least for now; Shaw told waiting reporters that Stalin had big black moustaches. Once out of Russia he declared the Soviets wonderful and the rest of Europe far behind them, and he added: "I am a confirmed Communist." He predicted that capitalism was doomed, encouraged all young men to migrate to the Soviet Union, and characterized Stalin as a giant and all the Western leaders pygmies by comparison. How much of this he believed and to what extent he was engaging in his favorite pursuit of taunting the English with irony may be open to question. Nancy and Waldorf issued no public statement upon their return, but she told friends she found Russia "wonderful and remarkable." Bobby, meanwhile, was still in jail.

A brief political storm now broke out. Lady Astor was attacked roundly and eloquently by none other than Churchill himself in the *Sunday Pictorial.* Churchill's chief complaint, echoing and focusing the complaints of other Conservatives, was that Nancy had not contradicted Bernard Shaw's account of the Soviet Union and the Soviets, and because she had not done so—had, in fact, said nothing at all—it was reasonable to assume that she too had become a disciple of Stalin and his system. (Waldorf had advised her to say nothing in public about the Soviet Union, no matter how provoked.) Could the member for Plymouth remain a Conservative?, Churchill asked. And he said this:

> She successfully exploits the best of both worlds. She reigns in the Old World and the New, and on both sides of the Atlantic, at once as a leader of smart fashionable society and of advanced feminist democracy. She combines a kindly heart with a sharp and wagging tongue. She embodies the historical portent of the first woman member of the

House of Commons. She applauds the policies of the Government from the benches of the Opposition. She denounces the vice of gambling and keeps an almost unrivalled racing stable. She accepts Communist hospitality and flattery, and remains the Conservative member for Plymouth.

Stalin, Churchill added, had to push aside "his morning budget of death warrants" before he could receive his distinguished guests in the Kremlin. And he went on to take Lady Astor and Bernard Shaw to task for saying nothing, not a syllable, about tyranny and the lack of free speech in the Soviet Union, or such atrocities as forced labor and death camps. Churchill was genuinely shocked that no one in the Shaw party should utter a critical sound about Stalin and his gang of cutthroats, and one can hardly blame him for his indignation. The Astors and the others couldn't have seemed more satisfied if they had just returned from Brighton. Of course they had promised to say nothing about their conversation with Stalin; but as Shaw himself had shown, they could in fact say anything they liked. Lady Astor's silence did suggest to some that she agreed with everything Shaw said. But the matter was not so important, and it had little lasting political significance. As a matter of fact, in this month (August 1931) the Plymouth Conservative association passed a vote of confidence in the member for the Sutton division.

Nancy Astor fought her sixth general election campaign in October 1931. The MacDonald government had resigned over economic measures taken and not taken as the Depression deepened; MacDonald wanted to curb spending and keep the budget balanced, while most of his Labour colleagues favored more rigorous spending measures to relieve suffering. MacDonald quickly came back at the head of what was called a National Government, which included Liberals and Conservatives as well as right-wing Labourites; the election would ratify or repudiate this arrangement. Nancy now wondered if perhaps her son William should stand for the seat in her place; she felt stale, and she knew that some unpopularity clung to her as a result of the Soviet fiasco. She was fifty-two and not quite as energetic as when she had first stood in 1919; and now there were plenty of women in Parliament—fifteen, to be exact—and she had nothing to prove.

Had she retired from Parliament in 1931 her posthumous reputation, prodigious and unstained, would have been the better for it. But instead she made one of the worst decisions of her life and decided to stand again, with results that would soon be catastrophic and indelible. For in just a few years her name would be associated with one of the most repellent, unsavory, and traitorous movements in the history of British politics.

She ran. In the beginning, she said later, "I was not feeling my usual lively self," but she perked up as the campaign swung into full gear. This time she faced only a Labour candidate—the Liberals having gone more or less out of business—who wound up carrying 78 percent of the Labour vote. But this was not nearly enough, and Lady Astor won a resounding victory. She increased her majority to over 10,000, the largest she ever had. Nationally, MacDonald's coalition romped home with an enormous vote, the Conservatives becoming its senior partner by regaining a huge number of seats in the Commons. Meanwhile, the Communist party of Great Britain, which in 1929 had just 3,200 registered members, had increased that number fivefold by 1931. In two by-elections in 1932 the party won, respectively, 32 percent and 34 percent of the constituency vote.

And so Lady Astor went back to the Commons in 1932, this time with a black eye, the result of a golfing accident. The M.P.s cheered. "My word, Nancy," said one of her nearby parliamentary colleagues, "what must the other bloke be like!" The other bloke was the Prince of Wales, whose caddie had made a mistake with a golf club.

One of the thorniest items of business during the 1932 sitting was the status of India. The MacDonald government wished to promote India to dominion status. Nancy, with her admiration for Gandhi, supported the government, further souring her relations with Churchill, an ardent opponent of Indian devolution and defender of the Empire.

The member for Plymouth and her husband visited America again late in 1932. Shortly after they returned to England—on 30 January 1933, to be exact—Adolf Hitler became the German Chancellor.

VII

Ten days later, on 9 February 1933, the Oxford Union passed, by a vote of 275 to 153, the following resolution: "That this House will in no circumstances fight for King and Country." What was striking, of course, was the phrase "in no circumstances." Not long afterward the Cambridge Union voted 213 to 138 for "uncompromising" pacifism. Churchill characterized these resolutions, masquerading as an expression of war weariness, as "abject, squalid, shameless, disquieting, and disgusting." In a by-election in October 1933 in East Fulham (London), a Conservative majority of 14,000 was dissolved by an unknown Labour candidate who, as William Manchester has described it in *The Last Lion,* promised the voters he would "close every recruiting station, disband the Army and disarm the Air Force," and who demanded that England "give the lead to the whole world by initiating immediately a policy of general disarmament." Labour won the election by 5,000 votes, a swing of 26 percent. When their pay was reduced from four shillings a day to three, Manchester reminds us, sailors from the Royal Navy mutinied: 13,000 of them, stationed in Scotland, defied their officers, sang "The Red Flag," and elected representatives to their own "soviet."

Their pay was restored. The *Observer*, still owned and conducted by the
Astors, said editorially that Eastern Europe should be reconstituted under
German leadership. Sir John Simon, an Asquithian Liberal and quite possi-
bly the worst foreign minister in English history—he served in that capacity
from 1931 to 1935—described Hitler to George V as "an Austrian Joan of
Arc with a moustache."

So it would be unfair to blame Nancy Astor or the "Cliveden Set," as it
came to be called, for thoughts held by many and policies pursued by several British governments. It is nonetheless true, however, that the thoughts
were discreditable and the governments not merely naive but, in some
instances, traitorous. And it is also a fact that because she chose to associate
herself with the most reactionary, cynical, dishonest, disloyal, and treacherous politicians of the day, possibly of any day, whatever their party—
though almost all of them were Tories—Nancy Astor is remembered now
not for her accomplishments, which in some areas were substantial, but
rather for the most glaring public debacle of her career. She was not just an
ardent appeaser; she and her circle became the arch-appeasers of the
moment and among the very last people on earth to tumble to the truth of
Hitler's aims and Churchill's warnings. The only other possibility is worse:
that she and her set understood Hitler very well from the start and only pretended not to.

In her defense, if one wanted to defend her, it might be said that she never
was cut out for politics at the highest level, that she was altogether too ignorant. But this is the field on which she chose to play; and the fact is that,
throughout the rest of the 1930s, she approved of every measure introduced
into Parliament, no matter how cowardly, craven, or treasonous, which
might prevent or postpone war and preparation for war; and she became
one of the country's staunchest and most persistent defenders of Hitler and
Mussolini. Lucy Kavaler makes this distinction: Nancy Astor, she says,
never saw the dictators for what they were, never read them until it was too
late; whereas Stanley Baldwin, Neville Chamberlain (who succeeded Baldwin as prime minister in 1937), Sir John Simon and his successor Lord Halifax, and others in the government (Sir Samuel Hoare comes to mind) did see
the dictators for what they were but acted as if they didn't, refusing to do or
say anything that might disturb or awaken the electorate. They embraced
disarmament to preserve their majority and lied to their constituents about
the true facts of Germany's growing power. Baldwin actually said that winning elections was more important than telling the truth or doing what was
right, especially if by doing so you risked your hold on office. That is why it
may be fair and fitting to characterize Baldwin, Chamberlain, Halifax,
Simon, and Hoare, and perhaps others who said and did what they did, as
traitors, but to withhold that characterization from Nancy Astor, who acted
out of ignorance and intolerance and prejudice rather than hope for personal,
political gain. That she probably never did—and so Kavaler's distinction

4.2 Lord and Lady Astor in 1935; by permission of the National Portrait Gallery.

may be plausible, though difficult to prove. Cliveden eventually became synonymous with appeasement and pro-Nazi sentiment (like Darlington Hall in *The Remains of the Day*), and it is a nice question, and perhaps finally an irrelevant one, as to whether the Astors were naive or actually disloyal. Certainly they provided hospitality, privacy, and a sympathetic setting for British politicians who were undoubtedly conspiring to betray Britain, whether the Astors understood this or not. In other words, they gave tangible aid and comfort to one of the true enemies of Britain in the 1930s: its own government.

And certain other facts should be remembered. As late as 1947 (as we shall see) Lady Astor was spouting pro-Nazi sentiments. Earlier—very early indeed, just a month after Hitler came to power—she signed a letter urging disarmament in the air. She saw the Italian rape of Ethiopia as the subjugation of a negro state by a white one; a daughter of the Confederacy, she approved on the whole. Her dislike of Jews, Catholics, and other minorities could be traced back to her upbringing in the American South, and it was reemphasized by the fanatical Protestantism induced in her chiefly by the works of Mary Baker Eddy. The Viscountess could find nothing to dislike in the Nazis; the imprisonment, torture, and murder of the socially unacceptable of the day left her undisturbed. As Kavaler has pointed out, the member for Plymouth reserved her real repugnance for the French: to her they embodied license, the sort of license she especially disliked, in their comparatively uncomplicated and uninhibited sexual behavior, their love of drinking, and their Catholicism. Her politics in this period were ludicrously shallow and superficial—and worse. From 1933 on almost all of the statements made by Nancy Astor about international policy read like products of the Nazi propaganda machine. The few contributions she made in the House on other issues during these years were often astonishingly inept. In 1934, for example, she told the Commons that brewers routinely bribed members and ministers to back their interests. Asked to produce evidence, she broke down. Indeed, as time went on she found that some of her colleagues in the Commons no longer paid any attention to her when she rose to speak but rather sauntered out of the chamber until she was finished, treatment reserved for parliamentary bores and fools.

So it is no accident that among the most frequent visitors to Cliveden in the mid- and late 1930s were four of the dictators' Conservative apologists, the appeasers Chamberlain, Halifax, Simon, and Hoare. Along with the Astors and others who joined the parties, this group became known as the Cliveden Set, a term of opprobrium to this day so much were they hated. Other habitual visitors in these years included Sir Oswald Mosley, leader of the British fascists, and Hitler's ambassador to Britain (and later Foreign Minister) Joachim von Ribbentrop, who always said he felt very much at home at Cliveden, as no doubt he did. Lady Astor did refuse to return the Nazi salute from von Ribbentrop. However, up to the beginning of the war she thought Hitler's demands were reasonable, and said so. The Astors' two newspapers, the *Observer* and *The Times* (edited by Geofferey Dawson, a sometimes member of the Cliveden Set), both took a consistently pro-fascist line. As Kavaler has noted, the pro-German propaganda in these two newspapers was much more effective than anything Joseph Goebbels and the Ministry of Propaganda in Berlin were able to produce. Other British newspapers of the day were fond of pointing this out.

So the phrase "Cliveden Set" was coined to describe those in and out of the government who were plotting the victory not of Britain but of appeasement and who formulated the pro-German policies followed by the British government until the outbreak of war, when Churchill's recall to power became inevitable. As is well known, for years his had been a voice in the wilderness. He understood the maniacal ambition of Hitler, and he understood that only strength, not words, could thwart it.

As we have seen, Nancy Astor up to now had been a progressive Conservative; there is nothing in her life to this point, except perhaps her roots, to prepare us for what, in her mid-fifties, she unfortunately became. It is easy to suggest that she might have been misled by others. But she was a mature woman, apparently well informed, a six-term M.P., and nobody's fool. Her family owned and ran newspapers; she had access to more information than most Britons. She should have known better, and she cannot escape blame. In giving the Cliveden Set a place to meet and talk and plan she did positive harm to her adopted country and to the country of her birth, in both of which she was denounced with good cause. Whether the Astors actually were pro-Nazi is hardly the point; they appeared to be pro-Nazi, and this cannot be forgiven. It is unlikely that, as some charged then and later, the Cliveden Set actually hatched conspiracies to deliver England into the hands of the Germans. But for a time in some quarters Nancy Astor was thought of and written about as a traitor, and deservedly so. Christopher Sykes, writing in 1972, parades a peculiar delusion before his readers when he declares in his life of Lady Astor that "The stand she took on most questions of the time is such as is easily approved today."

In June 1935 Ramsey MacDonald resigned his leadership of the National Government in favor of the senior partner, Baldwin, who called a general election that autumn. The major issue was the question of pacifism versus rearmament, the very question the unions of Oxford and of Cambridge had debated two years before. Each side, pacifists and disarmers, argued vehemently that it was the most committed to peace. No one advocated any measure that might have given the fascist dictators pause. Now in her seventh campaign at Plymouth, the Viscountess toed the Baldwin line, promising "There will be no great armaments." Her Labour opponent reduced her majority to a little over 6,000, but she was in again; her political folly and that of her friends would not be obvious until the war began. Nancy could not have known that the general election of November 1935 was to be her

last campaign; and of course she could not have known the associated fact
that a large part of her constituency a few years hence would wonder if she
was a traitor. The Conservatives came back with a reduced but substantial
majority. Ramsey MacDonald lost his seat, and Clement Atlee took over
leadership of the Labour party. The number of women members fell from
fifteen to nine; six of these were Conservatives. Nancy's son William carried
(barely) the infamous East Fulham constituency as the Conservative candidate. Addressing a rally for William, his mother took the opportunity to
remind the electors of East Fulham: "If you return him to Westminster, you
will be as unique as Plymouth, which returned the first woman, for he will
be the first young man in Parliament who has got his mother in the House
to look after him." He got in anyway.

One of Lady Astor's first acts after the results of the election were known
was to write to Baldwin. She said: "Don't put Winston in the Government—it will mean war at home and abroad. I know the depths of Winston's disloyalty—and you can't think how he is distrusted by *all* the
country." Which country did she mean? And disloyal to whom: his party,
or England? One cannot help wondering how a reasonably well-informed
person could write such drivel as this. And it was the Astors' loyalty that
deserved greater scrutiny, not Churchill's. Baldwin, of course, had no intention of giving Churchill any government job for the simple reason that if he
did, he would have to listen to endless talk about the necessity to rearm, and
his policy was not to rearm, not to listen, above all not to disturb the voters
by requesting money for armaments.

By 1936 Nazism had become fashionable in some circles of London's
West End society. As William Manchester reminds us, you could see ladies
wearing bracelets with swastika charms and young men combing their hair
to slant across their forehead in the manner of Hitler. Hitler had admirers in
Parliament and a very lofty one indeed on the throne, for Edward VIII had
now succeeded his father. Germanophilia in the British upper classes
refused to fade and in fact became more visible, more and more of an obsession.

In the summer of 1936 the weekly *Time and Tide* warned that dangerous
views were held by a number of upper-class Britons; Lady Astor was
named as one of them. She admired not only Hitler's politics, said the magazine, but also his personal habits: he was said to be a nondrinker and a
nonsmoker, and this was absurdly important to her. The French were too
self-indulgent, had too many bad habits, to suit her; never mind that France
was a democracy. Nancy did herself no good by publicly supporting
Hitler's Rhineland coup, wiring Baldwin that she and her friends "wholeheartedly" endorsed the Nazi action. In July of this year she told an interviewer that the backers of anti-German feeling were overplaying their
hands; "if the Jews are behind it they are going too far, and they need to take

heed," she declared. What did she have in mind: concentration camps? A few months later she admitted to a friend of her son David that she was "*prodeutsch*" because, after all, the Germans were surrounded by hostile Roman Catholic powers (such as the licentious French, who liked to drink and smoke), and thus it was only natural that they rearm. She told a correspondent in October 1937: "There is a strong right thought in Germany which should not be drowned by false propaganda."

Late in 1937 Anthony Eden resigned as Foreign Secretary; he could not reconcile his views with those of the pacifist Chamberlain. Eden was replaced by the arch-appeaser Halifax, much to Waldorf Astor's satisfaction. "Anthony's manner always gets Hitler and Musso on the raw," he wrote to Nancy, as if this were a capital crime. "It's no good lecturing people or talking down to them if you want to improve relations or avoid a war." Waldorf desired a foreign secretary who would crawl instead of lecture, and he got one in the unctuous, oleaginous Halifax. One wonders to what extent Nancy's views were an extension of her husband's—and vice versa. At any rate outside of Cliveden, indeed outside of the ruling classes, more and more people were starting to see that Hitler needed managing, and not by words alone. Churchill was finally beginning to bring home to the English the growing danger.

In November 1937 the journalist Claud Cockburn wrote in the left-wing journal *The Week* that Britain had in its midst a group, the "Cliveden Set," whose purpose it was to thwart Churchill and indeed the entire country and make rearmament impossible. Cockburn charged that the Astors and their newspapers were fomenting pro-Nazi intrigues at the highest levels of the British government. Their chief goals, he said, were to prevent England from going to war under any circumstances and to leave the great protestant power Germany unmolested at any cost. Sir Neville Henderson, Britain's pro-Nazi ambassador in Berlin, and Geoffrey Dawson, the pro-Nazi editor of *The Times,* had joined the others at a recent Cliveden conclave, said Cockburn, and all were of the same mind. Cockburn painted Chamberlain as the archfiend and the others as his loyal supporters. The ultimate goal of the group, he said, was to oversee the destruction and disappearance of socialism from the face of the earth. In the meantime, Cockburn concluded, the British government had promised Hitler that he would not be interfered with, that he had a free hand.

There was enough truth in all of this, and enough public interest in the piece, for the story to be carried and amplified rather than dropped. Other articles now appeared in the press. The members of the Cliveden Set, it was said, were friends of the Third Reich and constituted Britain's "other" Foreign Office. The Astors were denounced by Labour in 1938 as trying to force a pro-Hitler policy down the country's throat. The Astors, it was also said, had financial reasons for supporting the Axis. After all, they were the true leaders of the Cliveden Set; and the Cliveden Set, as all the world knew, gave the government its orders as well as its hospitality. Some people, perhaps a great many, now believed that Cliveden was at the center of a conspiracy—even so intelligent and well-informed a person as Sir Harold Nicolson, the future biographer of George V, who described Lady Astor as fighting "bravely for Hitler and Mussolini." And so when Hitler gobbled up Austria—and, later, Czechoslovakia—the Astors were denounced as "traitors in our midst" by large sections of the press (excluding, of course, *The Times* and the *Observer*). In Parliament the member for Plymouth was accused to her face of being a friend of the Nazis and wishing to turn Britain into a fascist state. The Astors were called *les Cagoulards,* the hooded ones, the name by which French fascists were known in France; and *The Times* in some quarters was called the *Clivedener Neueste Nachrichten.* News cameramen patrolled St. James's Square to photograph those going in and out of number 4.

For several years Nancy and her family lived in a glass bowl, and the publicity was unpleasant and hurtful. She was said to favor any sort of peace at any sort of price. The idea of a fascist clique at Cliveden was given additional buoyancy by the fact that there were now seven members of the Astor family, including several by marriage, in Parliament —five in the Commons and two in the Lords. Once only during this period was Nancy able to generate some favorable news about herself. U.S. Supreme Court Justice Felix Frankfurter had an aged uncle living in Vienna who, along with thousands of other Jews, was rounded up and interned after the Nazi *Anschluss.* Frankfurter asked Lady Astor to do what she could. Nancy got hold of von Ribbentrop and threatened to go to Vienna herself if Frankfurter's uncle wasn't released. Three days later he was freed. Such evidence of her influence with the Nazis is suggestive, to say the least; why didn't she use it more often? But the member for Plymouth was her own worst enemy. She still had not learned when to stop talking. Instead of saying clearly that she abhorred the Nazis she made mealy-mouthed statements in the United States in 1938, telling her audiences only that she was not a friend of Hitler and that she hoped a meeting of minds with him, a "settlement," was still possible. But she was an admirer of Hitler, and that's why she didn't denounce him. In the autumn of this year the Astors thought they had the settlement they wanted in the assurance of "peace in our time" brought back by Chamberlain from Munich. The famous piece of paper, they said publicly, was a justification and a vindication of all they stood for. It turned out to be a fatal admission. In the House of Commons Churchill denounced Munich as a sellout. He was constantly interrupted by shouts of "Nonsense!" from Lady Astor, who felt that anyone who opposed her beloved Chamberlain now, at his finest hour, was guilty of treason. Churchill resumed: "The noble lady cries 'Nonsense.' The terms which the Prime

Minister has been able to secure by all his immense exertions and by all the anguish and strain through which we have passed, the terms which he has gained . . . have been that the German dictator instead of snatching the victuals from the table has been content to have them served to him course by course." Again the Viscountess interrupted: "Don't be rude about the Prime Minister." Now she was in far over her head. The sixty-four-year-old Churchill turned to her and snapped: "No doubt Lady Astor has been receiving very recently a finishing course in manners." The Labour benches shouted that the finishing course had been given by von Ribbentrop.

Thus was Nancy Astor's esteem in the House of Commons reduced to zero by 1938, nineteen years after she had first entered it to world acclaim. Her political downfall came about as a result of reactionary politics, ignorance, intolerance, racism, and prejudice. Her behavior was unforgivable, and it was to put an end to her political career as well as those of her friends in government. Her popularity in America was also extinguished. In some ways she was the same sort of political ignoramus as Charles A. Lindbergh. Undoubtedly she believed the idiotic things she said, at least until the war began. The great irony was that, as Shaw said of Lady Astor in 1939, "She has no political philosophy." Even when it had become certain that war was inevitable she wrote in a published article that she had no regrets about trying "to the uttermost for peace." Peace at any price? Yes, she answered herself, for even now (1939) war might be avoided or postponed. And she claimed that Chamberlain had appeased Hitler in order to gain time for Britain to rearm. This was a spectacular lie; Chamberlain's goal was not to go to war but to keep Hitler from going to war so that Britain would not have to fight—a goal patently impossible and therefore ludicrous, not to mention dishonorable and cowardly. Even in 1939, before the invasion of Poland, Nancy Astor still understood nothing. Two days after Hitler marched into Prague, she rose in the House to ask whether the government would condemn the German action. A fellow Conservative shouted: "You caused it yourself!" Sir Stafford Cripps referred to her openly as "the honourable member for Berlin."

Because Nancy and her friends were so influential in the 1930s, as Maurice Collis, a writer friendly to the Astors, has observed, they must share with those directly responsible some of the blame for what happened—and for misleading the public about Hitler's ultimate aim and for supporting appeasement as a tenable policy. What little that can be said in Lady Astor's behalf is this. Once the war began she was one of the few former supporters of appeasement and disarmament who admitted publicly that she had been wrong. Her biographer Christopher Sykes, writing in 1972, may give us an idea how persistent in these matters British error and right-wing lunacy can be when he says: "The attempt to appease Hitler . . . is open to criticism and has been . . . perhaps justly condemned, but for all that it has not yet been proved to have been utterly in vain." One wonders what sort of proof Mr. Sykes requires beyond a world war, a holocaust, and millions of deaths. At least Nancy Astor finally acknowledged that appeasement was an error, and without using the word "perhaps."

One other event of these prewar years must be mentioned. During the Abdication Crisis of 1936 Lady Astor gets high marks for speaking her mind very directly indeed to her longtime golfing partner, now Edward VIII. She begged the King to give Mrs. Simpson up (as always, she and Churchill were on opposite sides). She told him plainly the objection was that the lady had been (twice) divorced, not that she was American. And she turned out to be right: for once she understood an issue perfectly. Upon George VI's ascent to the throne she was made a Companion of Honour. The universities of Birmingham and Reading gave her honorary degrees. The citizens of Plymouth showed what they thought of current political opinion touching their member and her family by electing her and Waldorf Mayoress and Mayor of the city, though it would be the last time they elected her to anything.

Nancy Astor was now sixty.

VIII

"Only I and Mr. Churchill enjoy the war," Lady Astor said, "but only I admit it." When the war began in earnest she was harshly and publicly critical of Chamberlain, and joined a group of Conservative M.P.s who combined with Labour to bring him down in the wake of a no-confidence vote (which Chamberlain narrowly won) in May 1940. And so the Viscountess played a small role in promoting to power her old nemesis Churchill, who was not "finished" after all.

Nancy and Waldorf spent the war years in Plymouth among their constituents. The area was badly and continually bombed because a major naval base was located there. Nancy threw herself into civil defense and nursing; she worked very hard. On some evenings pieces of glass sprayed by explosions had to be picked out of her hair. She and Waldorf added codicils to their wills expressing a desire to be buried together in a common grave with other casualties if they died in an air raid. (There would not have been much choice in the matter.) Lady Astor was fined £50 by a local judge when a censor came across a letter from her to a friend in the United States asking for various items unobtainable in England—nylons, gloves, shoes, dresses, even a fur jacket. This was tactless and embarrassing, to say the least. Nancy went up to London as often as she could in order to participate in parliamentary debates (she bought a motorcycle for the purpose, but Waldorf got rid of it; she went by train) and found her colleagues in an intolerant mood. On one occasion she was told in the House, to general cheering, that "the views of the noble lady have been almost invariably wrong"; no one wished to listen to her, and the newspapers for once gave her short shrift. She was associated in the public mind with Cliveden and appeasement.

Once again Cliveden was offered to the Canadians as a hospital, and the offer was gratefully accepted. Children evacuated from the larger cities also were accommodated in houses on the estate. Down in Plymouth air raids, which had commenced in July 1940, went on, with interruptions, almost to the end of the war. They slackened for a time after the Battle of Britain and the German air defeat in September 1940, but the bombing recommenced in earnest in March 1941, by which time there had already been thirty-seven raids on the coastal city. Watching Plymouth burn one night, as it did night after night for years, Nancy Astor declared: "There goes thirty years of our lives, but we'll rebuild it again." In the March raids the city center was nearly annihilated just two hours after King George VI and Queen Elizabeth had paid a visit there. The bombers returned and the *blitzkrieg* continued throughout much of the rest of the year.

Nancy and Waldorf tried to keep spirits high in Plymouth by walking through the streets at all hours and speaking cheerfully to everyone they met. The Viscountess could not bear to dress down; even on these nocturnal walks through the fires and the rubble she wore a ton of jewelry. One raid blew out all the windows in the Astors' Plymouth home. Nancy, who always slept with the windows thrown open whatever the season, was unmoved. The Plymouth house was badly damaged on several occasions, but the Astors refused to leave. They were now chiefly occupied with the plight of evacuees and the rebuilding of the city. Churchill came to look the place over and help cheer people up. Out of his hearing Nancy referred to him as "an old repertory actor." Even more was done for the morale of Plymouth when Lady Astor organized a series—they became nightly events—of dances in the center of the city, complete with band, until the light failed.

Bernard Shaw was feeling poorly—"85 and three quarters dead," as he wrote to Nancy; she found a place for him and his wife outside of London in the comparative safety of the Cliveden estate. The playwright remained there until the end of the war. "I have been reading Hitler's Mein Kampf," Shaw wrote to Lady Astor from Cliveden. "He is the greatest living Tory." When a huge package of chocolates arrived from America, addressed to the Lord Mayor of Plymouth, Waldorf ordered that the chocolates be taken out and distributed in the city. Nancy, who had a passion for chocolates, objected and lost her temper completely when Waldorf wouldn't give in to her selfish greed. A few minutes later he suffered a heart attack and possibly a mild stroke. He was flat on his back for six weeks. How this may have affected the Viscountess's passion for chocolates is not recorded.

In a radio broadcast in 1942 the member for Plymouth warned the nation and the world of the creeping danger of—Roman Catholicism. Hitler had invaded Russia, there were British troops in North Africa and the Far East, but Nancy Astor was worried about Catholic influences in the Foreign Office and the BBC. In the House she hinted at the penetration of the Foreign Office by papal agents. That such charges should be made against blameless public servants by one of the leaders of the Cliveden Set enraged M.P.s, not unnaturally. The speech was considered incompetent; now sixty-three, Nancy Astor remained a completely spent force in British politics. Nor did it help her reputation, then or later, given what was happening to the Jews in Europe, that many of her other speeches emphasized the so-called shared Christianity of the Allies. In Cheltenham, in September 1942, she was more gracious. For the first time in public, perhaps sensing the general impatience with her, she buried the Cliveden Set. "After the last war we were all striving for peace," Nancy said at Cheltenham. "The trouble was that we didn't understand Europe or the world as the admirals and generals did. I am afraid that I was one who was against those who didn't want us to disarm." Which is putting it mildly, but at least she said it. She also warned against placing too much reliance on the Soviets, who "are not fighting for us. They are fighting for themselves."

At the end of 1942 Waldorf Astor gave Cliveden to the National Trust along with a suitable endowment so that it could be maintained at his expense. It was at this time that Sir William Beveridge produced his famous report outlining the shape of the socialist state that Britain would become after the war. Typically, Lord Astor welcomed the Beveridge Report; equally typically, Lady Astor denounced it. Their children began to notice, to their astonishment, that their parents were not getting along. The wound caused by the great chocolate controversy, apparently the harbinger of more serious difficulties between them, did not heal.

The Astors lived in Plymouth until the end of the war. From 1943 Nancy billeted some American officers, one of them black, in their house there. In March, saying as usual more than was advisable, she made another moronic attack on Catholics in the Foreign Office, referring in a speech in the House to what she called its "Latin point of view" (i.e., pro-French). She did not know what she was talking about and had the misfortune to be followed by Harold Nicolson, who did, and who sent an amusing account to his sons. Lady Astor, he said, "has one of those minds that work from association to association, and therefore spreads sideways with extreme rapidity. Further and further did she diverge from the point. . . . 'Well, I come from Virginia,' said Lady Astor, 'and that reminds me, when I was in Washington. . . .' I was annoyed . . . as I knew that I was to be called after her. It was like playing squash with a dish of scrambled eggs."

Through 1943 and into 1944 the bombing raids on Plymouth continued and there remained much work for Nancy to do. She sometimes visited Cliveden, and on one occasion exhorted the American troops stationed in the neighborhood to carry the Anglo-Saxon biblical spirit to benighted

Europe, as Sykes puts it. It was a silly, ignorant sort of speech to give; she seemed to have lost the knack of making speeches as easily as she had acquired it. Equally silly, but of a piece, was her wild opposition to the marriage of her son John Jacob to the daughter of the Argentine ambassador on the grounds that, as a Latin and a Catholic, the girl was an unsuitable bride for the son of an English viscount. To his credit John Jacob paid her no attention and the marriage took place. Both Lord and Lady Astor boycotted the wedding, a ridiculous performance. They were both sixty-five now and should have known better. It was time they retired from public life.

As it turned out, retirement was exactly what the citizens of Plymouth had in mind for them. In November 1944 the city fathers decided to choose a new lord mayor from among themselves for the coming postwar period, and Waldorf was asked to step aside. An even more unwelcome fate awaited Lady Astor. A general election, put off because of the war, would be held as soon as it ended. Local Conservatives thought her a liability given her abysmal standing both within the party and in the country. Waldorf saw what she could or would not; that her prewar appeasement and her connection in everybody's mind with the discredited Cliveden Set had damaged her political reputation beyond repair. He thought she could avoid humiliation by simply withdrawing; it was unclear whether the Conservative association would even consider adopting her as a candidate. There was no hope at all of her being returned to Westminster. Waldorf also feared that if by some miracle she was re-elected, she might be laughed at or hissed in the House of Commons. Privately Nancy suggested that she be given a peerage in her own right so that she could sit with Waldorf in the House of Lords. As usual she had no idea how the political winds were blowing. Churchill, of course, vetoed the peerage. Stupidly, she then brought the matter up in public, asking Churchill to his face in April 1945 for a peerage. Waldorf grabbed her and made her stop talking. This happened just after Nancy had delivered one of the most rambling and incoherent speeches of her career. Harold Nicolson, who witnessed these back-to-back incidents, wrote in his diary: "I wish she would not make quite such an idiot of herself in public." Undoubtedly she was growing senile.

Nancy never recovered from her forced retirement. She had represented Plymouth for twenty-five years and thought she would go on doing so forever. What could she do now? She was not exactly addicted to needlepoint. "The House will lose its most historic figure," lamented *John Bull*, which some years earlier had trumpeted the facts of her American divorce. Most of the papers printed vague regrets of some sort, but she had not the standing in the country she used to have and the more usual response to her going was indifference. Borrowing the language Disraeli used about Gladstone in his seventies, the Viscountess described herself as an extinct volcano—but even this was self-flattery, for the volcanic personality that had pole-vaulted her into the House of Commons almost without warning a quarter century earlier had long since cooled and crumbled. And she was no Gladstone. What has sometimes been said of her home state of Virginia could now be said of Nancy Astor: "Not much future but oh what a past."

In a speech to a women's group Nancy went out of her way to avoid making a graceful exit. Her retirement, she declared bitterly, was "one of the hardest things I have ever done in my life, but a thing every man in the world will approve of." She was "bound to obey" her husband, who insisted that she stand down: "Isn't that a triumph for men?" Waldorf willingly took the blame for what in fact were the consequences of his wife's and his own disgraceful political conduct, telling their friends that he had asked her to stay at home with him because he was unwell. It was with great enthusiasm that she grabbed the chance to blame him; never once did she hint to anyone that any other ground existed for the decision to retire. But it was all clear enough. In the early months of 1945, as the war ground down, she let herself entertain second thoughts about standing again, but she was living in a delusion. The Plymouth Conservative association would not have her. It was she who was "finished."

The war in Europe ended in May 1945, that in Asia in August. The general election was fixed for July, and in June Lady Astor spoke several times in the House, as usual having to be called to order by the Speaker when she got off the subject. In a farewell speech to the House she said: "I don't think any other assembly in the world could have been more tolerant of a foreign-born woman, as I was, who fought against so many things they believed in"—and in favor of so many things they were against, as she might also have said. "I shall miss the House, but the House won't miss me," she told a colleague. "It never misses anybody. I have seen them all go—Lloyd George, Asquith, Baldwin, Snowden, MacDonald . . . and not one of them was missed. The House is like a sea. M.P.'s are like little ships that sail across it and disappear over the horizon. Some of them carry a light. Others don't."

As it turned out, she was well out of the general election of July 1945, a famous defeat for Churchill and the Conservatives. Labour took nearly two-thirds of the seats, and a socialist was returned for the Sutton division of Plymouth. But ever afterward Nancy blamed her political eclipse on Waldorf and his advice and refused to see the plain fact that her day had passed.

In September 1945 a document (the Black Book) written in 1940 and containing the names of over 2,300 resident Britons to be executed when the Germans invaded England was found to contain Lady Astor's name but not her husband's. Nancy claimed she could no longer be accounted a prewar friend of Germany. But at the end of the year von Ribbentrop's counsel at the Nuremburg trials requested the testimony of Lord and Lady Astor (Churchill's too) on behalf of his client. The incident passed, though some sections of the press claimed that the Astors would condemn themselves as traitors had they gone to Nuremburg.

Early in 1946 they visited the United States. "Any plans?" Nancy was asked. "I may run for Congress," she replied. She gave countless speeches, predicting accurately that the next menace in Europe would be Soviet and inaccurately that Churchill would never again be called back to the premiership. Her habit of burying him prematurely extended over many decades; now she chose to call him in public "no peace-time prime minister." Not content with this, in a New York speech she spoke scathingly of his wartime leadership. Her hearers were shocked. She was invited to meet General Eisenhower at the Pentagon, but no invitation to visit the White House came from President Truman. To black high school students in Washington she spoke with utter tactlessness, telling them how, like many Southerners, as Sykes describes it, she had learned to understand and admire the colored people through her "black mammy"; then she reminisced about a negro porter who had served her family in Virginia. She denounced the nightclubs and immorality of Harlem and asserted that "no race can develop beyond its moral character." And she urged a return to the simple faith of the "aunts" and "uncles" of the good old days in the South. The students looked at her as if she were a fossil, which is what she was.

Over the next two years she made several trips to the United States, where she still had an audience to lecture to, dwindling though it was. On one visit she addressed joint sessions of the legislatures of Virginia and of South Carolina. The American press was not as kind to her as it had been in the old days. "Like so much else of the '20s and '30s," declared the *New York Herald Tribune,* using the word Nancy had used about herself earlier, she has become "extinct." Some interest in her lingered, but she was no longer taken seriously by many people. She had been around too long and wrong too often. As much as anything else her continuing, compulsive, gratuitous, public criticism of Churchill, who was half American and revered in the United States, undermined her position in America. As usual, she did not know when to stop talking.

Back in London, Waldorf sold the house in St. James's Square to the government as a headquarters for the Arts Council. A smaller house was purchased at 35 Hill Street. Lady Astor's days as a grand hostess were over. But she was not completely extinguished. She complained bitterly about the liberal bias of the *Observer,* now edited by her son Michael. She continued to contemplate a political comeback, Waldorf continued to object, and their relations remained strained; they lived apart from one another during Waldorf's last years. In 1947 Nancy received more unwelcome publicity after making yet another series of tasteless statements, this time on Palestine. To win, she said, an American presidential candidate has to carry New York; and in order to carry New York he has to win "the Jewish and foreign vote.

There are too many people in New York that don't belong anywhere—they have no roots." The roots of some could be found in the substandard housing the Astor family was famous for building all over New York. And of course the briefest of history lessons would have enlightened her about the role of New York voters in presidential elections. She continued to see the Jews as foreigners; some sections of her speeches read like passages of *Mein Kampf*, and this was 1947. But on went the torrent. She accused the U.S. government of keeping the Jewish underground in Palestine going, and then as usual spoke one too many lines: "I don't mind how many Jews are killed in Palestine. My only interest is in the number of innocent British who are slaughtered." This was clear enough. The congressional delegation of New York urged the State Department to cancel her visa and deport her, and denounced her as "a vicious anti-Semite," which she certainly was and had been for years, and a "harridan," which is what she had turned into in old age. Now sixty-eight, she was not aging gracefully. Waldorf begged her to shut up. "Think of the historian," he wrote to her. "You cannot avoid being a historic personage and having played a historic part. The historian is now and in the future to write about you. Please do nothing—say nothing—which may mar the historian's account." Poor Waldorf; the warning came much too late and went unheeded. It is notable that in the general election of 1949, two of Lady Astor's sons stood as Conservative candidates for Parliament: her presence was requested in neither constituency. One son lost, the other won. Overall the Labour majority was reduced from over 200 seats to just a handful.

Near the end of 1950, after breaking a leg, Bernard Shaw, now ninety-five, began to fade away. He told Nancy, one of his few invited visitors, that he would like to die, "but . . . this confounded vitality won't let me." The Viscountess replied: "Yes, I know—I've got it too." On his deathbed Shaw spoke to her about the actress Ellen Ternan, who had had five husbands and two illegitimate children and was sustained throughout her life, Shaw said, by the conviction that she had never done anything she knew to be wrong. Shaw died on 2 November 1950. For Lady Astor it was perhaps the greatest of many losses she had suffered during these first five postwar years, the unhappiest years of her life since she had been Mrs. Robert Gould Shaw and lived in Boston.

IX

Waldorf Astor had suffered another stroke in 1950; after two years as an invalid he died in September 1952, aged seventy-three. His last words, uttered to a son, were "Look after mother." Nancy wrote to a friend: "We had 40 happy years together. No two people ever worked happier than we did—these last seven years have been heart breaking—but thank God he was like his old self for the last ten days and oh how it makes me grieve of the years wasted!" Though they had often quarreled in later years, he had been the great love of her life as well as her only companion and chief advisor. Always he had counseled moderation and caution, knowing Nancy as he did, but in his various social schemes for the protection of the disadvantaged he had rarely been cautious or moderate. Little has been written about the second Lord Astor, but until his appeasement period he was a force for good, and had been over many years—as a philanthropist, a public servant, a father, a husband. If Nancy had listened to him more often her reputation today would be much less clouded.

Lady Astor now lived in London for most of the year, first at the house in Hill Street and after that was sold at a flat (her first and only) in Eaton Square. There were occasional trips to North America and much shorter ones to the Strangers' Gallery of the House of Commons to hear her sons speak. (Two of them had been returned in the general election of 1951, which brought Churchill back to power.) Her relations with her eldest son, the third Lord Astor, were not good; thinking she had become impoverished with the death of her husband, Nancy badgered William Astor with questions about money. She continued to travel. During a trip to the United States in 1953 she suggested to Senator Joseph McCarthy that he drink poison. This represented a political advance. A few months later she was off to Rhodesia, startling the governor of Northern Rhodesia by answering his expression of welcome with the words, "Welcome to you, as one slave-owner to another!"

Throwing her old principles overboard, she now took a glass or two of Dubonnet every day and also drank eggnog; she declared both drinks to be non-alcoholic. She abandoned Christian Science and consulted doctors. In 1954-55 she joined in the effort to prevent Richard Aldington's debunking biography of her old motorcycle companion T. E. Lawrence from being published; it was published in Paris. In 1956 an official British government publication on German foreign policy revived the memory of the Cliveden Set in the public mind; the book was reviewed under such eye-catching headlines as "The Spy at Cliveden." Nancy, now seventy-seven, had no energy for another argument, and the moment passed.

By 1957 both of Nancy's sisters had died; the journey she made to the United Stated in 1958 was her last. She spent much of this year redecorating her new flat at 100 Eaton Square. In May 1959 she celebrated her eightieth birthday. "Years ago I thought that old age would be dreadful because I should not be able to do the things I want to do. Now I find there is nothing I want to do after all," she told an interviewer. She was battling depression and a fading memory. "I don't feel I have accomplished anything in life," she remarked to another interviewer. To yet another she said: "I have only one interest, really, the Bible." The city of Plymouth gave her the Freedom of the City. "They should have given it years ago and had I been a man, they would have done so," she told friends. At the public ceremony making her a

Freeman she remarked that she had always wanted to ride free on the Plymouth buses but supposed she would still have to pay. That evening at a dinner in her honor Nancy removed a long diamond necklace she was wearing and presented it to the Lord Mayoress, declaring it a gift to be worn by all future Lord Mayoresses of Plymouth in perpetuity. Not to be outdone, the Lord Mayor of Plymouth presented to the viscountess a free ticket *in perpetuum* to ride the city buses.

This perpetual bus ticket was the last public honor paid to her during her lifetime. She gave interviews to the BBC in the early 1960s, but by then her memory had all but faded out and she was more likely than ever to ramble. To help refresh her memory, Lady Astor got hold of the old visitors' book at Cliveden and grew fond of amusing guests in Eaton Square by flipping through it and characterizing the great and the famous in a tart sentence or two. She enjoyed telling a story about the Bishop of Exeter, who couldn't find his ticket at the barrier when going for his train. The ticket collector said that it didn't matter and waved him through. "It does matter," said the Bishop, still fumbling for his ticket. "It doesn't," the collector repeated. The Bishop replied at last: "It does because I don't know where I'm going." On the Henry Fords at Cliveden: "He loved dancing. . . . He wanted to send for his private orchestra from New York. When he left he gave each of the children a Ford motor car. Mrs. Ford lived very simply. She arrived at Cliveden without a maid and only six trunks." On dinner in New York with the Roosevelts and the Vanderbilts: "At table I was put ahead of Grace Vanderbilt. She was rather cross, I could see. So I said to her: 'The Astors skinned skunks a hundred years before the Vanderbilts worked ferries.'"

In 1963 William Astor got some unwelcome publicity. He had received at Cliveden on numerous occasions some of the protagonists of the Profumo scandal, and the press made a meal of it. What was not known and therefore not reported, as Alan Pryce-Jones has revealed in *The Bonus of Laughter*, is that Nancy Astor, who is usually and inaccurately portrayed as being kept in the dark about the story for weeks, had in fact taken a great fancy to Christine Keeler. She would be ravishing, the Viscountess declared, if only she were dressed up a little. One day after tea Christine was brought to Cliveden and sent upstairs to be dressed by the lady's maid, who sent her back to rejoin the party dripping in diamonds and applauded by Lady Astor. This was a matter of days before the Profumo scandal broke. And so Nancy remained at the heart of public affairs (so to speak) up to the year preceding her death. Appropriately, William Astor is at the heart of *Scandal*, a recent film version of the Profumo affair.

In March 1964 Bobby Shaw attempted suicide by taking an overdose of sleeping pills. Nancy went to see her son in the hospital and returned home shaken. On 18 April she suffered a stroke. As she lay dying she called for Waldorf; at times she would imagine she was back in Virginia. On 2 May, a few weeks before her eighty-fifth birthday, she died. She was buried next to

Waldorf at Cliveden. By her wish the casket containing her ashes was covered by a Confederate flag. Also by her direction, after her funeral all five of her sons received preselected (by her) packets of letters she had kept for the sole purpose of trying to make them feel guilty: each packet was connected to an argument or dispute the son had had with his mother in days gone by. She went out leaving a cruel and bitter legacy.

"She's all the time looking for a light she can never find," one of her longtime family retainers said of her. Nancy Astor did some good public work, especially in Plymouth during the Second World War; through ignorance, willful blindness, and irrational prejudice she also prevented herself from doing a great deal more. She had great, almost unlimited opportunities; she took advantage of some but missed many others. That the first woman to sit in the British parliament was a divorcée from Virginia is testimony to the power of her ambition and the tenaciousness of her passion for the limelight; that she did so little with the excellent cards fate dealt her is testimony to the poverty of her imagination and the shallowness of her intelligence. It is perhaps altogether fitting that she should go into eternity wrapped in a shroud symbolizing a bigoted and extinct society.

WORKS CONSULTED

CHAPTER 1

Aronson, Theo. *Prince Eddy and the Homosexual Underworld.* London: John Murray, 1994.

King George V. Diary. Unpublished: Royal Archives, Windsor.

Gore, John. *King George V: A Personal Memoir.* London: John Murray, 1941.

Judd, Denis. *The Life and Times of George V.* London: Weidenfeld and Nicolson, 1973.

MacDonald, Ramsey. MacDonald Papers, Public Record Office, London.

Nicolson, Harold. *King George V.: His Life and Reign.* London: Constable, 1952.

Pope-Hennessy, James. *Queen Mary, 1867-1953.* London: Allen and Unwin, 1959.

Rose, Kenneth. *King George V.* New York: Alfred Knopf, 1984.

Secrest, Merlye. *Kenneth Clark: A Biography.* New York: Holt, Rinehart and Winston, 1984.

Queen Victoria, *The Letters of Queen Victoria.* Edited by G. E. Buckle. Third Series, Vols. I-III, 1886-1901. London: John Murray, 1930-1932.

CHAPTER 2

Austin, Allen E. *Elizabeth Bowen.* New York: Twayne, 1971; rev. ed., 1989.

Bowen, Elizabeth. Letters to William Plomer (unpublished). University of Durham.

———. Letters to Virginia Woolf (unpublished). University of Sussex.

Brooke, Jocelyn. *Elizabeth Bowen.* London and New York: Longmans, Green, 1952.

Craig, Patricia. *Elizabeth Bowen.* Harmondsworth and New York: Penguin Books, 1986.

Devlin, Albert J. and Peggy Whitman Prenshaw. "Conversation with Eudora Welty." *Mississippi Quarterly* 39:4 (Fall 1986).

Dunleavy, Janet E. "Elizabeth Bowen," in *Dictionary of Literary Biography.* Vol. 15. Detroit: Gale Research, 1983.

Fisk, Robert. *In Time of War: Ireland, Ulster, and the Price of Neutrality.* Brandon, Ireland: André Deutsch, 1983.

Glendinning, Victoria. *Elizabeth Bowen: Portrait of A Writer.* London: Weidenfeld and Nicolson, 1977.

Halperin, John. "Elizabeth Bowen and Henry James." *Henry James Review* 7:1 (Autumn 1985).

———. "Maugham in Bondage." In *Novelists in Their Youth.* London: Chatto and Windus; New York: St. Martin's Press, 1990.

Heath, William Webster. *Elizabeth Bowen: An Introduction to Her Novels.* Madison: University of Wisconsin Press, 1961.

Jenkins, Elizabeth. Letters to John Halperin: 17 August 1986; 18 December 1987; 4 July 1993.

Keane Molly (M. J. Farrell). Letter to John Halperin: 16 July 1987.

Kenney, Edwin J., Jr. *Elizabeth Bowen.* Lewisburg, PA: Bucknell University Press, 1974.

Lassner, Phyllis. *Elizabeth Bowen.* Basingstoke: Macmillan, 1990.

Lee, Hermione. *Elizabeth Bowen: An Estimation.* London: Vision Press; Totowa, NJ: Barnes & Noble, 1981.

Lehmann, Rosamond. Letter to John Halperin: 2 October 1986.

Plomer, William. *At Home.* London: Jonathan Cape; New York: Noonday Press, 1958.

Ritchie, Charles. *The Siren Years: Undiplomatic Diaries 1937-45.* Toronto: Macmillan of Canada, 1974.

Rowse, A. L. *Glimpses of the Great.* London: Methuen, 1985.

Sarton, May. *A World of Light: Portraits and Celebrations.* New York: Norton, 1976.

Sarton, May. Conversation with John Halperin: 30 November 1986. Letters to John Halperin: 23 February 1987 and 23 August 1993.

White, Terence de Vere. *The Anglo-Irish.* London: Gallancz, 1972.

Wilson, Edmund. *Europe without Baedeker.* New York: Farrar, Straus and Giroux, 1966.

CHAPTER 3

Boyle, Andrew. *The Climate of Treason: Five Who Spied for Russia.* London: Hutchinson, 1979.

Brown, Anthony Cave. *Treason in the Blood.* Boston: Houghton Mifflin, 1994.

Halperin, John. "Between Two Worlds: The Novels of John le Carré." *South Atlantic Quarterly* 79:1 (Winter 1980).

Knightley, Phillip. *The Master Spy.* New York: Vintage Books, 1988.

Monroe, Elizabeth. *Philby of Arabia.* London: Faber and Faber, 1973.

Page, B. D. Leitch, and P. Knightley. *Philby: The Spy Who Betrayed A Generation.* London: Deutsch, 1968.

Philby, H. St. John. *Arabian Days.* London: R. Hale, 1948.

———. *Forty Years in the Wilderness.* London: R. Hale, 1957.

Philby, Kim. *My Secret War.* New York: Grove Press, 1968.

The Philby Papers (unpublished). Private Papers Collection, St. Antony's College, Oxford.

CHAPTER 4

Astor, Nancy. *My Two Countries.* Garden City, NY: Doubleday, 1923.

Collis, Maurice. *Nancy Astor: An Informal Biography.* London: Faber and Faber, 1960.

Gates, John D. *The Astor Family: A Unique Exploration of One of America's First Families.* Garden City, NY: Doubleday, 1981.

Kavaler, Lucy. *The Astors: A Family Chronicle of Pomp and Power.* New York: Dodd, Mead, 1966.

Manchester, William. *The Last Lion: Winston Spencer Churchill, Vol. I: Visions of Glory, 1874-1932.* Boston: Little, Brown, 1983.

———. *The Last Lion: Winston Spencer Churchill, Vol. II: Alone, 1932-1940.* Boston: Little, Brown, 1988.

Pryce-Jones, Alan. *The Bonus of Laughter.* London: Hamish Hamilton, 1987.

Rowse, A. L. "Nancy Astor," in *Memories of Men and Women.* London: Eyre Methuen, 1980.

Sykes, Christopher. *Nancy: The Life of Lady Astor.* London: Collins, 1972.

INDEX

George IV, 8, 14, 71
George V, 1-6, 7-72, 102, 113, 182, 183, 187, 200, 202, 212, 218; childhood of, 8-10; and Prince Albert Victor (Eddy), 10-16; career in Royal Navy, 10-15; and Eddy's death, 16-17; engagement and marriage to Princess May (Queen Mary), 18-21; birth of children, 21-22; life at Sandringham, 22-24, 33-35; death of Queen Victoria, 23-24; and the reign of Edward VII, 25-30; and the death of Edward VII, 30-31; accession to the throne, 31-32; and the Parliament Bill, 32-33; role in domestic crises, 1906-12, 33-37; trip to India, 37-38; role during the Great War, 38-46; decision to change family name to Windsor, 42-45; and Irish Home Rule, 48-49; and the politics of the 1920s, 50-53; and Ramsey MacDonald, 50-52, 57-59, 61, 65, 67; and the General Strike of 1926, 53-55; illness and recovery, 56-58; and National Government, 59-60, 61, 65; distrust of Hitler, 61-62; and Prince of Wales, 63-64; and his Silver Jubilee, 65-66; final months, 67-70; death of Princess Victoria, 69; death in 1936, 70; funeral, 70-72. See also Prince Albert Victor (Eddy); Edward VII; Edward VIII; "Georgian"; Queen Mary (Princess May); MacDonald, Ramsey
George VI, 22, 27, 40, 50, 64, 113, 220, 221
"Georgian," 1-6, 8, 31-32, 41, 44-45, 66-67, 71-72, 77, 86, 170-171, 182, 200, 228-29
Georgian Poetry, 2, 3, 4, 86
Georgian "revolt," 2
Gibson, Charles Dana, 174, 177
Gibson, Irene Langhorne, 174, 175
Gladstone, William, 8, 18, 19, 23, 49, 132, 213, 214
Glendinning, Victoria, 74, 80, 81, 84, 87, 88, 89, 90, 91, 93, 94, 96, 97, 100, 104, 109, 111, 112, 115, 116, 117, 119, 120, 121, 123, 124, 125
Goebbels, Joseph, 62, 215
Gore, John, 20, 22, 40, 46, 48, 66, 69, 70, 71
Goring, Hermann, 62
Gow, James, 132
Graves, Robert, 2
Great War (World War I), 1, 4, 5, 6, 31, 39-46, 49, 61, 64, 83, 85, 108, 112-13, 137, 138, 171, 181, 185-88, 199, 206
Green, Henry, 90, 96
Greene, Graham, 96, 109, 114; *A Sort of Life*, 115; *The Third Man*, 115
Grey, Edward, 28, 39, 40
Guevara, Ché, 129

H
Haggard, H. Rider, 84
Halifax, Lord, 85, 108, 212, 213, 217
Hammett, Dashiell, 127
Harding, Warren G., 198
Hardy, G. H., 158

Hardy, Thomas, 1, 35, 115
Hartley, L. P., 87, 90, 96, 120
Hawthorne, Nathaniel, 93
Heath, Edward, 126
Henderson, Neville, 217
Henry, Prince, 22, 27
Henry VIII, 18
Hitchcock, Alfred, 101
Hitler, Adolf, 5, 7, 27, 52, 61, 62, 155, 157, 158, 208, 211, 212, 215-19, 221; *Mein Kampf*, 221, 226. See also Nazism; World War II
Hoare, Samuel, 63, 212, 213
House, Humphry, 96, 100, 101
House, Madeleine, 100, 101
Huxley, Aldous, 50, 87

I
Ibn Saud, 139-41, 145-51, 154-57, 160, 161, 162, 164, 170, 171. See also Philby, Harry St. John Bridger
Ibsen, Henrik, 93
Irish Home Rule, 7, 18, 38-39, 48-49
Irish Literary Revival, 75, 85
Irish nationalism, 7, 29, 38-39, 48-49, 79, 83, 85, 108-9, 113, 183, 187
Irish Republican Army, 49

J
James I, 180
James, Henry, 31, 33, 73-77, 84, 87, 89, 90, 91-92, 94, 98-99, 101, 104, 106, 113, 114, 115, 116, 119, 120, 125, 181. WORKS: *The Portrait of A Lady*, 73, 92, 104; *The Spoils of Poynton*, 75; "The Beast in the Jungle," 76; *The Golden Bowl*, 76, and *Friends and Relations* (Bowen), 98-99; *What Maisie Knew*, 76; "The Pupil," 76; *The Ambassadors*, 77. See also Bowen, Elizabeth
James, P. D., 110
Jenkins, Elizabeth, 80, 84, 92, 96, 97, 100, 101, 103, 104, 120-21, 127
John, Augustus, 110, 203
John, Prince, 22
Johnston, Alexander, 135
Johnston, Dora. See Philby, Dora Johnston
Joyce, James, 1, 50
Judd, Denis, 8, 25, 52, 54, 59, 66

K
Kavaler, Lucy, 194, 198, 212, 214, 215
Keane, Molly (M. J. Farrell), 89, 121
Keats, John, 3-4
Keeler, Christine, 228
Keene, Nancy Witcher, 173, 175, 177
Kenney, Edwin J., 79, 80, 82, 87, 94
Keynes, J. M., 102, 133
Kiely, Benedict, 117
Kipling, Rudyard, 36, 38, 109, 136, 170, 182; *Plain Tales from the Hills*, 134; *Kim*, 136